SCOTTISH HISTORY SOCIETY

SIXTH SERIES

VOLUME 18

Personal Correspondence of Sir John Bellenden of Auchnoull and His Circle, 1560–1582

Personal Correspondence of
Sir John Bellenden of Auchnoull
and His Circle, 1560–1582

Edited by
† Peter D. Anderson and John H. Ballantyne

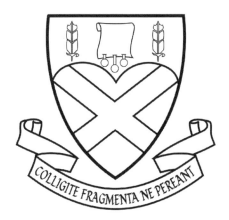

COLLIGITE FRAGMENTA NE PEREANT

SCOTTISH HISTORY SOCIETY
2023
THE BOYDELL PRESS

First published 2023

ISBN 978-0-906245-48-4

A Scottish History Society publication
in association with The Boydell Press.
The Boydell Press is an imprint of Boydell & Brewer Ltd
PO Box 9, Woodbridge, Suffolk IP12 3DF, UK
and of Boydell & Brewer Inc.
668 Mt Hope Avenue, Rochester, NY 14620–2731, USA

website: www.boydellandbrewer.com

A CIP catalogue record of this publication is available
from the British Library

The publisher has no responsibility for the continued existence or accuracy of URLs for
external or third-party internet websites referred to in this book, and does not guarantee
that any content on such websites is, or will remain, accurate or appropriate

This publication is printed on acid-free paper

MIX
Paper from
responsible sources
FSC® C013056

Printed and bound in Great Britain by
TJ Books Limited, Padstow, Cornwall

# CONTENTS

# PREFACE

Dr Peter Anderson, the lead editor, did not live to see the publication of this volume. He died in October 2022 after suffering from a debilitating illness for several years. Peter had a deep knowledge of the period of the Stewart earldom in Orkney and Shetland and published biographies of both Lord Robert Stewart and his son Patrick.

Thanks are given to a variety of individuals for assistance and, where necessary, permission to publish items from within the correspondence and related legal documents. Most notable are the duke of Roxburghe and the National Library of Scotland (NLS), who hold the bulk of the letters, and gave permission for their use. Thanks for liaison with the duke's archives at Floors Castle are due to the National Register of Archives of Scotland. Much background material in filling in the whole background to the period was derived from lengthy previous researches on the Stewart earls of Orkney, on the history of Orkney and Shetland, and the lands of the abbey of Holyroodhouse, in the National Archives (now Records) of Scotland, the National Library of Scotland, the Orkney Library and Archives, the Shetland Museum and Archives. Overall thanks are therefore due to successive Keepers of the Records of Scotland, National Librarians, the staff of their respective institutions, and the archivists of Orkney and Shetland.

# ABBREVIATIONS AND BIBLIOGRAPHY

| | |
|---|---|
| *Acct Bk of Sir John Foulis* | Cornelius Hallen, A. W. C. (ed.), *Account Book of Sir John Foulis of Ravelston, 1671–1707* (SHS), 1894 |
| *Accts of Thirds of Benefices* | Donaldson, G. (ed.), *Accounts of the Collectors of Thirds of Benefices* (SHS), Edinburgh, 1949 |
| Anderson, *Stewart Earls* | Anderson, P. D., *The Stewart Earls of Orkney*, Edinburgh, 2012 |
| Anderson, 'Cathedral, Palace and Castle' | Anderson, P. D., 'Cathedral, Palace and Castle: The Strongholds of Kirkwall', in *The Faces of Orkney: Stones, Skalds and Saints* (SSNS), Edinburgh, 2003 |
| *APS* | *Acts of the Parliaments of Scotland*, Edinburgh, 1844–75 |
| *Atlas of Scottish History* | McNeill, P. G. B., and MacQueen, H. L. (eds), *An Atlas of Scottish History to 1707*, Edinburgh, 1969; online in https://scotlandsplaces.gov.uk |
| Ballantyne and Smith | Ballantyne, J. H., and Smith, B. (eds), *Shetland Documents, 1195–1579, 1580–1611*, Lerwick, 1999, 1994 |
| *Barnbarroch Corresp.* | Vans Agnew, R. (ed.), *Correspondence of Sir Patrick Waus of Barnbarroch*, Edinburgh, 1887 |
| Blaeu, *Atlas* | Blaeu, J., *Atlas of Scotland*, Amsterdam, 1654 (online NLS) |
| *BUKS* | Thomson, T. (ed.), *Booke of the Universall Kirk of Scotland* (Acts and Proceedings of the General Assemblies of the Kirk of Scotland), (Bannatyne Club), i–iii, Edinburgh, 1839–45 |
| *Canongate Ct Bk* | Wood, M. (ed.), *Court Book of the Regality of Broughton and the Burgh of the Canongate, 1569–73*, Edinburgh and London, 1937 |
| *CSP Scot* | Bain, J. et al. (eds), *Calendar of State Papers relating to Scotland and Mary, Queen of Scots*, Edinburgh, 1898–1969 |

*CSP Spanish*

Tyler, R. (ed.), *Calendar of State Papers, Spain (Simancas), 1554–58*, Vol. xiii, 1954

Donaldson, *Reformed by Bishops*

Donaldson, G., *Reformed by Bishops: Galloway, Orkney and Caithness*, Edinburgh, 1987, 19–51

Donaldson, 'Some Shetland Parishes'

Donaldson, G., 'Some Shetland Parishes at the Reformation', in Barbara E. Crawford (ed.), *Essays in Shetland History*, Lerwick, 1984

*ER*

Mackay, J. G. *et al.* (eds), *The Exchequer Rolls of Scotland*, Edinburgh, 1897–1908

EUL

Edinburgh University Library

EUL Laing Mss

Laing Manuscripts

Fleming, *Mary, Queen of Scots*

Hay Fleming, D., *Mary, Queen of Scots*, London, 1898

*Fasti*

Watt, D. E. R., and Murray, A. L. (eds), *Fasti Ecclesiae Scotticanae Medii Aevi* (SRS), Edinburgh, 1983

Gore-Browne, *Lord Bothwell*

Gore-Browne, R., *Lord Bothwell*, London, 1937

*History of Peeblesshire*

Buchan, J. W., and Paton, H., *History of Peeblesshire*, Glasgow, 1925–7

HMC

Historical Manuscripts Commission

*James V Letters*

Hannay, R. K., and Hay, D. (eds), *Letters of James V*, Edinburgh, 1954

Keith, *Affairs*

Keith, R., *History of the Affairs of Church and State in Scotland*, Edinburgh, 1844

*Laing Chrs*

Anderson, J. (ed.), *Calendar of the Laing Charters, 854–1837*, Edinburgh, 1899

*Light in the North*

Cant, H. W. M., and Firth, H. N. (eds), *Light in the North: St Magnus Cathedral through the Centuries*, Kirkwall, 1989

*Mary of Lorraine Corresp.*

Cameron, A. (ed.), *The Scottish Correspondence of Mary of Lorraine* (SHS), Edinburgh, 1927

*Macfarlane's Geographical Collections*

Mitchell, A., and Clark, J. T. (eds), *Geographical Collections relating to Scotland made by Walter Macfarlane* (SHS), iii, Edinburgh, 1908

Melville, *Memoirs*

Melville of Halhill, Sir James, *Memoirs of His Own Life*, 263–4

| | |
|---|---|
| Murray, 'Sir John Skene and the Exchequer' | Murray, A. L., 'Sir John Skene and the Exchequer, 1594–1612', *Stair Society Miscellany One*, 1971 |
| Napier, *Memoirs* | Napier, M., *Memoirs of John Napier of Merchiston*, Edinburgh and London, 1834 |
| NLS | National Library of Scotland |
| NLS Adv. Mss | Advocates' Manuscripts |
| NLS Mss | NLS Manuscripts |
| NRAS | National Register of Archives of Scotland |
| NRAS 1100 | Roxburghe Muniments |
| NRS | National Records of Scotland |
| NRS CC8 | Commissariot of Edinburgh Register of Testaments |
| NRS CS7 | Register of Acts and Decrees of the Court of Session |
| NRS CS290 | Register of Cautions in Suspensions |
| NRS E14 | Abbreviates of Charters of Kirklands |
| NRS GD1/45 | Title Deeds to Lands in Orkney |
| NRS GD34 | Hay of Haystoun Papers |
| NRS GD96 | Sinclair of Mey Muniments |
| NRS GD106 | Craven Bequest |
| NRS GD107 | Tulloch of Tannachie Muniments |
| NRS GD263 | Heddle of Melsetter Papers |
| NRS JC1 | Justiciary Court Books, Old Series |
| NRS NP1/30 | Notarial Protocol Book of Alexander Lawson, 1570–90 |
| NRS NP1/36 | Notarial Protocol Book of Thomas Auchinleck, 1576–1615 |
| NRS RD1 | Register of Deeds, 1st Series |
| NRS RD11 | Register of Deeds Warrants, 1st Series |
| NRS RH2 | Miscellaneous Transcripts |
| NRS RH6 | Register House Charters, 1st Series |
| NRS RH9/15 | Papers relating to Orkney and Shetland |
| OA | Orkney Archives |
| OA D8 | Orkney Library Miscellaneous Collection |

| | |
|---|---|
| OA D23 | Joseph Storer Clouston Papers |
| OA D24 | Baikie of Tankerness Papers |
| OA D38 | Earldom of Orkney (Morton) Papers |
| OA SC11 | Orkney Sheriff Court |
| ODNB | *Oxford Dictionary of National Biography*, online |
| OSR | Johnston, A. W., and A. (eds), *Orkney and Shetland Records* (Viking Society), London, 1907 |
| Pitcairn, *Criminal Trials* | Pitcairn, R. (ed.), *Criminal Trials in Scotland*, Vols i–iii, Edinburgh, 1833 |
| Pitscottie, *Historie* | Lindsay of Pitscottie, R., *The Historie of Scotland* (STS), Edinburgh, 1899 |
| *Prot. Bk Gilbert Grote* | Angus, W. (ed.), *Protocol Book of Mr Gilbert Grote, 1552–1573* (SRS), Edinburgh, 1914 (NRAS NP1/15) |
| *Records of the Coinage of Scotland* | Cochran-Patrick, R. W., *Records of the Coinage of Scotland*, i, Edinburgh, 1876 |
| REO | Storer Clouston, J. (ed.), *Records of the Earldom of Orkney*, Edinburgh, 1914 |
| RMS | Balfour Paul, J. (ed.), *Registrum Magni Sigilli Regum Scotorum*, Edinburgh, 1882–90 |
| RPC | Burton, J. H. *et al.* (eds), *Register of the Privy Council of Scotland*, Edinburgh, 1877–82 |
| RSS | Livingstone, M. *et al.* (eds), *Registrum Secreti Sigilli Regum Scotorum*, 1908–66 |
| SA | Shetland Archives |
| SA SC12 | Lerwick Sheriff Court |
| Shaw, 'Adam Bothwell' | Shaw, D., 'Adam Bothwell: A Conserver of the Renaissance in Scotland', in Cowan, I. B., and Shaw, D. (eds), *The Renaissance and Reformation in Scotland: Essays in Honour of Gordon Donaldson*, Edinburgh, 1983 |
| *Scots Peerage* | Balfour Paul, J. (ed.), *The Scots Peerage*, Vols i–xi, Edinburgh, 1904–14 |
| SHS | Scottish History Society |
| Simpson, 'Noltland Castle' | Simpson, W. D., 'Noltland Castle, Westray: A Critical Study', in Mooney, J. (ed.), *Records of the City and Royal Burgh of Kirkwall* (Spalding Club), Aberdeen, 1952 |

Smith, *Toons and Tenants*    Smith, B., *Toons and Tenants: Settlement and Society in Shetland, 1299–1899*, Lerwick, 2000

'Some Notes on Early Tullochs'    'Some Notes on Early Tullochs', *The Scottish Genealogist*, xli, no. 1 (March 1994), 25–6

SRS    Scottish Record Society

SSNS    Scottish Society for Northern Studies

*TA*    Dickson, T. *et al.* (eds), *Accounts of the (Lord High) Treasurer of Scotland*, Vols i–xii, 1877–1970

# THE SINCLAIR FAMILY

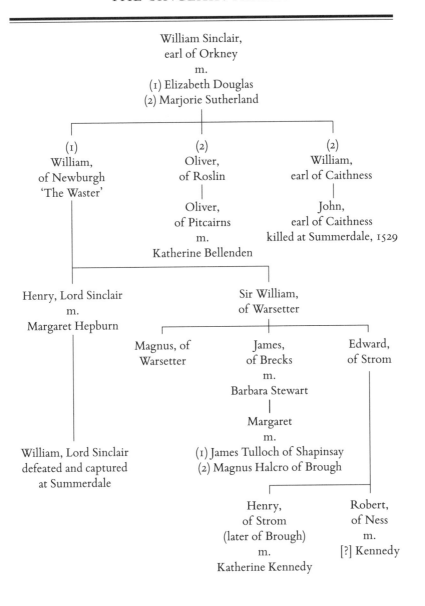

William Sinclair,
earl of Orkney
m.
(1) Elizabeth Douglas
(2) Marjorie Sutherland

(1)
William,
of Newburgh
'The Waster'

(2)
Oliver,
of Roslin

Oliver,
of Pitcairns
m.
Katherine Bellenden

(2)
William,
earl of Caithness

John,
earl of Caithness
killed at Summerdale, 1529

Henry, Lord Sinclair
m.
Margaret Hepburn

Sir William,
of Warsetter

Magnus, of
Warsetter

James,
of Brecks
m.
Barbara Stewart

Margaret
m.
(1) James Tulloch of Shapinsay
(2) Magnus Halcro of Brough

Edward,
of Strom

William, Lord Sinclair
defeated and captured
at Summerdale

Henry,
of Strom
(later of Brough)
m.
Katherine Kennedy

Robert,
of Ness
m.
[?] Kennedy

# THE BELLENDEN FAMILY

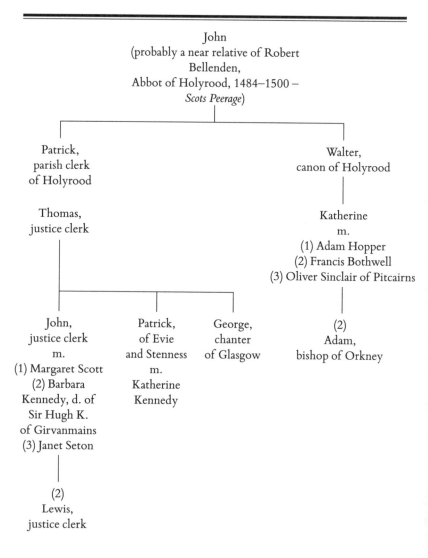

John
(probably a near relative of Robert
Bellenden,
Abbot of Holyrood, 1484–1500 –
*Scots Peerage*)

Patrick,
parish clerk
of Holyrood

Walter,
canon of Holyrood

Thomas,
justice clerk

Katherine
m.
(1) Adam Hopper
(2) Francis Bothwell
(3) Oliver Sinclair of Pitcairns

John,
justice clerk
m.
(1) Margaret Scott
(2) Barbara
Kennedy, d. of
Sir Hugh K.
of Girvanmains
(3) Janet Seton

Patrick,
of Evie
and Stenness
m.
Katherine
Kennedy

George,
chanter
of Glasgow

(2)
Adam,
bishop of Orkney

(2)
Lewis,
justice clerk

# THE BOTHWELL FAMILY

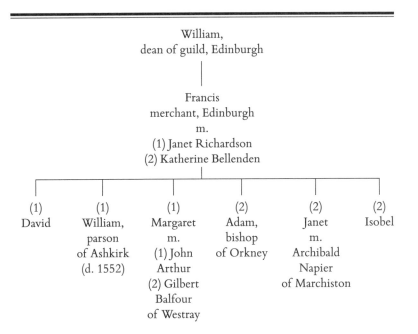

William,
dean of guild, Edinburgh

Francis
merchant, Edinburgh
m.
(1) Janet Richardson
(2) Katherine Bellenden

(1)
David

(1)
William,
parson
of Ashkirk
(d. 1552)

(1)
Margaret
m.
(1) John
Arthur
(2) Gilbert
Balfour
of Westray

(2)
Adam,
bishop
of Orkney

(2)
Janet
m.
Archibald
Napier
of Marchiston

(2)
Isobel

# CORRESPONDENCE SUMMARY

Letters from:

# INTRODUCTION

The editors of this work first encountered this run of correspondence in the course of their different researches into the history of Orkney and Shetland, John Ballantyne in his work with Brian Smith on Shetland documents, and Peter Anderson in his studies of the two Stewart earls of Orkney.[1] The first of these earls, as Lord Robert Stewart, features prominently in the letters. Peter Anderson had already made basic transcriptions of the letters for research purposes, but it was John Ballantyne who provided independently the rigorous versions which now form the subject of this work.

There are four main sources for this material: in the National Library of Scotland are Advocates' Manuscripts Adv. Mss 22.3.14 and 54.1.6, and manuscript Ms 1707. In the Roxburghe Muniments in Floors Castle are bundles 1104 and 1634. Those in Adv. Ms 54.1.6 are printed in Mark Napier, *Memoirs of John Napier of Merchiston*, 63–71, which also contains printed versions of nos. 7, 9 and 10 in the transcription, the original sources for which are unknown.

There are a variety of writers and recipients and none of the letters is in answer to any of the others, though other letters are mentioned, which do not survive. Despite this, and despite the variety of provenances, taken together each surviving epistle contributes to a coherent whole narrative. The run of correspondence, from 1560 to 1582, seems to form an almost continuous chronological sequence. There are gaps in the chronology – in particular, the last in line is separated from the rest by ten years – but most of these are at least partly explicable, with good reasons, other than simple loss, for interruptions in the action. They seem pauses rather than absences, in an ongoing account of a coherent, if contentious, body of affairs. Although of necessity telling only one side of the discussion, each letter tends to contain enough clues to infer the nature of replies and other points of view.

Pivotal to the story is the character of Sir John Bellenden of Auchnoull (1520?[2]–76). He, despite the name of this collection, in fact writes none of the letters, but is rather the recipient of the greater part of them, and

---

[1] See Abbreviations and Bibliography.
[2] *Acct Bk of Sir John Foulis*, xliii–iv, gives Bellenden's age at death as 56. Auchnoull is now Auchnoon, a farm to the north of Harperrig Reservoir and the Pentland Hills.

is a commanding presence throughout the correspondence, even when he is neither writer nor recipient. As justice clerk and noted legal writer, he was at the centre of royal and national affairs for much of his life, as well as pivotal to the complicated lives of his correspondents. He was the second of a trio of justice clerks, father, son and grandson, who held the office through most of the second half of the sixteenth century. Sir John's father, whom he succeeded in 1546, was Thomas Bellenden of Auchnoull; his son, Sir Lewis Bellenden, succeeded him in turn on his death in 1576, and is recipient of the last of the letters (letter no. 49, 2 September 1582). He was closely involved in the tumultuous events of Mary's brief reign, helping to facilitate the Darnley marriage, as well as being for a time one of the fringe suspects in the Riccio murder.[3]

He was thus a person of great and wide influence. What makes him central to this correspondence, apart from his clear authority, are his strong family and 'friendly' ties with the writers, and his close personal involvement in their affairs. Adam Bothwell, bishop of Orkney and writer of many of the letters, both to Bellenden and others, was well-heeled, well-educated and well-connected;[4] he was Bellenden's cousin and, perhaps awkward, protégé. Sir Patrick Bellenden of Evie and Stenness, turbulent in Edinburgh in the 1560s and later a controversial figure in Orkney and Shetland, was his brother. Also noteworthy was Gilbert Balfour of Westray who, like Patrick Bellenden, took his lairdly designation from Orkney, where he built a castle on the island, mighty for the area and still an impressive ruin. He was not a correspondent but plays a noteworthy part in events, though he had other adventures as well, and Noltland Castle has been described as in effect a bolt-hole.[5] He was married to Margaret, half-sister to Adam Bothwell. Bothwell's full sister, Janet, was married to Archibald Napier of Merchiston, and mother of the genius of logarithms. Looming over all but Bellenden himself was the figure of Lord Robert Stewart, illegitimate son of James V, later earl of Orkney, lord of Shetland. His family connections with the rest were more distant, but his other connections with Bellenden went back some years.

There are various themes dealt with in the letters – personal (notably the assertiveness of women), domestic (illness and bereavement), environmental (plague) – and these will be examined presently. But central is that of complex disputes over landed estates. On the one hand are those of the Northern Isles, in particular Orkney, in all its complexity, but also in Shetland and, to a lesser degree, in Caithness. On the other are the extensive temporal lands and the spiritualities – the appropriated churches and teinds – of the abbey of Holyrood. Much of the subject matter of the letters concerns the

[3]  Finlay, 'Sir John Bellenden of Auchnoull', *ODNB*, vii, no. 94.
[4]  Shaw, 'Adam Bothwell', 140–69; also Shaw, 'Adam Bothwell', *ODNB*.
[5]  Simpson, 'Noltland Castle', 144.

struggles of various of the individuals involved to lay hands on these lands, in the turbulent years surrounding the Reformation. The most prominent of these was to be Robert Stewart.

Since childhood, like his brothers, Robert had been a commendator – nominally interim abbot but in practice a conduit for the revenues of the great religious houses into the king's hands through his illegitimate sons – in his case of the abbey of Holyroodhouse. Post-Reformation, the adult Robert remained superior of a crescent of baronies across the Lothians and into Stirling – Whitekirk, Broughton (with the burgh of the Canongate), Ogilface, the Kerse – as well as that of Dunrod, on the Solway.[6] Coupled with this were the spiritualities of 25 churches appropriated to the abbey.[7] Adam Bothwell had inherited land in Corstorphine, and became vicar of the church there, which was appropriated to Holyrood.[8]

The Bellendens, moreover, had long had connections with the abbey of Holyrood. Robert Bellenden had been abbot in the late fifteenth century, Sir John's grandfather, whose brother had been a canon, had himself been parish clerk.[9] When Lord Robert Stewart, who had accompanied his sister to France in youth, returned there in 1557–8 for her wedding, Sir John Bellenden acted as his commissioner during his absence. On his return, Robert granted him, with his then spouse Barbara Kennedy, land in the barony of Broughton.[10] It was in the years up to this time that Bellenden also supported Robert's eldest brother James, 'abbot' of Kelso and Melrose (d. 1557) (letter no. 48, 17 September 1572). Later, Bellenden was to become guardian of Robert's eldest son, Henry (letter no. 23, 5 June 1569). This, coupled with Robert's occasional flattering remarks to Bellenden, (e.g. letter no. 48) might suggest a cordial relationship, even avuncular on Bellenden's part, but the unfolding of the correspondence suggests this was far from the case.

\* \* \*

When the widowed Mary herself came back to Scotland, a good passage brought her to Leith unexpectedly early, Robert being the only nobleman present to greet her. In the months that followed, he became a courtier, with his short-lived brother John, then for a time danced attendance upon Darnley, though later becoming more distant. He was an innocent guest at the queen's table when the murderers came looking for Riccio, while Patrick Bellenden was one of the attackers, presenting a gun at the pregnant queen.

---

[6] Anderson, *Stewart Earls*, 27–8.
[7] *Atlas of Scottish History*, 368.
[8] Shaw, 'Adam Bothwell', *ODNB*; Donaldson, *Reformed by Bishops*, 23.
[9] Unpublished article by John Ballantyne, 'Mr Thomas Bellenden of Auchnoull, c. 1490–1547' (NRS Library, ref. BIOG 117.000). See also genealogical tables.
[10] *RMS*, iv, no. 1385.

Robert flirted with the protestant Lords of the Congregation, led by, among others, his brother James, the later regent, but was generally regarded as untrustworthy and self-seeking.[11]

Even before the end of his sister's reign, Robert began seeking to transfer his interests in Holyrood to lands in Orkney and Shetland. He came to be the most prominent, but was neither the first nor the only significant figure to do so. Katherine Bellenden, Sir John's aunt and Adam Bothwell's mother, had married, as her second husband, Oliver Sinclair, grandson of William, the last Sinclair earl of Orkney. He provides a definite link between Lowland Scotland and the Northern Isles. Traditionally designated of Pitcairns, but by the 1550s feudatory of the Holyrood barony of Whitekirk, he had visited the islands during James V's circumnavigation of his dominions in 1540, and had briefly been made tacksman of the royal estates in the islands, as well as sheriff. After his humiliation at the battle of Solway Moss, followed by the death of the king, of whom he had been a favourite, he fell into financial difficulties. He owed money to Mary of Guise, who took over title to the royal estates as her widow's portion. She had a valuation made, which demonstrated that Orkney, at least, was wealthier and more fertile than had previously been assumed.[12] This may have attracted attention. Oliver, though now in eclipse, never relinquished his interests there; he was still referred to as 'sheriff' as late as 1560, and received a grant of bishopric land in Eday at that time.[13]

The major secular estates of Orkney and Shetland consisted of: the Norwegian/Danish royal lands pledged to the Scottish crown in lieu of dowry in 1468–9; the earldom estates aggressively acquired by James III from the last of the Sinclair earls in 1472; and the 'conquest lands' – lands acquired in a private capacity by Earl William, seemingly to retain a foothold in the islands after losing the earldom to the king of Scots.[14] These last had somehow, possibly at the end of Oliver Sinclair's brief prominence, been gathered up with the rest of the royal and earldom lands, and were the particular pursuit of William, Lord Sinclair, great-grandson of the last earl. He regarded himself as their rightful heir, and he was to continue to chase them, fruitlessly, through the whole period, including a remonstrance to the queen dowager over Oliver Sinclair's refusal to part with the lands Lord Sinclair claimed in Shetland.[15]

But the largest and wealthiest estates in the islands, with other possessions in Caithness, were those of the bishopric, centred notably on Birsay, an eleventh-century bequest of Earl Thorfinn, the first incontrovertibly Christian earl of Orkney. These were the temporalities; with them were lucrative spiritualities. It was to all this ecclesiastical wealth that southerners were first drawn, in

[11]   Anderson, *Stewart Earls*, 29–34.
[12]   Murray, 'Sir John Skene and the Exchequer', 141–2.
[13]   NRS GD96/80.
[14]   Anderson, *Stewart Earls*, 6, 9, 46.
[15]   *Mary of Lorraine Corresp.*, 85.

the persons of Sir John Bellenden, Adam Bothwell, and their followers. The story told by the letters begins on 26 October 1560 (letter no. 1), just over a year after the appointment of Adam Bothwell to the bishopric of Orkney, but it is clear that Bothwell at least had been involved in the Northern Isles for some years before. In 1555, he and William Moodie, chamberlain of the earldom lands of Orkney, were both in Orkney on an officially sponsored visit. They may have had separate reasons for being there, though both received expenses simultaneously from the treasury.[16]

Moodie was on the business of the dowager queen regent. On his way home, by land, he wrote her a letter, detailing difficult dealings with Monsieur Bonot, her French bailie of Orkney, as well as serious incursions by the English in the Northern Isles.[17] The latter seem to have been more than one of the periodic landings of the English fishing fleets, which were notorious for plundering supplies and impressing men from the Northern Isles on their way to their fishing grounds south of Iceland.[18] Relations between Scotland and England were uneasy at this time, and this seems to have been a genuine military attack, with the English threatening to return in greater numbers. They did so two years later, in 1557, when they suffered a heavy defeat at Papdale outside Kirkwall, at the hands of island forces, probably led by Edward Sinclair of Strom.[19]

Bothwell's business in the north is nowhere stated. His simultaneous visit with Moodie may have been pure coincidence, or it could have represented an inspection of the bishopric lands, parallel with that of Moodie.[20] On the other hand, given indications of Bellenden's interest in the islands at this time, it seems likely that the justice clerk had a hand in Bothwell's visit for his own reasons. He was perhaps anticipating that Bothwell would eventually become bishop, and saw opportunities to lay hands for himself on the income of the wealthy bishopric estates; he already seems to have been making plans. The current bishop of Orkney was Robert Reid, previously vigorous but by this time an absentee, greatly involved in national affairs. Shortly after Reid's death in 1558, Bellenden was awarded a temporary grant under the privy seal of the bishopric temporalities.[21] Not long after, Bothwell was presented as bishop.[22]

---

16  *TA*, x, 284.
17  *Mary of Lorraine Corresp.*, 398.
18  *ER*, xv, 151–2; *James V Letters*, 297.
19  *CSP Spanish*, xiii, 320; Pitscottie, *Historie*, ii, 118; there is a garbled version of this episode by writer 'Jo. Ben' (*Macfarlane's Geographical Collections*, 319), which specifically mentions Edward Sinclair.
20  Duncan Shaw, in his *ODNB* entry on Bothwell, suggests the influence of Gilbert Balfour or Oliver Sinclair on the bishop's preferment. Balfour was certainly involved in Bothwell's affairs, but Sinclair, despite his Orkney interests, remained a figure from the past. It is hoped to show that Bellenden has the strongest combination of prominence, interest and influence.
21  *RSS*, v, no. 589.
22  *Fasti*, 329.

Adam Bothwell set off for his diocese in February 1560. On the way, he was captured by an English ship and held prisoner for several weeks in St Andrews.[23] In April, he arrived in Orkney. Soon, he was under pressure. Within months, he and Balfour, his constable, were in dispute with Thomas Tulloch of Fluris, former constable of Bishop Reid and administrator since Reid's departure, regarding alleged spulyie of property in Kirkwall and Westray, actions that were to continue for some time.[24] Tulloch, despite his Scottish designation, had a long history in the area. Probably, like most of the Orkney Tullochs (the name remains common in Orkney to this day), he was related to or connected with the Tulloch bishops of the fifteenth century, and he had been a follower of Bishop Reid virtually from the beginning of his episcopate, at least since 1544.[25] He is variously referred to as bailie,[26] constable,[27] and later chamberlain.[28]

His activities do seem to have occasioned discontents among the bishop's tenants. In 1556 he was required to produce his victual-delivery weights for inspection,[29] a common sign of suspected sharp practice. He was exonerated of any wrongdoing,[30] but early in Bothwell's episcopate, there was a contract between the bishop and Gilbert Balfour concerning possible actions against him.[31] Balfour had supplanted Tulloch as constable of the bishopric, and some dispute regarding the outgoing constable's dues and liabilities from his tenure might be expected, but there clearly were other matters involved. He in turn raised his actions for spulyie in Kirkwall and Westray. The Westray lands were those of Noltland, and the action may well have been connected with Balfour's acquisition of lands in the island as a whole, but also his erection of a castle in Noltland itself. There was another element however. Bothwell was later to see Bellenden's hand in providing support for Tulloch in his actions (letter no. 5, 5 February 1561) as part of his general campaign for pensions from the bishopric. It seems probable that this desire for income, as well as being a venal ploy in itself, was also seeking recompense for a considerable outlay, by both Bellenden and Bothwell, in securing the see, from the pope and the Italian bankers who served him, for the relatively impecunious Bothwell.[32]

Bothwell's time in Orkney was not to prove easy. As he remarked in the first of the letters, to his brother-in-law, Archibald Napier of Merchiston,

[23]   Donaldson, *Reformed by Bishops*, 25–6.
[24]   NRS CS7/21¹, f. 8, 67; CS7/22, f. 85 (*bis*), 152; GD107 (calendar description only). See also letter no. 9.
[25]   *REO*, 363, no. ccxxxvi; *RMS*, iii, no. 3102; see also 'Some Notes on Early Tullochs', 25–6.
[26]   NRS CS7/4, f. 132.
[27]   NRS GD107 (calendar description only).
[28]   NRAS 1100, bdl 1612.
[29]   NRS GD107 (calendar description only).
[30]   NRS GD107 (calendar description only).
[31]   OA D23, Notebook 3, 106.
[32]   Donaldson, *Reformed by Bishops*, 23.

'My being … hes bene in continuall trawell and labour of bodye and mynd and evill helth thairthrow continualle sene my cumming in this cuntray.' He referred further details to the letter-carrier, who could 'reherss yow … quhat cummeris sume frendis hes sterit oup unto us' (letter no. 1, 26 October 1560). This passage draws attention to a partly hidden element throughout the correspondence. Not everything the writer had to say was committed to paper. Although the services of 'posts' or 'post boys' – dedicated messengers for public use – were available[33] most, if not all, these letters were conveyed by servants of the correspondents, some with instructions to amplify the contents. On occasion the bearers of both letter and reply are identified. Bothwell's letter to Napier was in response to one from his brother-in-law, brought by James King, who had told the bishop that Napier was concerned that he had written several letters without reply. Bothwell excused himself, saying that he had received nothing. This exchange was relatively trivial, but in other circumstances the device was used to convey additional details that sometimes we can only guess at. As becomes clear, it is by no. means impossible to work out who Bothwell's troublesome 'frendis' are, but this is the first example of a frustratingly elliptical element in the correspondence. Much interpretation and consultation of other sources is required to understand quite what is going on.

One element about which the bishop was happy to be explicit was the pressure he was under from Bellenden. As bishop, 'all the cummer that can be maid me sall not caus me to geif ouer that thing suld be my supple in tyme of neid, and that otheris weill deserving suld bruik efter me.' He sought Napier's assistance in conveying to all involved how hard he, Bothwell, was working to meet Bellenden's pension demands. These – 1100 merks yearly, to be derived from 20 chalders of bere – were more than he had to sustain himself, particularly given current grain prices. He asked Napier to persuade him to be reasonable and remind him 'that he that wald haif all, all is able to tyne'. This was accompanied by the vaguely threatening comment that 'gif he continowis as he hes begown I may find rameid thairfor sik as I best may, althocht it stand not with his plesuir'.

Bothwell now made a number of small grants to followers: William Moodie, the bishopric chamberlain, his companion in Orkney in 1555, received Orkney bishopric land in Caithness, his own home area.[34] John Cullen and John Brown, burgess of Kirkwall, received lands in St Ola.[35] Much more important, however, was the fulfilment of what were clearly obligations, evolved over the previous few years, to relatives he had brought with him to Orkney. On 30 June 1560, he granted Gilbert Balfour charters of enormous estates, one

---

[33] Anderson, *Stewart Earls*, 243–4 etc.
[34] NRS E14, i, 107.
[35] NRS E14, i, 205, RH6/1819; *OSR*, i, 121, no. lxiii.

of lands in Birsay, one of properties in Westray.[36] The stated reason for these grants was the 'great danger' Balfour had braved in travelling to Rome to pay for and bring back Bothwell's bulls of provision to the see. There was more to it than that. The latter of these possessions Balfour thenceforth used as his territorial designation, and the Westray lands were to remain in the hands of the Balfour family for centuries. Birsay was a different matter. Despite the charter, Balfour's powers there were not unchallenged, and the lands were to be the subject of complex and longstanding disputes. The 1560 charter itself was endorsed 'The first charter of few of Birsaye and this wes nevir usitt.' This was followed on 16 January 1561, at the beginning of the following year, by letters of reversion and obligation, by Balfour and his wife, to the bishop.[37] The precise nature of this manoeuvre is unclear but, as will be seen, Bellenden clearly had some designs on the lands himself. Gilbert Balfour was to draw some revenues from Birsay, but for the most part he remained 'of Westray'.

Balfour, although ostensibly a follower of Bothwell, was also self-seeking. In a second letter to Napier on 1 December the same year (letter no. 2), Bothwell went on to repeat his complaints about his treatment, but Bellenden was not his sole tormentor. The bearer of this letter south appears to have been Margaret Bothwell, the bishop's half-sister, wife of Gilbert Balfour, with whom he was 'continualle at debait ... becaus I wald not geiff hym all that I haid quhill I gat mair'. He wanted Napier to try to keep Balfour's wife in the south, since he suspected 'hyr causing' behind the dispute. This was only the first instance in the correspondence where women were to show formidable involvement in their husbands' affairs, as well as being agents in their own right. Bothwell's third letter to Napier, written only days later (letter no. 3, 5 December 1560), stated that he intended to entrust several individuals with 'power and commission' in his interests to try and settle his differences with the justice clerk since, being in Orkney, he could not do so himself. These – Napier's 'collegis' – included his 'nyghbuir' the laird of Roslin, a Sinclair and brother to Oliver of Pitcairns (Whitekirk); Oliver was described as 'sheriff', presumably from his grant of 1540, and as Bothwell's 'guidfather' (step-father); as well as Alexander King, described elsewhere (letter no. 2) as the bishop's 'gossop' (godfather), as well as his legal adviser.

In his closing remarks, Bothwell strongly recommended that Napier send his son John abroad, either to France or Flanders, 'for he can leyr na guid at hame nor get na proffeit in this maist perullus worlde'. The future mathematical genius, though only about ten years old at the time, may already have been manifesting his abilities, which could profit from more advanced study abroad, but this was not the only reason for leaving the perilous world of Scotland. Plague, endemic in Scotland, was shortly to become rampant,

---

[36]  NRAS 1100, bdl 1625; *RMS*, iv, no. 1668.
[37]  NRAS 1100, bdl 1612.

as we shall see. Napier and Bothwell were to talk of it again and, three years later, John Napier did indeed leave Scotland.

Bothwell now received another letter from his sister, Lady Merchiston. His response (letter no. 4, 19 January [1560–1]) was neither long nor wide-ranging, but was perhaps the most intimate and personal of the entire series, personal counsel from one sibling to another. Janet Bothwell had complained that there was a 'variance' between herself and her husband, and she was, in her brother's words, 'not sua luiffet of him as ye war wont'. He was sorry, particularly since he was so far away, and at a very difficult time for him to provide his best support. The bishop's response, though clearly designed to provide appropriate comfort, was distinctly clerical in tone. Janet's troubles were 'the visitatione of God to pruif yow, to try yow gif ye luif him … quhome as he hes beyne protectour, guvernour and defendar of in tymes passit, sua dout not bot he will be in tymes cumming; and reconsall yow with your housband in gayning tyme, to your gryt contentment … Prayand yow to tak the samin thairfor in patience; saying with godle Job, gif we haif ressavit guid owt of the hand of the lord, quhai suld we not alsua ressave evill, and geiffin him maist hartle thankis thairfor.'[38]

He sent his reply by the same unnamed bearer who had brought his sister's letter. The latter carried with him 30 pounds for her, sent by her brother despite his inability to help further 'throw frendis mysusing' (of which the bearer could give details). As matters eased, he would send her husband some token 'for intertynement of amite'. Nothing is said regarding the nature of the differences between Janet and her husband, nor are they referred to in any other letter. Bishop Adam's last remarks, however, may suggest that money was involved, and the bishop regarded himself as somehow under some obligation. Whatever the truth of the matter, there is perhaps more humanity in this letter than in any of the others.

On 24 December, Bothwell received a letter from Napier. He replied on 5 February 1561 (letter no. 5). In addition to his other difficulties, Bothwell had had to face trouble from two Sinclair brothers, Henry and Robert, probably part of the unspecified 'cummers' of his first letter. According to Bothwell, Henry and Robert had both been provided with wives by Bellenden, 'quha maryet with thaime twa sisteris'. Apparently under Bellenden's influence, one of these, probably Henry, had met the regent Lord James in Strathbogy and made representations against the bishop with the purpose of stirring up trouble. Also at Bellenden's instigation, the brothers had proceeded 'to lowp in ane off my plaices callet Birsay, quhilk thai kepit; and thaireftyr onbesset the way quhairbe I was to cum haime from my visitatioun, with gret number off commonis quhem thai pat than in beleiff to leiff frelie, and to knaw na superiouris in na tymis cumyn; quhilkis be Goddis graice haid na powair to

---

[38] Book of Job, e.g. Job 2, 10.

hairme me, althocht thair uttir purpos was at thair hethir cumyn, to haiff alder slaine me, or taiken me.' Bothwell had then asked Henry, 'cheiff off that conjuratioun', what their motivation was, and what he had done to them or anyone else in the country to provoke their opposition.

The question of motivation, apart from Bellenden's attempts to discomfit Bothwell, is a complex one. The mention of land-holding, with talk of living freely and knowing no superiors, suggested that any dismembering of the bishopric estates could have involved the creation of allodial, or rather udal, holdings according to the Norse, rather than the Scots, feudal pattern. In circumstances where the old bishopric estates were to be dismembered, this might mean land being distributed in udal parcels, rather than the clearly feudal form demonstrated by Bothwell's charters of lands in Birsay and Westray. Exactly how a udal arrangement would serve the ends of Bellenden is unclear. This was not the only issue, however. Much more important on this, the cusp of the Reformation, was religion. Bothwell was avowedly a member of the reformers, and the changes he brought had their objectors, perhaps mainly in Birsay, ancient bishopric centre and site of Orkney's original cathedral.

At the first head court after Yule 1560 'ane gret multitude off the commonis', gathered outside the cathedral, were confronted by the bishop's messengers, who asked if they would be content 'off mutatioun off religioun'. This they refused; nevertheless the reformist Bothwell closed the kirk doors and thenceforth forbade mass to be said there. This 'irritat' them so much that they repeatedly demanded that they be let in, and appear to have invaded the bishop's palace. Bothwell's seemingly persistent illness now hit him and he was forced to take to his bed and lie listening, humiliated, as a priest was brought to 'ane chapell hard at the scheik' of his bedchamber in The Yards to 'do mess, and marye certaine pairis in the auld maner … quhilk I culd not stoppe withowt I wald haiff committit slauchter'.

Henry Sinclair agreed to answer for his actions in writing; but his response, when it came, did not give any justification, but instead offered a series of 'petitions'. These came from both the Sinclair brothers as well as some others, and totalled 18–20. Finding his queries unanswered as to 'quhatt mowet' Henry Sinclair 'to do syk thingis to me', Bothwell referred the petitions to 'the schireff', demanding justice. Bishop and sheriff examined them together. The sheriff was willing to settle matters, and asked the bishop first to make an answer. The bishop refused 'quhill I haid my houss againe'. The actual subject matter of the petitions is not given, but in the end 'the said Henry fader gainestowd', calling Henry and his followers fools who did not know what they were doing, and said he 'wald on na sort consent the mess wer doune'. What this suggests is that the petitions concerned the prospect of udal tenure, which the sheriff thought was an illusion, and religion, in which he, like the bishop, was firmly for reform.

\* \* \*

Throughout all this, the issues, and the main personalities – Bellenden, Bothwell, Balfour – are clear enough, but there are a number of questions which seem obscure, even enigmatic. Partly this could be due to familiarity among the correspondents, but also because of what may be a prudent vagueness. Who exactly were all these Sinclairs? Who was 'the said Henry fader'? Who was 'the schiref'? What exactly was their connection, both to each other and to Bellenden's tormenting of Adam Bothwell? And who were the 'twa sisteris'? In point of fact, the answers are not hard to find; only the elliptical nature of the references prompts the questions.

Edward Sinclair of Strom was a formidable figure, victor over the English at Papdale in 1557 and, with his brother James, over the Caithness Sinclairs at the battle of Summerdale back in 1529; the latter made him the sworn foe of Lord Sinclair.[39] He was sheriff of Orkney, depute to the longstanding absentee, Oliver Sinclair, and father of Henry, younger of Strom (later of Brough), and Robert, of Ness. Bellenden, in his quest to channel to himself assets from the bishopric, had clearly sought to establish clients in the islands, particularly among the Sinclairs. He had thus linked his cause to the interests of one of the two Sinclair factions. If inferences are correct, Sir John did this by marrying Henry and Robert to his own sisters-in-law.

Henry Sinclair's wife was Katherine Kennedy. Henry, as it happened, had only a year or two to live after the arrival of Adam Bothwell. Katherine shortly afterwards married Patrick Bellenden.[40] He, in a later letter to his brother, Sir John (letter no. 27, 24 July 1569), incidentally relayed the good wishes of 'Your lordship and my gud fader Sir Hew and my wife'. 'Sir Hew' was Sir Hugh Kennedy of Girvanmains, father to Sir John's second wife, Barbara Kennedy (mother of Sir Lewis Bellenden).[41] If Sir Hugh was father-in-law to both Bellenden brothers, then it suggests that Barbara and Katherine Kennedy were sisters. One must suppose that a third Kennedy sister was married to Robert of Ness, though she is unnamed and so far untraced; Robert did have sons,[42] but his history, as well as his part in these events, is little known. It should be noted too that Sir Hugh was closely related to the earl of Cassillis, whose daughter Jean was to marry Robert Stewart;[43] she, like Robert, will appear presently. If Sir John's match-making was a ploy in his plans to lay hands on pensions from the Orkney bishopric lands, then it was part of a long game, dating back to Bothwell's early visit to Orkney before July 1556,

---

[39] OA D8/5, 621; *REO*, 57, no. xxv.
[40] 16 August 1561 x 12 July 1563 (*RSS*, v, nos. 1419, 2642).
[41] *Scots Peerage*, ii, 65.
[42] NRS RD1/34, ff. 105–7.
[43] Anderson, *Stewart Earls*, 35.

at least in the case of Henry, who was already married to Katherine Kennedy by 31 July of that year.[44]

The correspondence does give a somewhat one-sided view of the bishop's struggles. Apart from Napier himself, he was not without allies and supporters, both among other factions within the Sinclairs and his own dignitaries. In December 1561, bonds of caution had to be found before the Justiciary Court for the principal members of a band of 80 persons led by Magnus Halcro who, among other crimes, had issued from the castle of Kirkwall in pursuit of Henry Sinclair and William Moodie for their slaughter. Besides Magnus himself were his brother William; Edward Sinclair, brother of the laird of Roslin; and churchmen 'Freir' Francis Bothwell, Alexander Dick, Magnus Murray and Duncan Ramsay.[45] All were required to find cautioners that they would underlie the law; Oliver Sinclair of Whitekirk stood for his kinsman Edward, two Sinclair kinsmen and ten of his main henchmen; Gilbert Balfour for Magnus and William Halcro, as well as Thomas Chalmer; and William Bothwell, burgess of Edinburgh, for Francis Bothwell.[46]

So far as we know, those pursued survived (Moodie certainly did), but Sir Patrick Bellenden, on succeeding Henry Sinclair as Katherine Kennedy's husband by March 1563,[47] began to take a role in the power struggles of the north. In July of that year, from Magnus Halcro with the consent of Bishop Bothwell,[48] he received the lands in Stenness from which he derived his territorial designation. About a year later, the bishop granted him land in Evie, with teindsheaves in Stenness.[49] He became sheriff principal.[50] The significance of his appearance in Orkney, and his relationship with his brother Auchnoull, are difficult to define. As early as March 1556 he had granted a procuratory to Sir John to represent him in any legal process,[51] but there is nothing more (other than the marriage business) to suggest anything other than a brotherly relationship between the two. Patrick is mentioned in association with his brother in a decreet arbitral by Maitland of Lethington of 30 June 1564,[52] settling the dispute between Sir John and Bothwell. Both Bellenden brothers agree to 'intromit no further with the bishop's living' beyond the assignation to Sir John of teinds and other duties in a wide variety of areas in Orkney – the islands of Rousay, Egilsay, Sanday; the parishes of Deerness and Holm – although Patrick does not appear personally in the assignation itself.

[44]   SA SC12/65/1/8; Ballantyne and Smith 1195–1579, 70, no. 105.
[45]   NRS JC1/11; Pitcairn, *Criminal Trials*, i, 213.
[46]   NRS JC1/11.
[47]   NRS RH2/1/20/145. *Northern Notes and Queries*, i–ii (Edinburgh, 1888), 104, gives 11 April 1563 as the date of their marriage.
[48]   *RSS*, v, no. 2642.
[49]   NRAS 1100, bdl 1093.
[50]   NRAS 1100, bdl 1093; NRS GD106/258.
[51]   NRAS 1100, bdl 1612.
[52]   NRAS 1100, bdl 1612; NRS RD11/3.

It is possible that Patrick was intended to succeed Sinclair as his brother's chief troublemaker in Orkney and Shetland but, as we shall see, his part in the turbulent events to follow was more complex than that. Moreover, his appearance and activities in Orkney, in the early 1560s, run concurrently for some years with his doings in Edinburgh, notably his attendance upon Darnley and involvement in the death of Riccio. For his part in this he was remitted in 1566,[53] but his notoriety may have prompted his attempts to set up a more permanent, prosperous base in Orkney and Shetland, provoking in turn his struggles with Lord Robert.

This was some time in the future. Though asked to do so more than once, Sir John Bellenden never visited Orkney or Shetland, but remained throughout this period in regular contact with his allies there. Bothwell was certain that his 'small frend the justice clerk' was stirring up trouble, not only through the Sinclairs, but also the longer-standing irritant Thomas Tulloch. At the same time, his letter of 5 February 1561 thanked Napier for his assistance in approaching the lords of council, to counteract falsehoods against him, 'and mak me frendis amangis thaime'. Lying sick in the north, he could not do so himself; but since Napier's efforts were succeeding, he would come south as soon as he could. He was anxious that Napier should keep him informed 'that I may provid for my affairis in caice thair wraith may not be mitigat, for I will not commit me to ane angry multitud'.

The remainder of this letter was confined to family business, concerning lands that Bothwell had inherited years before in the south, notably those of Briglands in Peebles and Dunsyre in Lanarkshire.[54] On his behalf Alexander King, his godfather, was to seek his entry into these lands. (This is also referred to in letter no. 2, 1 December 1560.) Much more important was a charter now granted to Napier by the bishop, of 'syk thing I haiff', for which he sent a reversion, asking that it be subscribed and sealed. This suggests that the bishop had placed what remained to him of the bishopric in Napier's hands, under reversion, in order to keep it from the clutches of his unfriendly 'frends'. Bothwell's next letter, no. 6, on 25 March 1561, again thanked Napier for his efforts in mollifying the lords, though he remained unspecific about the nature of complaints against him, whether by Bellenden or any associates. One, emanating from the Sinclair brothers, Bothwell felt was already answered; about a second, 'I nay it utterlie that the samin can ever be verefeitt, altoght I haid guid caus to haif done the samin to our soverane.' Bothwell, clearly, was reluctant to meet the full demands, in the form of lands and pensions, from the Bellendens, Balfour and others, but if, as he believed, this was the

[53] Fleming, *Mary, Queen of Scots*, 502.
[54] Dunsyre: lands on the upper ward of Lanark, eight miles or so east of Carstairs. Briglands is in Peebles (*History of Peeblesshire*, ii, 365; Napier, *Memoirs*, 49). In Bothwell's seising in the lands of Dunsyre, Alexander King acted as notary.

reason he was being traduced in the south, it remains difficult to determine the precise nature of the alleged complaints.

It would hardly seem to be about religion. The regent was a firmly convinced supporter of the reformed church and Bothwell, though appointed under the old dispensation by papal bull, had nevertheless stood as firmly as he could against the opponents of reformation in the islands (apparently led by clients of Bellenden – curiously, since Bellenden, like his father Thomas before him, as well as Bothwell, was a determined reformer). Bothwell was to institute a thorough-going introduction of the new religion. He was later to take part in many of the more national activities of the new church, as well as becoming a lord of session. His future actions on the public stage were indeed to be the subject of controversy, including on matters of religion. These will be examined; but for the moment, the letter-writing does not help to illuminate the exact nature of the ongoing disputes.

\* \* \*

By 20 April, the bishop was seeking a more powerful ally than Merchiston. His servant James Alexander told Napier (letter no. 7) that Bothwell had left his palace and boarded a ship in Kirkwall harbour. He intended to remain there, awaiting fair wind and weather for France, where he intended to complain to the queen about Bellenden's treatment of himself and others – 'hys lordschipis extorsyone'. His illness had persisted – 'mervallis seiks and beleefit nocht to haif recuverit' – and he was unable to stay in the north 'because of the evil air and weakness of his body'. In anticipation of the perils of the voyage, he had made his will, naming Napier as an executor and Napier's son as his heir … 'and intendis, gyf God prolongis his … dayis to agment that airschyp to the gret weill and prophit of your mastership and your airis and his'.

Bothwell's expedition to France, begun after a few days on board ship, marked the end of his longest sojourn in Orkney. Thereafter, for the next few years, his visits were restricted to the summer months. His activities were vigorous enough, though the periodic nature of his attention to his see was later to excite adverse comment from the General Assembly. He had clearly not enjoyed his stay. According to Alexander, in a separate letter to Lady Merchiston (letter no. 8, 20 April 1561), Bellenden was not his only problem; there were others involved, and 'gyf your ladyschip had knawyne be quhat personyss thai war moifit, ye wald nocht beleifit. I wil expreme na namyss bot the occasyone of the trybill that mufit his lordschip maist was nocht done be na Orknanaye borne.' The Orcadians, in particular the Sinclairs, were therefore merely pawns in a game played by greater, Scottish figures, though why her ladyship should have been surprised at who they were is unclear. If they were not the obvious usual suspects – Bellenden, Balfour, etc. – then we too must remain ignorant.

In writing to Lady Merchiston of his master's travails, Alexander re-empha-sised Bothwell's remarks – made while labouring under an illness thought possibly fatal at the time – about his friendship with her husband, naming him as executor and his son as heir in all heritage matters. Shortly after, she received another letter (no. 9, 25 April 1561), this time from Francis Bothwell, a relative (he addresses her as 'darrest antt') of her and the bishop, who had made him treasurer of Orkney. He too stressed Bothwell's 'greit luiff' for the Napiers – the bishop's will had also included bequests to her daughter and son, John Napier's siblings – and urged her to seek her husband's support for the bishop in his absence, in a case to be pursued against him before the session by Tulloch of Fluris. He said however that he could not 'latt you gang without repruiff'. He had previously shown her some things concerning certain persons 'towart thair misbehavor towart my lord', which he had asked her to keep secret. Instead, she showed these to her half-sister Margaret, the wife of Gilbert Balfour, whom Bothwell already suspected of aiding her husband in their disputes. She 'vrait agane heir despitfullie, and causit cummaris to be amang us, of the quhilk my lord was gretlie offendat at you for the tyme'. Perhaps she was one of those that Francis Bothwell was thinking of when he referred to other hidden unbelievable troublemakers.

About five months later, Francis Bothwell wrote again to Lady Merchiston (letter no. 10, 28 August 1561). He had heard of Queen Mary's return to Scotland, in which she had been accompanied by the bishop. He counselled her and her husband to treat the bishop wisely and kindly; her husband should never leave his side, 'and that for your greit weill and profeit'. This was important, not merely for Bothwell's sake but for their own, because there were those that will seek 'to obteine that thyng the quhilk ye haiff Goddis rycht of. It is nocht neidfull to expreim the personis to you, for ye knaw them.' One must presume he meant Bellenden and Balfour, though we cannot be certain, and the characteristic tact is noteworthy. Francis himself, being in Orkney while the bishop remained in the south, was at a disadvantage. If he were with the bishop, he would help him to safeguard the Napiers' rights, because he knew well the trouble that could be caused, both by their opponents and by the lords. If the bishop decided to remain in the south, then Francis wished to be sent for, not because he was looking for trouble, but for the bishop's sake. She was not to tell the bishop of what he was saying, since he wrote as a friend, to offer a friendly warning.

\* \* \*

There now occurs a gap in the correspondence (or at least that which we know to have survived) of nearly four years. During this time, despite Adam Bothwell's intermittent presence in his diocese, which occasionally raised eyebrows within the kirk, his ecclesiastical activities have earned praise.[55] He preached personally.[56] He made a number of important church appointments; Gilbert Foulsie, his secretary, became archdeacon and remained a kenspeckle figure thereafter;[57] Francis Bothwell was treasurer of the cathedral.[58] Adam's one failure in his quest for preferred officials seems to have been John Kincaid, possibly John Kincaid of Warriston, a kinsman of Janet Bothwell. Kincaid first appears in 1561, in the early months of Bothwell's episcopate, and had expectations of succeeding Thomas Tulloch as chamberlain as well as becoming constable. However he left soon after, refusing to remain in Orkney as long as the bishop tolerated the interference of Balfour, who had already replaced Tulloch as constable, and would give no account of what he had been up to with the bishopric revenues. According to James Alexander, Bothwell was exceedingly displeased (letter no. 7, 20 April 1561). John Kincaid was no more seen in Orkney, though an Alexander Kincaid appeared a few years later and became vicar of Walls.[59]

Bothwell 'disponed benefices and gave out stipends out of his rents to ministers, exhorters and readers', and by 1567 almost every parish in Orkney and Shetland was served by a minister or reader.[60] Quite a number of Bothwell's other followers also appear at this time, some lay, some in holy orders. Moodie, Cullen and Brown have already been mentioned. They joined, in the bishop's immediate service, Duncan Scollay, an existing servant, his surname suggesting a native Orcadian, who became a burgess of Kirkwall, and was granted property in Work and in Kirkwall by the bishop.[61] To this group was added John Gifford, a longstanding bishop's man, who held land in Gorn in Sandwick. Bishop Adam famously visited Shetland, accompanying Kirkcaldy of Grange in their unavailing attempt to capture the fleeing earl of Bothwell, coming close to losing his life in the process when Kirkcaldy's ship the *Unicorn* struck a rock and sank, in Bressay Sound.[62]

Apart from the Kincaid affair, practically no sign of these events appears in the existing correspondence, so perhaps the gap is particularly significant. As during a later apparent lacuna in the sequence, which will be looked at presently, the potential writers are not in the islands. They have all made their way south, and they are far from idle. Bothwell, before his troubles, and besides his energetic pastoral activities, was seeking to settle differences between himself, Balfour and Bellenden. On 10 March 1564, he and Balfour of

[55]   Shaw, 'Adam Bothwell', 141.
[56]   *CSP Scot*, i, 523.
[57]   *REO*, 269, no. cliv.
[58]   NRAS 1100, bdl 1625; *REO*, 342, no. ccxx.
[59]   *RMS*, iv, 2472; *REO*, 287, no. clxx; Donaldson, 'Some Shetland Parishes', 158.
[60]   Shaw, 'Adam Bothwell', *ODNB*.
[61]   *REO*, 263, no. cxlviii.
[62]   Gore-Brown, *Lord Bothwell*, 405.

Westray chose respectively Sir John Bellenden and James Balfour of Pittendreich (Gilbert's brother, designated parson of Flysk) to arbitrate between them.[63] This document mentioned many 'controversies', but chiefly concerned various lands in Westray and Birsay. Balfour's rights in Westray were guaranteed. The lands in Birsay were not specified, but it became clear that they were those mentioned in Bothwell's charter to Balfour of 30 June 1560 – more than 150 pennylands in Birsay itself and 35 pennylands in Marwick.[64] These were noted in a number of documents following upon the arbiters' decreet – a contract between the two disputants,[65] with a procuratory of resignation of those same lands, dated at Edinburgh on 16 March 1564, by Gilbert Balfour in the hands of Adam Bothwell,[66] and an executing instrument following thereupon, concluded at Perth the following May (it also contained reference to letters of resignation and obligation granted to the bishop by Balfour and his wife, only about six months after Balfour's 1560 charter).[67]

Several months later, on 30 June 1564, William Maitland of Lethington, the Scottish secretary, produced a decreet arbitral to seal a further agreement between Bothwell and Bellenden.[68] This showed that Bothwell, at the outset, had granted Bellenden a pension of £400 (600 merks). This was less than the 1100 merks he had previously been pressing for, but was supplemented by the promise of half of two other bishopric pensions, to Lord John Stewart, and to Archibald, son of Patrick, Lord Ruthven, should they be ended for any reason. The recent death of Lord John[69] therefore brought Bellenden a further £200. Bothwell also had to assign to Bellenden duties from lands in Rousay, Egilsay, Sanday, Deerness and Holm (though the bishop could redeem those of Deerness and Holm for the sum of £162 2s 4d, using the duties 'for sustentation of the ministry').

Perhaps the most curious element in the decreet was the ordinance that Bellenden, who by now had apparently come into possession of the bishopric lands of Birsay, following upon Balfour's resignation to the bishop, was to assign these back to Bothwell for his lifetime, though Bellenden retained possession of the feu, which would return to his heirs in due time. To facilitate this, Bellenden had sought a transumpt – a fully authenticated copy version – of Balfour's 1560 charter. The original document had specified just what properties, conditions and payments were involved, but since that document does not appear to have taken effect, we must assume that the destination of these lands had remained the subject of dispute from early

---

[63] NRS RH9/15/75.
[64] NRAS 1100, bdl 1625.
[65] Ibid.
[66] Ibid.
[67] Ibid.
[68] NRAS 1100, bdl 1612 (draft copy); NRS CS7/31, f. 64.
[69] Keith, *Affairs*, ii, 202.

in the whole deconstruction of the old Orkney bishopric establishment. Bellenden's transumpt was forthcoming on 31 July 1564, following acts of the lords of council compelling Gilbert Foulsie, keeper of the regality register, to provide one.[70] In October 1564, Bellenden received his own charter of the Birsay lands, paying yearly the same sum as noted in Balfour's original.[71] It is far from clear why, firstly, Balfour's original charter was never activated (or enacted in the first place) nor, secondly, why Bellenden's possession of them was resigned to the bishop for his lifetime. And all this, as we shall see, was far from the last word on these lands.

* * *

These details sketch in the background to the matters discussed as the correspondence resumes. When that happens, on 6 August 1565 (letter no. 11), a new voice is heard. William Henderson wrote to Bellenden from Kirkwall concerning the justice clerk's affairs. He appended the title 'Dingwall pursuivant' to his signature. He had been an Edinburgh-based officer of arms for some years, and is found acting in that capacity as late as March 1564, when he gave out a proclamation at the mercat cross of Orkney, on a wide variety of customary matters – violation of the Sabbath, 'makand mercattis, adulteries, fornicatioun, and swering of aithis conforme to the act of parliament'.[72] Nevertheless he was already involved in Orkney affairs, and was later to be appointed messenger-at-arms specifically for Orkney.[73] He was ostensibly factor for Bellenden, but later acted for and liaised between both Bellenden and Robert (e.g. letters nos. 11–15 *passim*). He had been a witness the previous year to the charter by Magnus Halcro to Patrick Bellenden of lands in Stenness,[74] and later he is found acting as a notary, including before the sheriff and commissary courts.[75] In time he was to become treasurer of Orkney, parson of Stronsay and collector of thirds.[76] His brother, Cuthbert Henderson, was a notary who ultimately became minister in Rousay and Stronsay, and vicar of North Ronaldsay.[77]

William Henderson was also to be a major witness to the rumbustious events which were about to unfold. When we first meet him however, he speaks to Bellenden chiefly of the business, and problems, of gathering the justice clerk's income from the Orkney lands, in accordance with Maitland's decreet. In the intervening years since the previous letter, affairs in the north have

[70]  NRS CS7/31, ff. 140–1.
[71]  *OSR*, 146, no. 66.
[72]  *TA*, xi, 356.
[73]  *RPC*, i, 658–60.
[74]  *OSR*, 135, no. 165.
[75]  E.g. *REO*, 277, no. clxi; NRS GD1/45/4.
[76]  *RPC*, iii, 53; NRS RH2/1/20/165.
[77]  *RSS*, liv, f. 91; *RSS*, vii, no. 2445; NRS CS290/9 (30 August 1589).

plainly settled down. There was no reference to the lands of Birsay, though they were shortly to be the subject of a new dispute. Henderson enclosed an extract account of Bellenden's 'portion' of Orkney for the previous year, and mentioned his progress in gathering of rents from the tenants of Rousay, Sanday and Egilsay. They were complaining about the state of the crops – 'I dreid thair be less payit this yeir.' There was a dispute between James Annand, chancellor of the bishopric, and John Grahame, parson of Sanday and servitor of the justice clerk, concerning teinds. Henderson suggested that Bellenden should make Grahame 'provid thairfor'.

Duncan Scollay and John Gifford were also mentioned in connection with the bishop's affairs, as was Gifford's wife, Margaret Dunbar.[78] It was intended that she be responsible for the conveyance of Bellenden's rental goods from the island of Sanday to Kirkwall, for onward shipment south. Henderson had already paid her for this.[79]

In fact, whether or not she had brought the goods to Kirkwall, she had declared herself unable to come south, being heavy with child, and had no intention of going beyond Kirkwall until she be delivered (letter no. 11). Margaret Dunbar's career was particularly notable among the activities of women in this place and period, who were far from being ciphers, or chattels of their husbands. We have already encountered the agitations of Balfour's wife; presently we will encounter those of Lady Bellenden, the activities of Margaret Sinclair, and meet Jean Kennedy, Lord Robert's wife, the future Lady Orkney. It is true that much of their activities indeed lay in the furthering of their husbands' affairs, though they also had personal interests. Margaret Dunbar had in addition a story of her own.

She had previously been the spouse of John Wemyss, who had gone overseas, not returned, and was presumed to be dead. She was also one of the sisters and heirs of the deceased Andro Dunbar of Loch and Kilconquhar, and on 22 February 1564, she concluded a contract with Patrick Bellenden of Stenness and Gilbert Balfour of Westray, agreeing to sell them her portion of the lands of Loch in Wigtownshire and Kilconquhar in Fife for certain sums of money and a yearly payment of six chalders of Orkney bere for life. The contract was registered in the Books of Council and Session, and the commissary books of Orkney.[80] In November 1565, Bellenden and Balfour assigned the contract to Sir John Bellenden.[81] Margaret Dunbar was thus now a pensioner of the

---

[78] *RSS*, v, no. 2839; the date of her marriage to Gifford is unknown, but must have been some time in the early 1560s. By 6 August she was with child (letter no. 11).

[79] It is not clear whether the transfer actually happened, but Henderson speaks of conveying goods in future directly from Sanday to Leith. There are other instances of goods being shipped directly south from particular islands, without passing through Kirkwall (*Prot. Bk Gilbert Grote*, 80–1, no. 319).

[80] NRS RD1/8, f. 30.

[81] NRS CS7/35, f. 97.

bishopric in her own right, and she would not allow this to be forgotten, particularly since she had plans of her own. In fact, one reason that she was responsible for conveyance of Bellenden's rents from Sanday was that she was herself due her six chalders from them. She had duly received this, but the whole had been transported to Kirkwall at the considerable loss of eight pounds-worth of natural shrinkage in transit. The hapless Henderson had had to deal with this, and to meet the cost from his own purse (as well as other sums to John Gifford, converted into cash from oats and bere). Henderson hoped that Bellenden would compensate him for this, and sought advice as to what would be done in future, since 'or I cair it furth of Sanday yeirle to Kirkwa I had lever cair it to Leith furth of Sanday'.

* * *

It is more than two years before we hear from William Henderson again (letters nos. 12, 16 November 1567; 13, 4 February 1568). Writing to Bellenden, he speaks further of his problems in gathering up of the justice clerk's rents, with the prices obtained being the subject of complaint from Bellenden's wife. Much more important, however, was his first mention of a figure who had just appeared for the first time in the north.

It is difficult to arrive at precise details of the origins of Lord Robert Stewart's interest in Orkney and Shetland. The Holyrood and Orkney connections of both Oliver Sinclair and the Bellendens, and the consequent connection with Robert Stewart, have been noted. The wealth and fertility of Orkney in particular, no doubt observed by James V during his unique royal visit, and certainly revealed by his widow's valuation of the royal lands, may also be what attracted the Bellendens to the bishopric lands, using Bothwell as an instrument to lay hands on some of that wealth. This in turn drew in Robert Stewart.

There is a charter by Robert, dated and signed at Kirkwall, apparently on 20 January 1564, to William Moodie of land in Stromness,[82] but this is almost certainly a mis-date, and it is not until mid-1565 that there is clear evidence of Robert acting in the north. On 26 May 1565, shortly before Henderson reopened the correspondence, Lord Robert Stewart, designated 'of Strathdon', received a charter under the privy seal of lands in Orkney and Shetland. These were essentially the earldom and kingsland granted to Mary of Guise as her marriage portion, with all pertinents, including Kirkwall Castle, advocation of churches and benefices, and the offices of sheriff of Orkney and its equivalent *foudrie* of Shetland. At that time Robert was at the high point of his transient favour with Darnley 'whome he serves with his cappe in hys hand …'. Darnley knighted him, and he was said to be on the

82   *REO*, 271, no. clvi.

point of being invested as earl of Orkney.[83] This did not happen at this time, but on 7 December 1565 he granted a charter, significantly in overtly feudal form, 'notwithstanding of the laws and customs of the country of Orkney to the contrary', to John Mowat of land in Rendall.[84] Not long before, the other aspect of Robert's plans began to manifest itself. On 23 August 1565, he granted Bellenden a charter of Holyrood lands, with the office of justiciar and bailie of Broughton, the justiciary jurisdiction extending to other parts of the abbey lands, notably Abbotsgrange in the Kerse – hitherto his wife's marriage portion.[85]

There was something of a blip in this progress. In May 1567, as the queen's relationship with the earl of Bothwell developed, the earl was granted a *blenche ferme* charter of the earldom of Orkney and lordship of Shetland, all erected into a 'whole free dukedom',[86] and the following month letters from the earl to William Cecil and Queen Elizabeth styled him 'Duke' of Orkney.[87] Shortly afterwards, there was an action against Robert before the session, requiring him to present before the lords his 'pretended charter' of the lands of Orkney and Shetland 'to hear and see the same revoked and annulled by decreet of the lords of council … the lands … to remain perpetually with the sovereign … and the said commendator to refund, content and pay to the queen all profits he has taken up thereof'.[88] Robert did not appear, but in July he sat in with the lords, as they discussed measures on Bothwell's flight.[89] He played no part in Kirkcaldy and Bishop Adam's pursuit of Bothwell. Probably he made preparations for his own first journey to the north. Once there he was to remain for some time.[90]

Robert first arrived in Orkney in the second half of 1567, and swiftly took overall charge. According to Henderson, he was 'deligent in the furthsetting of justice and hes put gud ordour and rewle in the cuntre. God gif him grace to continew' (letter no. 12, 16 November 1567). He rewarded those who had assisted him in his coming north. He had already granted pensions to the Balfours, Gilbert, and Sir James of Pittendreich,[91] and now he gave a charter to Gilbert Balfour of further lands in Westray and Papa Westray, and a sum in victual from the lands of Whitekirk (as well as to his own brother-in-law, Laurence Bruce of Cultmalindie). William Pennycuke, parson of Penicuik, received a monk's pension, and Sir William Kirkcaldy of Grange, who had

---

83  *CSP Scot*, ii, 157.
84  *REO*, 282, no. clxiv.
85  *RMS*, iv, no. 1985; *RSS*, v, no. 2311.
86  *RSS*, v, nos. 3530, 3535.
87  *CSP Scot*, ii, 329–30.
88  NRS CS7/40, f. 139.
89  *CSP Scot*, ii, 354.
90  *REO*, 123, no. lvi.
91  *Canongate Ct Bk*, 132.

recently returned from his and the bishop's unsuccessful attempt to intercept Bothwell, received 'ane teynd besyd himself' in Fife. In accordance with his charter, Gilbert had surrendered to Robert the sheriffship of Orkney and Shetland and the keeping of the castle of Kirkwall. It was planned to formalise these dealings shortly in Edinburgh as well as resolving a dispute between Auchnoull and Robert over the teinds of Dalry, part of Holyrood's spiritualities in Edinburgh.

Quite different was Robert's treatment of Patrick Bellenden, who had 'departit furth of this cuntre in ane strange maner, for I persaif that my Lord Robert is myndit to do him na plesour'. This was the start of a longstanding feud between Patrick and both Stewart earls, father and son, lasting right through to Sir Patrick's death early the following century. Patrick had fallen out with both Robert and Gilbert Balfour, who complained that Patrick 'did nocht his dewtie to him'. The nature of this dispute is not mentioned but, as became apparent, Robert's appearance had supplanted Patrick's own efforts to be a figure in Orkney and Shetland. He had briefly held the sheriffship, which he now lost permanently, and he was later described as having long 'envied Lord Robert for dispossessing him of sumquhat he enjoyed in Orkney'.[92] If Sir John could not solve the dispute, then Henderson did not wish to see Patrick returning to the north. He ended these comments with another frustrating observation: 'Farder in this purpois I wil nocht wrytt bot referis to the beirar.' Details of what was actually happening, however, were eventually to become clear. Henderson ended his letter by stating that he was bound for the North Isles of Orkney. This was early evidence of an interest in the area which survived his death in the 1580s through his wife, Margaret Bonar, another doughty lady, who was in due course to inherit her husband's lands in Stronsay and North Ronaldsay, as a landowner in her own right.[93] If any of Bellenden's goods were to come to hand before his return, he had deputed her to arrange for its shipping south. Margaret Bonar was clearly acting in a similar capacity to Margaret Dunbar.

Henderson's next letter (no. 13) was written to Bellenden from Kirkwall on 4 February 1568. It was a lengthy piece on the same themes as its predecessor: Bellenden's affairs in Orkney and the ongoing dissension between Lord Robert and Sir Patrick Bellenden, as well as disputes between Robert and the bishop. Henderson had received a letter from Bellenden, as well as two from Bellenden's (third) wife, Janet Seton, both complaining that they had received few reports in any detail about the ingathering of income. Janet Seton seems to have been the chief instigator in this and she had given Henderson 'veray heych repruiffis', doubting his good faith. The chief problem was the delay in the transmission south of all the Martinmas (11 November)

92    *CSP Scot*, iv, 322.
93    *RMS*, v, no. 1895.

instalment of Bellenden's pension income, in meat and butter as well as cash. Henderson said that he had sent south as much as he could gather, including £120 of money, in Gilbert Balfour's bark. The difficulty was that negotiable quantities of meat and butter did not tend to come into the tenants' hands until Allhallowmas (1 November), and then had to be gathered from scattered isles in particularly tempestuous weather. As regards cash, Lady Bellenden complained about exchange rates, and her losses in converting gold and 'yopindalis' (silver coins of 15s–£1 Scots in value) into 'quhyt silver' (coins containing an agreed proportion of silver, used as negotiable units of cash). Henderson's brother Cuthbert seems to have handled the conversion, and Henderson suggested Bellenden inquire of him. For his own part, Henderson defended himself stoutly, stating that the rentals he had used to procure the rents were well known to both his lordship and the tenants, as were his own actions in gathering them, so he could not see how he would be able to 'defraud' his lordship.

Henderson defended Robert against several accusations of oppression made against him by Sir Patrick Bellenden to his brother. Besides his effective banishment of Patrick from Orkney, Robert was said to have evicted Patrick's servants from their lands, including Robert Sinclair (son of Robert Sinclair of Ness)[94] from Campston in St Andrews, as well as possessing John Houston in the subdeanery, from which Archibald Douglas had been evicted (temporarily, as a fringe suspect in the murder of David Riccio). He had also sacked William Halcro as bailie of Firth and Harray. Henderson stated that either these evictions had never taken place or, as in the case of the subdeanery, were to ameliorate oppression by others. In the case of Halcro, it was because of conviction *de crimine falsi*, unspecified. For his part, Robert was 'veray heychly offendit' at comments Patrick had made to the regent.

But the most troublesome of Robert's doings concerned his relations with the bishop. Of recent times, all Adam Bothwell's heroics, pacifications and undoubted pastoral achievements had not served him well in his troubles. Again, the details can only be background to the correspondence. Principal among them were questions about religion. Bothwell's participation in the pursuit of his fleeing namesake might have been intended to counter ecclesiastical criticism from another quarter. At the fifteenth general assembly, in December 1567, the 'haill Kirk' found that he, 'called bishop of Orkney', had 'transgressed the act of the Kirk in marrying the divorced adulterer (Bothwell, to Queen Mary)', and was therefore deprived of 'all functione of the ministrie'.[95] He was also accused of not visiting kirks of 'his country, allowing his sheep to wander without a pastor'. His relative and apparent

[94] *REO*, 468.
[95] *BUKS*, i, 112.

protégé, Francis Bothwell, was alleged to be a papist.[96] Later, in 1570, he was again accused of neglecting his diocese and failing to preach, rather spending his time as a lord of session. His use of monastic lands to fund his episcopal offices was alleged to be 'simoniacal', and his retention of the title of bishop and especially 'Roman titles as Reverend Father in God' which 'pertaineth to no Ministers of Jesus Christ, nor is given them in Scriptures'. Bothwell defended himself on all but one of these charges, though he abased himself on the question of his style. He remained a titular bishop for the rest of his life, but was never again appointed by the assembly to oversee his diocese; he was superseded in his functions by local ministers acting as commissioners. James Annand, Gilbert Foulsie and, later, Thomas Swinton were all to perform this office.[97]

Now, he was to be confronted by pressure from a new and sinister figure. According to William Henderson (letter no. 14, 20 March 1568), Robert Stewart had been travelling round his new domain, and on 16 March 1568 he rode from Kirkwall, accompanied by Henderson and Gilbert Foulsie, to John Gifford's house at Gorn in Sandwick. The following morning, in Kirkwall, one of his servants, John Brown, newly arrived in Orkney, went to morning prayers in the cathedral. When the service was over, he made to ascend the turnpyke stair to the 'pends' (*triforium*) of the cathedral. The bishop's men, guarding the building, warned him to leave or be fired on. He, 'nocht knawand that it was kepit gaif thame sharp words agane and thocht that it was done in dispyt'. He told his colleagues in the castle, and a group of Robert's servants – later named as James and Patrick Monteith, George Dundas, Thomas Robeson, Walter Bruce, David Scollay and William Sclater[98] – 'in ane angir ruschit' from the castle, in company with Brown. The bishop's men, seeing them, shot Brown fatally in the head. Robert's men entered the cathedral and opened fire, killing bishop's men Nicol Alexander and James Moir. The others fled, lowering themselves out of the building on a rope, leaving Robert's men in possession.

This at any rate was Henderson's story when he and Robert both wrote to Auchnoull three days later. About three o'clock on the afternoon of the 17th, hearing what had happened, Robert had immediately returned the ten miles or so to Kirkwall, arriving after dark. When he heard the details he 'wald nocht pass to the castell nor suffir his servands to speik wyth him', but went to the house of Hugh Gordon, a servant, and remained there two days. He investigated the incident and conferred with the 'honest men of the cuntrie' on what to do. When he and Henderson wrote on 20 March, Robert left the narrative to Henderson, who also wrote to Patrick Bellenden (letters nos.

[96]  *BUKS*, i, 162–3.
[97]  *BUKS*, i, 190–1; NLS Adv. Ms 35.5.1.
[98]  *RSS*, vi, no. 306.

14–16). Both emphasised Robert's lack of responsibility for what had happened. For Robert, the incident was 'chanceit by [without] his expectatioun and sair aganis his will'. It had taken place in his absence 'but ony motyve bot of suddantye'. Both noted Robert's desire to make recompense, with particular regret at the death of Nicol Alexander, who was a kinsman. Robert desired Henderson to remind Auchnoull of their own kinship. Their wives, both from the Kennedy family, were the reason for the longstanding affection and 'kyndness' that had been between Robert and Bellenden (as well as his brother Patrick); that and the fact that Robert and Sir John's bairns were thus in the fourth degree of kinship 'ferds of kyne' which should move the justice clerk 'to luf and favor wyth us', and thus to use his good offices in settling matters.

These letters might seem to sound a sincere note of regret. The incident in the cathedral hardly served Robert's desire for respectability as ruler in the islands, and might have jeopardised his further plans. But what were these plans? He and Henderson now set out explicitly in their letters what were surely Robert's intentions from the first. In Henderson's words, Robert was 'bent to haif superiorite of this cuntrie alswel of the bishopryc as the rest' – in other words to add the bishopric lands to the royal and earldom estates he already had in his possession. Robert himself stated that he hoped to achieve this by 'the interchance and cois [exchange] of … [the bishop's] leiffing and myne and of the lands of Birsay with your self and my lands of the Kerss'.

In a further lengthy letter of 31 March 1568 (letter no. 17), Robert amplified these thoughts. He thought his Kerse lands to be 'als gud as' those of Birsay and the superiority and bailiary of the Canongate to be a match for the Orkney bishopric lands. The bishop was very unwilling to contemplate the exchange Robert proposed, and Robert would deny the justice clerk nothing should he help him effect it. To satisfy Auchnoull he was prepared to 'augment' him with the bailiary of the Kerse (in addition to that of Broughton) 'swa that ye haiffand thai twa bailyereis thair is na man in Lowthean may do bettir service to thair prynce nor ye'. He was also keen to expedite a further exchange with the bishop involving the superiority of Leith, and sought Bellenden's influence with the regent.

To advance matters, he would send south his wife and his chamberlain. Robert himself could not come south in person 'wythout I war suir'. But Jean Kennedy was not merely being sent to do her husband's work for him. As part of her marriage settlement, in late 1561, she had been granted a liferent right in the lands of Abbotsgrange and Newbiggings in the barony of the Kerse.[99] She had therefore a personal interest in these affairs, guarding her own stake in any Kerse/Birsay excambion.

The reason for Robert's need to stay in the north was the hostility stirred up against him by Sir Patrick Bellenden at court. He had put Robert in

[99] NRS CS7/24, f. 442.

'hatrent and indignatioun with my lord regent and the consale'. If he wished to regain Robert's favour, Patrick should use his good offices, with his own friends and Lord Morton, to cause the regent to accept Robert's feu mails for Orkney – to recognise his rights in the islands. Robert refused to deal directly with Patrick, but was content that Sir John should do so in his name. He suggested that Sir John's personal presence in the north 'mycht bring all thing to ane perfectioun'.

Robert may have been hoping vainly to bring the Bellenden brothers together in Orkney to reach some agreement. This never happened, but an examination of events from Robert's first appearance in the north and the assault on the cathedral suggests that a storm had been brewing for some time, in which a whole host of individuals, Scots and Orcadians, were involved.

Patrick Bellenden seems to have been both independent agent in search of his own sources of wealth in the islands, and facilitator for his brother. The two roles may not always have been compatible. On the one hand, he had acquired land from the bishop in the parishes of Stenness, Evie and St Ola, as well as the island of Eynhallow[100] and the office of sheriff. This was part of the decreet arbitral by Maitland of Lethington, mediating between the bishop and, among others, the Bellenden brothers, who were to intromit no further with the bishop's living. Despite this, shortly after, on 29 April 1566, Patrick had been named as a leader of 'rebels' who had sought to control the palace and castle of Kirkwall, as well as the cathedral steeple, all of which should be guaranteed to the bishop.[101] A bond of caution in £1000 by Lord Somerville undertook that the strongholds, having been returned to the bishop, would be surely kept. This suggests that Patrick and his followers were attempting to seize power at the bishop's expense, whether for himself or for his brother. Yet the actual story seems much more complicated. In his letter of 31 March 1568, Robert stated that Patrick had convened a band of 'certane of this cuntre men ... to persew me in my body and to rute me and all myne perpetually furth of this cuntrie gif it may ly in thair power'. When the cathedral was stormed, it was the bishop's men who were in charge and from whom it was wrested by Robert's followers.

A letter from Henderson to Sir John, written from Scalloway in Shetland on 1 June 1568 (letter no. 19), stated that Patrick Bellenden, Gilbert Balfour, William Moodie and 'uther Orkney men' had banded together against Robert, all at the bishop's behest. Their intention was to invade Orkney and take the 'stepill'. Whether this was the plot Robert had mentioned in his March letter (though he had not been specific about the identity of the 'cuntre men') or even that of 1566 (when his appearance in the north was imminent) is not clear.

---

[100] *RMS*, iv, no. 1710; Donaldson, *Reformed by Bishops*, 36–7.
[101] *RPC*, i, 455.

There are a number of unanswered questions. William Moodie, as a Caithness man, was undoubtedly local, but Balfour and Patrick Bellenden, though both Orkney proprietors, were hardly 'Orkney men'. Henderson's knowledge of the plot apparently came from learning that Mr Magnus Halcro had written of it to his kinsman William Halcro of Aikers. How Henderson knew of this is unclear. Magnus Halcro was no lover of Robert, and was undoubtedly a bishop's man (letter no. 22, 2 June 1569). He had had his own hand in events hitherto. As early as July 1560, on the eve of Bothwell's episcopate, with several Orkney followers, including William Halcro of Aikers, he had concluded a contract with the earl of Caithness seeking his protection, in return for support for the earl, should he invade Orkney in pursuit of his 'auld ennymies'.[102]

Exactly who the Halcros' foes were is unknown (perhaps, to supporters of the bishop, it was Sir John Bellenden), but the interest of Caithness is noteworthy. Later, in 1572, an English observer was to note that Patrick Bellenden had mustered 300 men against Robert, as he had done in 1568.[103] He too enlisted the aid of the earl of Caithness 'in revenge'. Caithness's desire for vengeance on elements in Orkney derived from the disaster at Summerdale in 1529. It was still evident in the earl's attitude as late as 1614 amid the death throes of the Stewart earldom.[104] In part it was an ongoing Sinclair family squabble, confronting Caithness and Lord Sinclair on the one hand, with Oliver Sinclair and the descendants of the Summerdale victors on the other. However, the antagonism extended to whoever held significant power in Orkney over the Sinclairs' lost patrimony.

We have already seen how, in December 1561, Magnus Halcro, in support of the bishop against the importunities of Sir John Bellenden, had led a band against the Sinclairs enlisted by Sir John. Seeking allies where he could, it seems probable therefore that he was to enlist the same kind of support from Sir Patrick Bellenden against Lord Robert. Sir Patrick, though exacting land and wealth at the expense of the bishopric, may have been regarded by Halcro as a lesser evil than Robert, or even than Sir John Bellenden. But there was another, more mundane, reason for a relationship between Magnus and Sir Patrick. While the latter was sheriff, in the mid-1560s, he had been pursued before the session in Edinburgh by James Tulloch of Shapinsay, accusing him of oppression. It was stated that he had 'adherit, assistit and tane part with Mr Mawnis Halcro quha maist shamefully abusit Margaret Sinclare, spouse to the said James in manifest adulterie'.[105] 'Abusit' is a misleading term; Margaret Sinclair was clearly a willing participant in these high jinks, and Tulloch

[102] NRS GD96/78.
[103] *CSP Scot*, vi, 322 (Sir William Drury, marshal of Berwick, to Lord Burghley).
[104] Anderson, *Stewart Earls*, 268.
[105] NRS CS7/30, f. 321.

obtained a divorce, both in Orkney and in Edinburgh, receiving a final decreet on 31 March 1565.[106] This was however at the end of much wrangling, with Sinclair designated Halcro's spouse as early as March 1563.[107] They went on to have two daughters, to add to Magnus's own three natural sons.[108]

Margaret Sinclair was the daughter of James Sinclair of Sanday, brother of Edward Sinclair of Strom and acknowledged, if mercurial and brutal, leader of the victorious forces at Summerdale. By this time, March 1563, she had been involved in dealings of her own. She was to remain a landowner in her own right, designated 'of Linksness', her father's old estate and the site of his distracted suicide.[109] She renounced her liferent and conjunct fee in lands in Stenness to Patrick Bellenden, the actual formalities to be the responsibility of Magnus Halcro.[110] Halcro for his part assigned to her the remainder of a 19-year tack, dated 22 October, of a wide variety of lands in Rousay, as well as the Bu of Cairston and the island of Cava.[111] This, for Halcro, concluded a deal with Bellenden and a settlement for his new wife.

* * *

The rest of Robert's long letter of 31 March 1568 was a catalogue of complaints: Archibald Douglas, subdean of Orkney, had granted Patrick Bellenden a charter of the lands of his subdeanery, despite Robert having 'first promiss thairof'; the lords of session had decreed payment of pension to the parson of Penicuik for services which Robert felt he had not performed, as well as denying him *thirds* (the proportion of income paid to landowners from the spiritualities of ecclesiastical land now in their possession) for undisclosed reasons; Bellenden owed him six chalders of wheat, bere and oats for the teinds of Dalry, and he agreed to receive them in the form of six lasts of *cost* (a mixture of ⅔ malt and ⅓ meal, and a common element in Orkney payment). He was also highly displeased with Robert Boswall, a skipper, for letting two suspects of the Darnley murder slip through his hands. He had handed over to Boswall the laird of Beanston (Patrick Hepburn) and his followers, to be taken to Leith under guard to meet their fate; Boswall had instead turned them loose on the south coast of the Moray Firth.[112] He also,

[106]  NRS CS7/34, f. 15; CC8/2/1.
[107]  *Prot. Bk Gilbert Grote*, 229.
[108]  *REO*, 448.
[109]  Anderson, *Stewart Earls*, 10–11.
[110]  NRS RH2/1/20/145.
[111]  *Pro. Bk Gilbert Grote*, 229.
[112]  Patrick Hepburn of Beanston, follower of Bothwell in his flight to the Northern Isles, captured by Robert Stewart in Shetland. Alleged to be one of the murderers of Darnley 'with the hands' (*CSP Scot*, ii, 321).

unknown to Robert, 'tuke away' Edmund Blackadder, a notorious pirate,[113] for whom Gilbert Balfour had to answer. All this had been reported to the regent as Robert's fault.

Bellenden ignored the letter, at which Robert marvelled 'greitulye'. The justice clerk had already written to William Henderson, from Glasgow on 17 April, nine days before the date of the letter he had received from Robert, and it was clear that Bellenden's view was that his own letter stood, and required an answer. Robert's next approach to him spoke with Henderson's voice (letter no. 19, 1 June 1568). This extraordinary letter has already been referred to for mentioning Patrick Bellenden's attempt to convene a band, together with Magnus Halcro *et al.*, against Lord Robert. It included a few lines about the justice clerk's financial affairs; but then, almost certainly with Robert at his elbow, Henderson outlined new concrete reasons for what had happened. These give a different slant on events, and embed the cathedral doings in the whole power struggle Robert was waging against the bishop, as well as Patrick Bellenden's role in this. Patrick's and Halcro's intention was now given as 'the hail motyve and occasioun of the takyng of the kirk'; this was a far cry from Robert's initial response that events were without his control or consent. What had happened was a clear pre-emption of a possible assault on the steeple by Patrick, and a more explicit explanation of the indignation against him expressed in Robert's earlier letters.

Particular stress was laid on these events which would, in Henderson's words, put both Robert and the bishop to great 'inconvenientis' if not quickly remedied. Henderson had shown Bellenden's remarks to Robert, and had found that his lordship, on the one hand, was prepared to offer as much satisfaction for what had happened as had ever been made in Scotland, provided that his servants' safety was guaranteed. On the other hand, he would not allow those servants to be harmed by legal action, nor would he restore the steeple. Robert might have made a whole array of enemies, but he remained intransigent in the face of the bishop and his supporters. He was confident that the bishop could not harm him without Bellenden's assistance. In Henderson's words to the justice clerk , 'ye ar the man only that he feiris and nocht the bischop'. Robert was happy to negotiate with Bellenden through his chamberlain, Adam Bell, if the bishop would do the same.

Then the narrative takes an extraordinary turn. Still through the mouth of Henderson, Robert's own voice can be heard even more plainly. He was willing to negotiate:

---

[113] Edmund Blackadder, occasional servant of the earl of Bothwell and Robert Stewart (noted in the 1575 complaints against Robert (Ballantyne and Smith 1195–1579, 163)). Alleged to be one of the murderers of Darnley 'with the hands' (*CSP Scot*, ii, 321).

bot gif he persavis na thing bot rigour usit aganis him, he wil do all the displesour that he dow or may aganes the bischop and his parttakars, and wil caus him to be evil answerit of his lyffyng. And sayis planely that he douttis nocht quha cumis in his contrar gif my lord regent wil stand equal till him, and or he be put fra his rycht and title quhilk he hes of Orknay he will wair his lyff as he affeirmis. And all that wil pretend to depryfe him thairof he wil nocht spair to tak thair lyiffis and he may. And he is ane man that wil get money assistars and it is dangerous deilying wyth him.

It seems unlikely that Henderson thought this tirade up for himself.

The letter calmed down, and Henderson returned to Robert's familiar themes, seeking Bellenden's mediation, particularly in the matter of exchange of estates between himself and the bishop, and repeating his request that Bellenden speak to the regent, enabling him to come south without hindrance. This he hoped to do on his return from Shetland when he would speak personally to the regent, as well as settling matters with the bishop and 'satisfie him be your lordships advysing and mak ane end of all things bayth with him and you and your broder (whom he also intended to invite to Orkney), and wyth my lord regent for his awin effairs'. He would also seek to have the men held responsible for the cathedral incident relaxed from the horning which the bishop had taken out against them.

* * *

There is now another gap in the sequence of the letters, between 1 June 1568 (letter no. 19) and 21 May 1569 (letter no. 21). As previously, this may reflect the facts of the matter, there being little need for correspondence at a distance. For almost a year there is only one letter, but one which indicates that a quite separate, more urgent, matter had arisen. In Edinburgh, on 21 September 1568, Adam Bothwell wrote to Napier of Merchiston (letter no. 20). He spoke to Napier of 'the rigorous answer and refuiss that ye gat quhairof I wes not wele apayit'. What had displeased Bothwell was a refusal by the authorities to allow Napier to leave Edinburgh, due to his involvement with the curious affair of Sir William Stewart of Luthrie, Lord Lyon, who was charged, and ultimately executed, for treason and using witchcraft to conspire against the Regent Moray. Napier was said to be involved (as was Gilbert Balfour). He was cleared, but was bound over to remain within two miles of the capital.[114]

There was more to Bothwell's letter than a mere expression of frustration or disappointment, and the rest of it gives a clue to a particular state of affairs which has echoes at the present time of writing (January 2022). The capital was in the throes of the 'pest', and Napier, having seemingly avoided a charge

---

[114]  Goodare, 'Archibald Napier', *ODNB*.

of treason, remained in potential personal danger. The plague was endemic in Scotland throughout the sixteenth century, but this outbreak, which occurred in the 1560s, according to Lindsay of Pitscottie, spread and lingered. Lindsay states it arrived in Leith, probably from the continent, then spread to Kirkcaldy, where many died, as well as to Burntisland, Dysart, Anstruther and beyond. It then re-crossed the Forth to Edinburgh. Fairs and market were 'cryit doon' and, as will be seen, the session did not meet because of the 'contagious pest'.[115] As regards Napier's position, Bothwell spoke darkly of 'evil favoraris' who had put him there, trapped between 'twa grete inconvenientis'. These were, firstly, his forced confinement to his 'awin place' – Merchiston Castle, the tower house which still exists today at the heart of Napier University's Merchiston Campus – and, secondly, the danger that, as the plague raged, the whole open country south of Edinburgh would attract large numbers of the poorest people of the town who, fleeing the burgh, would overrun Napier's lands and infect his servants, putting all in 'maist extreme danger', particularly his children, because it was the young 'quhais bluid is in maist perrell to be infectit first'. Bothwell noted that it had been Napier's intention to send his own children away to lands which he possessed near Menteith, where Bothwell wished Napier could retire 'without offence of authoritie … sua that your houss gat na skaith'.

With this option forbidden, Bothwell saw a middle way. Without leaving the Edinburgh area, Napier should evacuate Merchiston, and lease a house north of the burgh, in country districts like Craigcrook (Gray Cruik), Inverleith or Wardie. He should close up 'your houssis, your grangis, your barnis and all, and suffer na man cum thairin' until the danger was past – in other words, self-isolate himself and his family, and quarantine his house. In the meantime, he would have to live on his normal revenues, and such funds as he could gather from his lands in Menteith or the Lennox. Failure to do so would bring ruin.

What Napier actually did, we do not know. A year later, according to the correspondence, the situation may have calmed somewhat, but there were still problems. These were not so much in Edinburgh as in the neighbouring and independent burgh of the Canongate, of which Bothwell was now superior. Here, the behaviour of individuals was endangering all. Bothwell wrote from Holyroodhouse on 26 September 1569 (letter no. 28) to Bellenden of Auchnoull, also a superior of the Canongate. In a postscript, he complained that those who lived in the area were in danger of their lives through 'the licentius using of tham that hes the pest upone tham, and yit laifis nocht of to repair in all cumpaneis as thocht thay had na infirmetie'. Immediately on closing his previous letter and dispatching the messenger, he had been approached by a deputation of the 'haill honest men' of the Canongate, and he wrote to Bellenden again the very next day (letter no. 29, 27 September 1569).

---

[115] Pitscottie, *Historie*, ii, 213.

The worthy townsfolk emphasised 'haivelie' that neither their lives nor those of their children were safe, so long as there was no punishment for those, infected but somehow not afflicted, who wilfully spread the pest. They cited as an example the sister of one John Hart, a merchant burgess of the Canongate and prominent citizen, with whom Bellenden had had previous dealings.[116] His sister was thought responsible for the infecting of his house, the death of his three children and the 'gypertie' of John Hart himself. She had done this, it was alleged, because she had lately 'reparit to and fra with honest men nochtwithstanding that scho had the pest upone hir'.

Bothwell had previously approached Mr David McGill, bailie of the Canongate, on the matter, and was seeking a public proclamation by the regent requiring all who knew themselves to be infected to report to magistrates within hours *under the pane of deith*, since there was no law that could threaten the capital penalty. Bothwell and his burghers at length secured a letter from the regent, allowing that if any of the offenders mentioned by Bothwell were put to death, this would be allowable, even though they had not in fact committed a capital offence.

Bothwell also offered a stark contrast between 'the Canongate' and 'our nychtburs the toune off Edinburgh'. In the capital, the inhabitants had been so well 'preservit' that 'thair haill foull folk' were to be brought back into town, many with their 'clengeour' (cleanser, one deemed to have the power of curing those suffering from the plague), leaving none behind on the 'mure', i.e. the open country to the south, perhaps what are now the Meadows, Bruntsfield Links, as well as Merchiston and beyond. In the lands of the regality of the Canongate on the other hand, there were more than 40 'foull personis' in Leith, more than 80 beside Bellenden's 'awin toune of the Cannomillis', and others who had come to the regality 'quhilkis all ar infectit be sick lawless and godless persons'. He sought assistance, since he was under pressure either to put all offenders to an assize, or suffer a mass exodus from the regality, with the uproar this would cause elsewhere. He was forced to spend large sums for the upkeep of persons that he dared not commit to a common prison, and would appreciate word by Thursday evening (two days thence), as he did not know how to proceed till he heard from the lords. Whether Bothwell got what he desired, or whether anyone, such as John Hart's sister, ever suffered the supreme penalty for alleged wilful spreading of the plague, is not disclosed. The desire for extreme deterrence may seem excessive, but the need to isolate and to quarantine, and the possibility that the disease could somehow be 'cleansed' from its victims, is with us still.

During the time of plague, and of the letter describing it, between Bothwell's two letters to Bellenden, June 1568 and May 1569, much had changed which

---

[116] NRAS 1100 bdl 1612, item 4. He and other merchants were to conclude a contract with Robert in the 1580s (NRS RD1/34, ff. 278–80).

does not surface in the letters. Adam Bothwell had managed to pursue Robert before the lords of session about the cathedral incident. Robert was put to the horn[117] and, on 11 June 1568, Bothwell had received a privy seal gift of Lord Robert's escheat for failure to present a number of his servants before the privy council in connection with the cathedral affair and taking of the bishop's 'place and yairdis thairof'.[118] These men, their names noted earlier, were plainly for the most part clients of Robert. James and Patrick Monteith were nephews of James Monteith in Easter Kerse; Walter Bruce was a natural son of the laird of Clackmannan and thus a relative of Robert's half-brother Laurence Bruce of Cultmalindie. Bruce, and Thomas Robeson, were to remain servants of Lord Robert for many years. David Scollay and William Sclater were Orcadians, named in the court action with a number of other 'cuntrie' men. Only George Dundas, son of the laird of Dundas, is without any traceable link to Robert, whether through Holyrood or the north.[119]

This response by the bishop to the rant in letter no. 19 was resolute enough, but the reference to Robert's 'money assistars' was not idle, and Robert's reply was swift. By July, he had appeared in the Canongate, and in the course of September 1568, he achieved almost everything he desired. On the 17th, he concluded a contract with Bellenden whereby the latter relinquished his Birsay lands in favour of Jean Kennedy in liferent, and their daughter Mary, in fee, in exchange for the lands of the Kerse. There was a charter of excambion the following day.[120] On the 26th, James Monteith, designated of Nether Saltcoats, was granted a respite for his part in the cathedral shootings.[121]

On the following days, 27 and 30 September, Robert in Edinburgh, and Adam Bothwell, at Fastcastle on his way south on royal business, concluded a detailed contract regarding an exchange of their respective lands, each element hedged about with conditions.[122] Robert took burden for his wife and children, legitimate and natural, who received a pension from the Holyrood thirds. Bothwell granted to Robert in liferent and Henry Stewart in fee all the lands, mills and fishings of the bishopric not already feued to Bellenden, Balfour and the rest. He also agreed to grant Robert a lifetime tack of the bishopric teinds, and would also deliver to him the castle and 'place of the Yairds', and grant Robert the offices of bailiary and justiciary within the bishopric, as well as the constabulary and keeping of the 'Yairds', in this case referred to as 'the castle'. In exchange, Robert granted to the bishop all his family's rights to the teinds of the abbey of Holyroodhouse, particularly those

---

[117] NRS JC1/13/99, 100.
[118] *RSS*, vi, no. 306.
[119] A George Dundas does appear later, but not until the end of the century, in Earl Patrick's time (NRS NP1/36, f. 67).
[120] NRS CS7/42, ff. 344–7, RH6/2129; printed *OSR*, 162, no. 68.
[121] *RSS*, vi, no. 505.
[122] NRS CS7/42, ff. 340–4.

of Broughton, Inverleith and Wardie, and disclaimed all right to a pension of £1000 reserved to him from the abbey, though he retained the right to take up the pension if the bishop should predecease him. It was also agreed that any revenues already uptaken by either side at the time of excambion would be refunded. Robert was to 'put into oblivioun forever' any antipathy to named followers of the bishop. These included, predictably enough, Patrick Bellenden and Magnus Halcro of Brough, but also a number of others. He would not only be reconciled with them, but would maintain them in peaceful possession of their lands and be a good lord and master. All this was to have an increasingly hollow ring.

The documents laying this out were inserted into the register of acts and decreets of the court of session on 3 October. In them, there was no reference to the transfer of Holyrood lands to Bothwell, matching the granting of those of the bishopric to Robert, but on the same day, at Ayton on the bishop's progress south, a precept was granted under the privy seal for a letter to the said Adam granting him 'the abbey of Holyrood, vacant by the resignation of Lord Robert Stewart, and appointing him commendator for life, reserving to the said Lord Robert a yearly pension of £1000'.[123] By July the following year, Bothwell was designating himself commendator of Holyroodhouse (letter no. 26, 8 July 1569). Finally, on 28 February 1570, Bothwell granted Robert (in liferent, his son Henry in fee) a charter of the bishopric lands of Orkney,[124] together with the teindsheaves. He also granted a tack of the teinds of the bishopric, for which Lord Robert agreed to various conditions, including upholding the kirk of Kirkwall, the school and the castle of the Yards, and payment to the bishop of 500 merks yearly.[125] The business of exchange, of excambion, was now seemingly complete. However, the charter from Bothwell to Robert was unsubscribed by the chapter at Kirkwall, and it was some time – two years in fact – before a new and final version was issued.

Not till 21 May 1569 do we encounter a new personal letter from Robert himself, now back in Kirkwall, to Sir John Bellenden (letter no. 21). It was a response to one from the justice clerk, which sought for Robert to implement the escheat of John Houston to his servant George Bellenden[126] of the goods of the subdeanery of Orkney, forfeited by Houston as the result of a dispute, and

---

[123] *RSS*, vi, no. 506.

[124] NRAS 1100, bdl 1625.

[125] NRS RH6/2131; *BUKS*, i, 166–7.

[126] Servant of Sir John Bellenden's brother (letter no. 21), presumably Sir Patrick. He should not be confused with Mr George Bellenden, chanter of Glasgow, and vicar of Dunrossness (see Appendix). George Bellenden, simply designated 'ane honorabill man', appears as sheriff depute of Orkney 'for the tym' on 21 December 1563 (*REO*, 117, no. lii), presumably as understudy for Sir Patrick, who briefly held the office of sheriff. Patrick, on the other hand, acted as factor to Mr George as vicar of Dunrossness during his absence from Scotland, 11 August 1565 (Ballantyne and Smith 1195–1579, 109, no. 148).

the subject of a gift to him of some weeks earlier.[127] Robert was intransigent. As far as he was concerned, he was now infeft with all the escheats of Orkney and Shetland 'as the kyng or queine mycht gif the samin'. If Bellenden had been mindful of this 'undoutit rycht', he would not have asked. The same applied to continuing complaints of the bishop. Robert stated that Bellenden knew his powers, 'quhilk I wilbe werreay layth to pas fra', and he intended to waste no more paper and ink in correspondence, since it did little good.

It was clear however that, while he had achieved much of what he wanted, there were still problems, and he believed that Bellenden should have worked harder to put him 'furtht of cummers', since he was willing to fulfil all the conditions of the contracts with Sir Patrick and Bishop Bothwell. If he was not sent documents, sealed and subscribed, so that he could take sasine, it would be to his great 'hinderance', and of no help to Bellenden or the bishop. He had heard that all his procurators had refused to handle his cases, but any action against him was unnecessary, for when he came south, after his customary summer visit to Shetland, he would fulfil all his parts of the contract made in the sight of the regent and Bellenden himself 'but ony proces of law'. If any part was disputed it would be 'of nane availl becaus of null defence', Bellenden's response would let Robert know 'gif your lordship be my assurit frend or nocht'.

A few days later, on 2 June 1569 (letter no. 22), came the voice of Magnus Halcro, writing to Bellenden from Kirkwall with 'angir and ane impatient hart'. His feelings were the reason he had not written for some time since this 'blak excambioun' was made, because his part in what had happened was 'mair hevyar' than he was prepared to express in writing. We have already seen something of those activities. Halcro had been chanter (precentor) of Orkney since at least 1556,[128] and had remained a loyal servant of the bishop and Bellenden throughout. He had had no desire to have 'changit maistiris'; his allegiance remained with the bishop 'nochtwythstanding all biganis' and the uncompensated troubles he had encountered in the bishop's service. Nevertheless, it was best to accept all that happened, and he looked for his lordship's 'gud mynd and support quhairin he may nocht hurt him self'. That said, he did not regret all his efforts on Bellenden's behalf. Fulsomely, he said that even if what he had done 'war ane hundreth tymes mair', it would have been time well spent 'for I had nevir samekle of ony mannis geir as I haif had of youris' – beyond his deserving. He therefore, without wishing to seem to flatter, pledged his continued faith to give Bellenden such service as he could. These comments, coupled with the date Halcro appears to have received advancement in Orkney, might suggest that he, the Orcadian churchman, had formed part of Bellenden's designs on bishopric wealth from the start,

---

serving both justice clerk and bishop, and had been gratefully rewarded for his efforts.

He still required Bellenden's assistance, however. Back in 1555, he had received the lands of Brough, on the south coast of the island of Rousay (whence he took his territorial designation)[129], as well as others in Rousay, Cairston in Stromness, and the island of Cava, in 1563.[130] The original Brough grant, from its previous proprietor Magnus Craigie, was of udal land,[131] and was thus Halcro's possession outright. Halcro had added to this a tack, received from the bishop, of further Rousay lands in nearby Skaill and Westness, worth five pennylands each. The Rousay parts of the two grants, udal and tack, were close together, and now lay run-rig (in strips, to be redistributed annually to ensure fair shares to tenants of fertile and poorer land). Halcro now understood that the lands of the tack were to be feued to Lord Robert, as superior of the whole bishopric estate. Halcro sought Bellenden's assistance to retain the tack lands, or at least the 5d of Skaill. He had no desire to be in 'rig and rendell' with Robert, though typically he did not commit any details to paper – saying only darkly, 'gif your lordship knew quhat is and apperantlie wilbe amang us'. If Bellenden did indeed help, Halcro would come south with Lord Robert when he came back from Shetland. In the meantime, he could let Robert know what Halcro was thinking – possibly because he feared telling the noble lord himself.

* * *

Robert must have returned from Shetland very soon after, since he is found writing to Bellenden from Kirkwall three days later, on 5 June (letter no. 23). He had sent a female servant, Janet Livingston, south on his business, in particular to fetch his eldest son, Henry (Hary), and bring him north from the guardianship of Bellenden, who was asked to deliver him to her. Robert was still at pains to settle affairs with Patrick Bellenden. He had dismissed James Monteith from his service, since he had heard from George Bellenden that if he did this Patrick was prepared to do his 'dewtie' to Robert and 'sal find me to be ane gud maister to him'. He sought Bellenden's help, should Monteith complain to the regent about his treatment. In fact Monteith, a member of the Monteith family who occupied various lands in the barony of the Kerse (notably Saltcoats, now swallowed up in the Grangemouth refinery), was a longstanding follower of Robert's, probably arrived in Orkney with him, and has already been noted as implicated in the attack on the cathedral. In fact,

[129]  NRS GD1/45/1.
[130]  *Prot. Bk Gilbert Grote*, 229.
[131]  NRS E108/6.

despite Robert's protestations, Monteith was later to reappear in the north, as was Edmund Blackadder, the subject of one of Robert's earlier complaints.

The remainder of Robert's letter was concerned with the continuing disputes with Bothwell over his obligations under the terms of the exchange of estates. A particular bone of contention was the conversion of annual payments in the charters from kind into cash. One particular case was the charter Robert had prepared of the lands of Shetland, which the bishop had complained was 'in deminusion of the rentall'. In Shetland (and Orkney), payment of rents and duties was reckoned in units of what has been described as 'coinless currency'.[132] What appear in written texts to be currency units – the Shetland merk, which contained 12 shillings, each of which was worth in turn 12 pennies – in fact stood for quantities of commodities in kind. The arithmetic of Shetland denominations was not unlike that of Scotland, though the Scots merk was worth 13s 4d. By the period in question, there were 'pounds' in use, each presumably worth 20s. The annual payment for the rents and duties of Shetland was reckoned as 19 pounds and 10 shillings in time-honoured Shetland reckoning. The commodities which this 'currency' represented consisted of two thirds of the whole (value 260 shillings) in *packs* of *wadmell*, coarse cloth peculiar to Shetland and the Faroes, the rest in barrels of butter. In quantity of wadmell, this amounted to 26 packs (10s a pack). The quantity of the other third, in butter (value 130s), is less exact. Robert refers to butter measure as being in *lispunds*, each shilling in butter being two lispunds. Each lispund was approximately one twelfth of a barrel. If therefore the remainder, in butter, amounted to 130s, this represented 260 lispunds, or 21⅔ barrels.

Translation of this 'coinless' currency into hard Scots cash seems to have been by a straight conversion of the Shetland sums, using an unknown exchange rate, rather than by looking at how much the quantities might fetch at market. The charter stated that each pound in Shetland coinless currency would fetch 35s 6½d and a third part of a halfpenny usual money of the realm of Scotland. Robert justified this to Bellenden by referring to 'all few chartours' in the rest of Scotland, where the *reddendo* was couched in bolls and chalders of produce, and yet the value this represented was quoted in 'sobir' (reasonably calculated) money. This might be diminution of any *profit* this could fetch on an open market, even though it was not diminution of the sum of the *rental*. The return noted in the charter contained the whole sum of the rental 'albeit the pryce of siluer be sett less nor may be gottin for it'. If that was a cause to reject his charter then the same could be said of all the feu charters in Scotland where victual was turned into cash. Let any future bishop seek to reduce it, he would stand by it.

---

[132] Smith, *Toons and Tenants*, xvi–ii.

Five days later, Robert wrote again to Bellenden (letter no. 24, 10 June 1569). Since his previous letter he had understood that Bishop Bothwell would do nothing about his charters. As a result he had written to the regent to pressure Bothwell to seal and subscribe the documents and give them either into his own custody or that of Bellenden, to remain while he performed his other obligations. In the meantime, Robert was losing much more money from his former Holyrood lands, including the teinds of Broughton, than he was receiving in recompense. Rather than lose out altogether, 'I sall rather pass to my awin and lat the bischop pass to his.' As far as Bellenden himself was concerned, he repeated the matter of his relations with Patrick Bellenden, and again sought the justice clerk's assistance, should the disgraced James Monteith make complaint to the regent, as Robert had lost £400 through James's 'intromission with my geir', among other actions. He assured Bellenden that he would fulfil all obligations to him, but there was another matter. Now Robert heard that the justice clerk's son Lewis had been 'seasit' in the Birsay lands, which were supposed to be the subject of the exchange with Sir John for the Holyrood Kerse lands. This placed Bellenden's part of the Holyrood-Kerse deal in doubt, unless there was a condition that Lewis revoke the charter on reaching maturity.

* * *

The next letter in the series is from Bishop Bothwell to Sir John Bellenden, on 14 June 1569 (no. 25). Bellenden was in Inverness, probably on a justice-ayre. The business of the excambion was far from over, yet it was clear that Bothwell had other important issues on his mind, while Robert's activities continued in the background. Some of these issues were personal, others connected with his work as a lord of session. In both capacities, like Robert, he sought from Bellenden assistance and advice, as well as representations with the regent. He was anxious for word.

Firstly, he was in a legal dispute with the laird of Dundas. Its nature is not disclosed, though the laird's son, George, had been named as one of the cathedral party. There were not enough lords of session in town to hear the action (their absence possibly due to the plague), but within eight days he understood that 'my Lord of Colddingame' – John Maitland of Thirlestane[133] – would arrive to provide a quorum, and it was important that Bellenden help him to prepare materials for his defence, since he was assured that the lords would proceed in the case without him 'to my gret hurte'.

Secondly, since Sir John had left town, some Edinburgh bailies, 'young men ... inexpert of sic officis', had three times trespassed on the jurisdiction of the Canongate, in order to make arrests. This would have meant great

---

[133] Lee, 'Maitland of Thirlestane', *ODNB*.

dishonour to him but, knowing the regent, who was absent, would find disorder 'oncouth', he had managed quietly to settle matters. He again sought Bellenden's offices in making representations to the regent, this time seeking a 'wretting' to Edinburgh's officials, preventing them from interference in his jurisdictions of Leith and the Canongate.

Thirdly, he sought further assistance from the justice clerk in supporting his friend, the dean of Moray, against the oppressions of his own relative the sheriff (of Moray) and his followers. Finally, after a matter regarding Robert, to which we will return shortly, he was in dispute with Edward Prestoun, barber burgess of the Canongate, concerning his pension as barber of the abbey and convent of Holyrood, granted by Robert Stewart as commendator on 6 June 1560.[134]

His one piece of business with Lord Robert was a simple vexation. He had issued a summons, seeking recompense for the intromissions of Robert and his chamberlain in 'this yeiris leving' of Holyrood. This had met with no success, and he had raised a further action. He wanted Bellenden to write to Robert as quickly as possible, warning him that the bishop had put letters in the hands of the clerk of session. Such was Bothwell's impatience that he wished that the bearer of his letter would not stay more than one night with Bellenden, before bringing the letter to Robert.

Bothwell had still not finished his catalogue of 'besynes'. The letter itself, written for most of the first two pages in a neat script, probably that of a clerk, suddenly changes into what may be his own, much looser hand for the rest of the letter and on into a lengthy postscript, this time on yet another matter. Bothwell had agreed to arbitrate on a dispute between 'my Lord of Newbottell' (Mr Mark Ker, the commendator)[135] and the laird of Traquair (John Stewart)[136] concerning a piece of land called Jonstoun.[137] This was not a success, and Bothwell announced his intention of referring the matter to the regent. Traquair was not happy, but said he would 'mak na truble'; nevertheless, the bishop understood that, on their way home from the encounter, Traquair's brother slew Newbattle's shepherd on the debated land. The character of the postscript, its length and the apparent haste in writing, suggests that the bishop was greatly exercised by what had happened.

On 8 July he wrote again to Bellenden, now in Aberdeen, on familiar issues (letter no. 26). Regarding his ongoing problems with the town of Edinburgh, he reproached Bellenden for not sending him a copy of a letter from the regent to the town, whose leaders were still causing him problems. More important were the activities of Lord Robert, who was clearly increasing his grip on the

---

[134] NRS CS7/45, f. 40.

[135] *Scots Peerage*, v, 455.

[136] Ibid., viii, 401.

[137] Unidentified, though it has been suggested that these were the lands now occupied by Johnstounburn House, near Fala.

Northern Isles. Bothwell's servant and former bishopric chamberlain,[138] William Bothwell (of Quhelpsyde),[139] had come south to tell the bishop that, while Robert had spoken 'fair wordis', he had forbidden him to take up revenues still owed to the bishop, or allowed the commons to make any payment in Orkney or, probably, in Shetland, 'sua that I may be eittin up be my creditors' (letter no. 26, 8 July 1569). Bishop Adam had raised letters against Robert, but William Bothwell had been unable to find a notary in the whole of Orkney to serve them. The bishop had sought from Robert whether he would 'poynd for my dettis or nocht', i.e. enforce payments still owed to him from his time as bishop. This Robert could easily do, 'for he is becum terrable to all that is within that boindis'. This appeal had had no effect, and the bishop had finally had letters served. Robert replied 'put me to the horne quhen ye will, ye sall get na thing of me'. He had also made revocations, on his own behalf and that of his wife and children, intending to annul all that had been done previously. 'Ye knaw your man and his humour', Bothwell said to Bellenden. It would be in the justice clerk's interests to provide such remedy as he could. Later (letter no. 28, 26 September 1569) Bothwell was to thank his relative for letters he had written to Orkney regarding the gathering of estate arrears. Unfortunately the selected messenger charged with their uptake 'hes na haist', for whatever reason, and was now so 'cankrait' (ill-natured) that he will do nothing. The bishop now regarded the matter as out of his hands and in those of the justice clerk.

In his letter of 8 July, the last paragraph, like the end of his previous letter, spilled over into a postscript in a different hand, again possibly his own. It was much shorter, however, and merely seemed to add information that had more recently come to hand. It did not seek any particular assistance from Bellenden, but it did move to a wholly different matter – Bothwell's own difficulties in governance of the abbey. He was seeking permission from the kirk to allow the return of 'channonis' (former Augustinians of the pre-Reformation abbey) to serve in his kirks, which were in great need. The first *Book of Discipline* had been accepted by the Protestant lords on the proviso that 'beneficed men who conformed should enjoy their livings for life provided that they supported ministers from their revenues'.[140] This arrangement, as it turned out unsatisfactory, was superseded by the system of collection of 'thirds of benefices' (a third each of the fruits of every benefice for the upkeep of the kirk, the crown and 'old possessors'). Bothwell had already made moves in Orkney, where he had used his cathedral dignitaries as ministers of the new kirk. Such a process had been far from smooth. There were doubts over the true religious allegiance of the former friar Francis Bothwell,[141] and it is possible that John Kincaid's differ-

---

[138] NRS RD1/19, ff. 95–9.
[139] Whelpside – lands west of Balerno, near Edinburgh.
[140] *Accts of Thirds of Benefices*, ix.
[141] *BUKS*, 112.

ences with the new dispensation had not solely been caused by antipathy to Gilbert Balfour. Nevertheless, Bothwell now sought to do something similar in the new benefice he had been forced to accept. In the case of Holyrood, this proved unworkable; according to Bothwell's postscript, those canons who had embraced reform had refused to serve as ministers, while the 'papistis' had said they would as soon swear allegiance to 'Mr Knox' as to Bothwell.

These problems were to continue. On 26 September 1569, Bishop Bothwell wrote to Sir John (letter no. 28) on his difficulties in actually paying his ministers. The minister of the abbey of Holyrood complained that he could not obtain his stipend. He was not concerned that the amount involved was less than it had been (though it was), but that previous procedure was not being followed. In the past, he had received 200 merks, of which the bishop paid 120 merks and the 'collectour' (of thirds of benefices) paid the rest. Now John Knox and 'ane of his collegis' had stopped payment by the collector and told the minister to seek the rest of his stipend from Bothwell 'in quhais kirk he did the service'. It was true that Bothwell's predecessor (presumably the abbot or, more recently and ironically, Robert Stewart as commendator) had authorised this sum, but Bothwell complained that 'my leving was mekle less than it was in his tyme'. Arguments about the disposition of the old church revenues between the kirk and the various landed interests, as well as Robert and Bellenden's manoeuvres concerning the ecclesiastical estates north and south, notably Birsay in Orkney and Kerse in the Holyrood lands, were having their effect.

Being urged to come to some agreement, Bothwell sought to show that payment was in fact the responsibility of the burgh of the Canongate 'quha ever of befoir, ya in the middis off papistrie' contributed large sums. Because Bellenden was out of town, Bothwell had written for advice to 'my Lord General', who happened to be an elder in the abbey kirk.[142] He also consulted the ministers of Glasgow and St Johnstone. All agreed that it was necessary to ask the regent to issue a commission, similar to that by the former queen directed to various notables, including Bellenden, Napier and Bothwell himself, to determine what burghs should contribute for the upkeep of their minister. Until such could be procured, there was little to be done, though he pitied the poverty of the minister and hoped for a quick conclusion.

\* \* \*

We now hear, for the first and only time, from Patrick Bellenden in person, writing to his brother (letter no. 27, 24 July 1569). He was in Ayrshire, at

---

[142] This was presumably the current 'Generall' (chief administrator) of the mint – a post Archibald Napier was later to occupy. David Forrest was general of the mint between 1564 and 1572 (*Records of the Coinage of Scotland*, 85, 244).

Dalquharran in Carrick, no doubt at the dwelling of Sir Hugh Kennedy of Girvanmains. (This letter has already been referred to as indicating that the Bellenden brothers were both married to daughters of Sir Hugh.) Patrick's main theme was his continuing efforts to come to an agreement with Robert Stewart. He spoke of Robert's desire that he return to Orkney, for which he, rather sardonically, relayed his thanks to Robert through Sir John 'for in deid I do esteime (as of necessitie I man) Orknay to be my peculiar dwelling', adding that his absence from the islands was 'nocht for feir of ony enemy I had in thay partis'. Like Bothwell, he sought his brother's assistance in dealing with Robert, who had fulfilled no part of previous agreements, 'sen ye ken the natour of the man, and how oft he is able to brek promiss', causing him great financial losses. If these could be fulfilled, particularly regarding the sheriffship of Orkney and the lands of Stenness, he could promise faithful service to his lordship, and seek Sir John's surety for this. A later postscript urged Sir John to approach Lord Robert at the earliest opportunity.

Then, suddenly and incongruously, Patrick passed to a quite different matter —condolences on the death of Sir John's daughter Katharine: 'I assuir your lordship I wes sa sare as in all my lyf I never wes sa havely oppressit.' This is a curious interpolation, as he then quickly passes on to other diverse matters. It is not, however, the only example of these unlooked-for priorities. On 6 October of the same year, Bothwell wrote to Bellenden, mainly concerning his woes in gathering arrears in the north (letter no. 32). In his last lines, he remarked: 'Margaret your dauchter is verray seik and hes hir hartlie to your lordship, bot I trw it be hir moderis seknes.'

This comment might seem slightly ominous, suggesting that Sir John's daughter was suffering from the same malady that had carried off Barbara Kennedy, his second wife, almost five years before. He gives no further details. The curiously inconsequential treatment of her indisposition is striking. There are a number of issues surrounding these daughters of Sir John;[143] but the letter, when seen against letter no. 34 (14 October 1569), is misleading. In the later writing, Margaret is again mentioned as sending her regards, but now she is referred to as 'your dauchter, my wyif'. Bellenden had no daughter Margaret. Bothwell's wife (d. 1608) was indeed called Margaret, but was in fact the daughter of John Murray of Touchadam.[144] The inference therefore is that she was Bellenden's god-daughter. It suggests too that Bothwell, as a close relative of Bellenden, might have known his wife from a relatively young age. Also, given that Margaret Murray still had 40 years to live, her malady,

---

[143] The *Scots Peerage* mentions only one daughter Catherine (sic), the daughter of Sir John's first wife, said to have died young. If Katharine is the same individual, dying as she did in mid-1569, she must have been in her teens or more, since her mother had predeceased her by at least 15 years. There is no mention at all of a daughter Margaret.

[144] Shaw, 'Adam Bothwell', *ODNB*.

inherited from her mother the lady of Touchadam, and known about by Bothwell, was chronic, possibly feminine in origin, but not life-threatening.

Sir Patrick's letter then mentioned the position of Sanders Purves, who had been a servant of Sir Patrick in the latter's capacity as clerk of the cocquet for Edinburgh. This post, in charge of the whole customs, weights and measures for the capital, had been granted for life to Sir John Bellenden in 1556.[145] So far as Sir John was concerned, this was largely a sinecure, and his brother seems to have been more directly involved in administration; he was himself named as clerk in 1572, prior to his brother's death.[146] Sanders Purves (elsewhere [letter no. 34] he is Alexander) was presumably responsible for the day-to-day routine of the office, but he had now been excommunicated 'for non adhering to the religioun'. This had plainly displeased Patrick, who would replace him 'sen the office is myne and I man answer for it', and he would rely on a personally-appointed deputy who would serve him appropriately. Again, he sought his brother's support, asking him to send a ticket that would enable him to claim his pension from the clerkship, 'for I haif bene lang fra hame and hes mekill to do thairwith'.

* * *

The postscript to Bothwell's previous letter to Bellenden had concerned the perils of the plague, as noted before; much of his next, written the following day (letter no. 29, 27 September 1569), continued the theme. Then it abruptly moved the discussion back to more 'bissines of my Lord Robertis'. Bellenden had suggested that his cousin 'consult with wyiss men' on the matter. Unfortunately, Bothwell could only find one advocate in town, Clement Little, a considerable figure in his own right,[147] but one who would not give advice lest the matter 'sall cum befoir him'. He had been in that position for two to three weeks. Bishop Adam's account of Robert's particular 'bissines' is somewhat obscure, but appears to have involved Robert's attempt to extract receipts for money he had paid to the bishop, possibly for outstanding debts arising from the excambion, but also regarding augmentation 'of the pensioun for the houses sustentatioun' – money for upkeep of Kirkwall Castle and the Yards – and complications arising therefrom.

Despite Bellenden's desire that the bishop seek advice elsewhere, Bothwell still pursued his counsel, not only because he was of 'als guid judgment as ony of the eldest practisars in Edinburgh', but also to ensure that the regent find no fault with him 'that the schakar is nocht set down' – possible blame that the exchequer rolls for the year had not been completed (perhaps again

[145] Finlay, 'Sir John Bellenden of Auchnoull', *ODNB*.
[146] 146 *RPC*, ii, 446.
[147] Kirk, 'Clement Little', *ODNB*.

because those responsible were avoiding the plague). The bishop was ready to play his part, but the Lord Clerk Register for his own reasons had delayed matters until 2 October next. In the meantime, it was his intention, if he was not otherwise needed, to retire to the country for as long as the continuing 'devoring' plague should last.

On 1 October Bothwell wrote again to Bellenden (letter no. 30). He spoke of his servant, James Hay, recently arrived from Shetland, who had been 'mervallous bissie, bot hes nocht gottin gret expeditioun'. Hay had achieved little in his task of gathering up for the bishop of arrears of rents and mails for all years up to the crop of 1567, because Lord Robert had pre-empted him and instead employed Mr William Lauder, chamberlain of the bishopric.[148] In fact, Robert had already been charged in the contract of September 1568 to require Lauder to account to the bishop for all his previous intromissions with the bishopric revenues.[149] The bishop's employment of James Hay may have been an attempt to meet perceived delay in Robert's performing of his obligations. Hay had assured Bothwell that, according to 'the honest men of Orknay', it was 'Williams wilfulness in uptaking boll for boll' that had caused the bishop to have so much owing in arrears. Robert had been quick to respond to Hay's efforts to intervene. He had not only made Lauder solely responsible for dealing with the arrears, but had closely supervised his activities. When Lauder's work was done, he was escorted south by Robert's servants William Gifford, James Kennedy,[150] the laird of Penicuik, and others. They had put into Montrose on Monday past (26 September), and were due in Edinburgh five days later, on the day the letter was written.

So far as the bishop securing final settlement from Lauder was concerned, this was just the beginning. Bothwell did not know how to make sure of payment 'bot the keping of his persoun' – securing letters of caption to enforce imprisonment. Bothwell had not been able to secure a decreet from 'the ordinar justice' but he was sure that he could receive one from the 'exterordinar', through the intercession of the regent. Inevitably, he sought Bellenden's help (looking also incidentally for a commission against malicious spreaders of the pest). Lauder was also due arrears from Orkney to Bellenden, and the justice clerk should tell Bothwell what he wanted to do.

Bothwell suggested the sending north of a previously unmentioned figure in whom he seems to have had particular confidence. He 'allanerlie suld get us all that is awand'. This was William Rynd. Little is known about Rynd, but he appears to have been a servant of the bishop as superior of Holyrood.

---

[148] Lauder had appeared in Orkney in the early years of Bothwell's episcopate and became deputy chamberlain to Tulloch of Fluris shortly afterwards; he probably became chamberlain in the mid-1560s (NRS CS7/21², ff. 253, 258).

[149] NRS CS7/42, f. 340.

[150] 'my ladeis brother' – difficult to identify, but possibly an illegitimate brother-in-law of Robert.

This introduction was amplified two days later by a further letter to Bellenden (no. 31, 3 October 1569), this time from William Bothwell of Quhelpsyde, former chamberlain of Orkney. It suggested a rather more vigorous approach. Quhelpsyde was ready to make his way north, provided he was accompanied by Rynd, or by Peter Loch, another servant who had assisted him in making up accounts. Either of these should be created officer, with power to impound and confiscate – 'poynd and strenye' – goods, with 'scharp chargis' to Lord Robert to obey, and also an order to William Henderson to assist.

Three days later (letter no. 32, 6 October 1569), Adam Bothwell's letter to Bellenden noted that William Bothwell would indeed go to Orkney, accompanied not by Rynd[151] or Loch, but by Malcolm Sinclair, provided he could get him authorisation, 'armis ... that he may use the office of messinger or pursuvant', with accompanying letters of poinding. A further letter from William Bothwell (letter no. 33, 13 October 1569) emphasised the virtues of Sinclair, described as 'my lordis [Adam Bothwell's] servand'. As his surname suggested, he was a native of the north. He knew it well, and was best fitted 'to do our besynes'. This was Malcolm Sinclair, later of Quendale. Malcolm had various interests in Orkney throughout his life[152] as well as being a notary[153] who became vicar, then parson, of Dunrossness.[154] The letter of the 6th confirmed Bothwell's discussions that led to this proposed arrangement. They had not been easy, but Mr Francis Bothwell had been successful as mediator. Again Bellenden's assistance was sought in ensuring Lord Robert's co-operation, while he sought letters of poinding 'quhairby na excuis may be justlie pretendit'. Bothwell was frustrated, by the magnitude of his debts and the lack of means to extricate himself. He attributed this to the 'wicked using' of his chamberlains and the reluctance of his debtors to pay.

By the former, he clearly meant Lauder in particular (though he may also have meant William Bothwell who, as a former chamberlain, was still responsible for further arrears). He sought Bellenden's assistance in securing caption against Lauder. He secured Lauder's warding from 9–17 October,

---

[151] William Rynd did appear in Orkney not long after: he assisted Bothwell in settling Bothwell's arrears for 1567, the book containing details being in Rynd's handwriting (NRS RD1/19, ff. 95–9), and was witness to a discharge by Halcro to Bellenden for payment of the latter's pension for 1568 (NRAS 1100, bdl 1097). He was witness to a charter by Magnus Halcro to Henry, his natural son, Kirkwall, 2 August 1571 (NRS GD1/45/7), and was present on an assize at a sheriff court held by Lord Robert in Birsay, 31 March 1574 (*REO*, 135, no. lxi). Peter Loch may be the individual of that name, said to be from 'St Reinold's (?St Ninian's) Isle', describing himself as a servant of Patrick Bellenden, and implicated in an attack against Hanseatic merchants in Shetland in 1566 (see below). He is otherwise unknown.

[152] E.g. Westray, 1578 (NRS RD1/17, ff. 47–9), 1617 (*REO*, 402); South Ronaldsay, 1590 (OA D23, Notebook 2, 62, NRS GD263/58), 1594 (GD263/58); Sanday, 1597 (*RMS*, vi, no. 1081), etc. Despite his later Shetland dignity (1575) and designation 'of Quendale' (1587x1590), he was almost certainly an Orcadian.

[153] Ballantyne and Smith 1580–1611, nos. 39, 51, 178.

[154] OA GD150/1652.

and was later in dispute with him specifically over the duties of Shetland (perhaps a particular reason for James Hay's visit there), as well as debts on the regality of Broughton.

By the arrival of William Bothwell's letter of 13 October, all was ready for him and Malcolm Sinclair to make their way to Orkney. They were to travel on Robert Stewart's own ship, within the next eight days; this was said to be the only possibility of getting there and the bishop was especially keen that Bellenden help him with 'sufficient provesioun' to make it happen. He also wanted that the justice clerk should not fail to get special charges from the regent to Robert that he offer every assistance possible, and that no man should offer any impediment.

But it was clearly Robert that was the main problem, whatever the short-comings of the bishop's servants. William Bothwell had had difficulty raising the arrears that as chamberlain he was bound to collect, and it seems likely that Lauder was pulled between the desires of the bishop and Bellenden on the one hand, and the manipulations of Robert on the other. In the bishop's next letter to Bellenden (letter no. 34, 14 October 1569), he understood that the justice clerk had hoped to have his dues from Orkney by means of the money which Lauder was to bring to Bothwell out of Shetland. Robert however had told him that all such money had already been paid. If true, this left both Bellenden and Bothwell in such poverty that neither could help the other. To Bothwell, Bellenden's distress was more grievous than his own, but he himself was faced with giving up his house, despite having agreed accounts with Lauder, who 'de claro' owed the sum of 306½ angel-nobles (£153 sterling)[155] for the duties of Shetland, and for which Bothwell had secured caption for Lauder to be warded at Holyrood Abbey from 9 to 17 October 1569. Of this he had received 120 angel-nobles (£60 sterling) and 40 yopindales (£30–40 Scots) which he had already spent, with other sums, to settle an urgent debt of £100 sterling he had incurred in London (on a visit as part of a commission bringing accusations against Queen Mary in England[156]). This meant that he was unable to use the money he had received from Shetland to pay Bellenden what he was owed.

Having thus excused himself, Bothwell offered Bellenden a security which he would have William Bothwell draw up regarding his debts to the justice clerk, as well as an assignation of what he was owed in Orkney. These would be sent to him as quickly as possible and, in his view, would do more good for his lordship than anything the bishop himself had yet acquired. He hoped that the regent would grant him 'ane armis' to command the handover of the remaining arrears, in order to repay Bellenden. The Lord Lyon had assured

---

[155] Lauder revoked his obligation two days later, on 17 October 1569 (Ballantyne and Smith 1195–1579, no. 183).

[156] Shaw, 'Adam Bothwell', ODNB.

him that he would grant authorisation for such power on receiving permission from the regent; here Bellenden could use his influence.

The rest of his letter was a long catalogue of the woes of both. Bellenden's servant John Graham had told him of his master's 'distres', which matched his own. Bothwell could get nothing from his tenants or feuars, nor could he get any more of the credit which had sustained him since his return from England. His own servant James Alexander, a long-time follower, now commissary of Orkney, would not furnish him with accounts without legal compulsion. The problem of paying the Holyrood Abbey minister rumbled on, and Bothwell repeated his pleas for assistance, seeking a commission from Bellenden to help him. Difficulties persisted with getting the lords of exchequer together; although Bothwell was waiting on the treasurer's arrival, as were the clerk register and the (lord) advocate, 'Mr Henry' [Lauder]. No others who had been convened had yet arrived. Also continuing was the problem with Alexander 'Sanders' Purves, servant to the clerk of the cocquet, and his excommunication. He was out of town (in fact near to Bellenden 'in the Merss', the justice clerk having spent the last few days in Kelso). Given his physical closeness to Bellenden, the latter should order his return to the capital.

Bothwell then favoured Bellenden with three more letters. The first was three days later (letter no. 35, 17 October 1569), then on the 30th (letter no. 36). The third gives no year, though it is dated 24 February (and can be fairly confidently ascribed to the following year, and numbered 37).[157] There then follows a further gap in the sequence. Not until 18 April 1572 does Bothwell write again to Bellenden (letter no. 38). In the meantime, it is clear that the ongoing matters of 1569 are at last moving to a resolution. Partly, these centred round the conditions of the decreet arbitral by Maitland of Lethington of 30 June 1564, in particular the pension to Bellenden of Auchnoull with all its complications. Gathering and payment of this was proving difficult, predictably as a result of the activities of Lord Robert.

It was not Bothwell's intention to send William Bothwell north again, leaving his direction to Bellenden, whose business in Orkney was William's particular task. There was some delay in the appointment of an officer of arms, but the bishop was sure that a temporary officer would be appointed. It was to become clear that Bothwell was actually referring to Malcolm Sinclair. He does not mention him by name at this time, but it was increasingly obvious that it was he that was wanted, partly because the work of gathering arrears would take some time, more than a month (not '*opus unius mensis*', in Bothwell's slightly pretentious phrase), but also because his status as a northerner made him much more fitted to endure the rigours of the country. He could stay

---

[157] See the 'heiddis and articlis' agreed by Robert (through his commissioners) with Bellenden and Bothwell, and charter from the bishop to Robert following thereupon, both dated 28 February 1569–70 (NRAS 1100, bdls 811, 1625; OA D24, box 10, no. 3).

longer, travel further and be better received, 'quhair as men that ar not accustumat will not jeopard and induir Heland bedding and Hieland feding, quhilk na man heiraway, nor uther nor ane Orknay man, will not tak wele with'. Bothwell clearly remembered his previous discomforts in Orkney.

Nearly a fortnight later, on 30 October (letter no. 36), Bothwell had heard nothing from Bellenden, most notably about the appointment of an officer of arms, and Robert's ship had departed. This was not in itself a problem, since another was due to sail in eight days' time, and he would indeed send William Bothwell as well as 'the said Malcolme', provided he received the authorisation he needed. Bothwell then changed the subject of his ongoing pleas to Bellenden for assistance. The justice clerk, at the time of Bothwell's previous letter, had been in Kelso, and was clearly still in the borders, being 'in the pairtis quhair your lordship may help me greatlie anent thame quha hes maid me veray evill payment this haill yeir bygane'. 'Thame' were the tenants to whom he had set the churches appropriated to the abbey of Holyroodhouse in Galloway, associated with the barony of Dunrod, namely the lairds of Closeburn, Bombie, Nuntoun, and 'ane Gordoun', who held a lease of the kirk of Balmaghie from the laird of Richardtoun. The details of this were listed in an enclosed note. All these kirks were in the Dumfries and Kirkcudbright areas.

Clearly Bothwell was having the same problems, south and north, of non-payment of rental, teind and feu arrears. Ironically, the person he had charged with 'creaving in' of these debts, 'our cusing, Thomas McClellane of Blakcraig', had not been resolute in his duties 'for fear to displease men', those from his own area, whom he knew well – in fact the reverse of the hopes the bishop had for Malcolm Sinclair as a native of the north. McClellane had prevented Bothwell's demands from being made clear, forcing him to do so himself. All this meant that he was shamed by his creditors of the past year – his baker, brewer and butcher – to whom he owed more than 500 merks. Bellenden's assistance was again sought. He should either order McClellane to hand over whatever cash he had gathered to Thomas Kincaid, Bothwell's servant, or provide letters of horning if the debtors refused. At the same time, the bishop complained that the kirk had insisted that he pay the minister of Liberton out of his own third of the old church finances, and with 80 merks more than had ever been given to any of the ministers. A hearing regarding this was due on Monday next, and thus Bothwell had been compelled to present his case in Bellenden's absence.

Bothwell's next fully dated letter to Bellenden was not written until 18 April 1572 (letter no. 38). The letter of 24 February 1569–70 is labelled as 'concerning the [?service] of the regality', and in it Bothwell continues unashamed in seeking Bellenden's assistance. With the session in recess, it would be an ideal time for the justice clerk to make a long-awaited visit to Edinburgh and 'gif sum attendance to put my effaris in ordour'. These affairs

concerned the broken-up remnants of the temporalities of Holyroodhouse –
Bellenden as superior of the barony of the Kerse, with interests in Broughton
and the Canongate, and Bothwell as superior of the rump. Bothwell had
continual troubles. He and his servants had worked hard for the good of
those who remained in the 'convent' of the abbey, but in vain, since they
are 'reddy to gratifie all men bot [except] onlie me'. Despite a request from
Bellenden, and a promise extracted from them thereupon, on being asked to
do anything 'in the contrair', they 'expeid all thingis that thai ar requyrit of'.
The bishop was in despair whether to hold back, or to remedy any wrongs
in the future. If Bellenden was there, Bothwell could show him more than
he would commit to writing.

Bothwell also sought Bellenden's advice on how to deal with 'the nychtbouris
of the Canyget', in deterring those who had no need 'to gang furth at this
present tyme'. This may have been a reference to spreaders of the pest, but
Bothwell also sought to know when Bellenden would arrive, and for him to
sound out the regent (now Lennox, following the assassination of Moray in
January 1570) whether he wanted the people 'of the baronie' to wait upon
himself, or upon one of them. The latter course would enable them to remain
in the Canongate and wait upon the session, as well as relieving him of his
difficulties.

* * *

The period between letters no. 36 (30 October 1569) and no. 38 (18 April 1572)
saw major developments in negotiation. Early in 1570, two agreements were
drawn up, seeking to settle the simmering discontents which had plagued
the previous years. First, a list of 'thingis to be performit be my Lord and
Lady Orknay to the justice clerk'; then, probably about the same time – 28
February 1570 – came 'The heiddis and articlis concordit, aggreit and thocht
ressonable to be past be my Lord Robert ... upon all differencis betuix his
Lordship and the Bischop of Orkney.'[158]

By the terms of the first of these agreements, Lady Orkney was to ratify a
contract concluded between her husband and Bellenden, and the consequent
charter to the latter of the lands of Abbotsgrange, within the lands of the
Kerse. As grantee, Bellenden was also to receive a number of associated
documents: Jean Kennedy's own previous charter of these lands 'of lyiffrent
or conjunctfie', with its associated precept and instrument of sasine; a previous
charter of Abbotsgrange by Lord Robert in 1560 to Alexander Chalmer, vicar
of Baro, later chamberlain of Holyrood, also with precept and instrument;
resignations by Chalmer in favour of Lady Orkney and Mary, the Stewarts'
daughter, as well as a charter, precept and instrument in Mary's favour.

---

[158] NRAS 1100, bdls 723, 811.

This was all in accordance with Robert's wish to grant to Bellenden his Holyrood properties of the Kerse and the bailiary of the Canongate, in exchange for Bellenden's lands in Birsay, as he had noted in letters nos. 15 and 17. What remain confusing, however, are the details of Bellenden's rights in Birsay. The first explicit grant of lands there by Bishop Bothwell was that to Gilbert Balfour and his wife on 30 June 1560, at the same time as a similar grant to them of land in Westray. As previously noted, this was endorsed as 'nevir usitt', and was followed shortly afterwards by letters of reversion and obligation to the bishop. Nevertheless, it was this grant which formed the basis of Bellenden's rights. What Bellenden appears to have been seeking was a grant of the Birsay lands for himself but, for whatever reason, this was not simply a matter of the bishop rescinding Balfour's grant and re-issuing it to Bellenden. Rather it was by means of a transumpt – a fully authenticated copy version of the original charter (as well as an instrument following thereupon) – secured by means of an action at Bellenden's instance before the lords in July 1564[159] against Gilbert Foulsie, the archdeacon, who had refused to produce one from the regality register. This opposition may reflect reluctance on Bothwell's part to grant Bellenden the charter, but obstruction was of no avail, and a charter was granted to Bellenden in October 1564, the conditions following those of the transumpted charter of 1560.

One of the conditions of the first agreement of 1570, however, still required that Bellenden be provided with the transumpts of all the relevant documents relating to Birsay, as well as cancellation of an obligation that he had made to Robert 'concernyng the procuring and obteyning of the fewis and takkis of Orkney (Orknay) at the bishoppis hands respective', with a 'wrytting' that he had done everything he was obliged to do. On the other, Holyrood, side of the exchange, Bellenden sought compensation for the lands of Grange, north-west of modern Grangemouth, Coillhewchburne (Colloche Burne,[160] between modern Westquarter and Hallglen) and Couperland (identity obscure, but no doubt close by).

By the second of the 1570 agreements, Robert Stewart also agreed to settle all matters of dispute between himself and the bishop. He was to deliver an authentic copy of the bishopric tack of September 1568. He would exhibit before a judge Gilbert Balfour's obligation of 30 June 1560; this was an obscure document, but obviously connected to the charter of the same date, whereby Adam Bothwell had transferred to Balfour, albeit temporarily, the lands of Birsay; interestingly, he refused to transfer the document itself to the bishop. He would provide a receipt to the bishop for the transfer of the palace of the Yards and its contents. He would secure for the bishop the thirds of Holyrood, at present arrested in the hands of the tenants, an ongoing complaint of the

[159] NRS CS7/31, f. 140–1.
[160] Blaeu, *Atlas*.

bishop. Robert was also to choose curators to 'his bairnis' to clarify their rights to thirds in Orkney, under the contract; he would 'warrand, acqueit and defend' an obligation made with James Johnston of Elphinstone six years before; Lady Orkney was to ratify the contract, particularly with regard to tacks of land in what is now North Edinburgh – Broughton, Inverleith, Wardie – as well as Inveravon out in the barony of the Kerse; all these to be made over by the bishop. There were attempts at settlement of various arrears of pensions and crop from both the lands of Holyrood, and Orkney and Shetland, as well as undertakings to Patrick Bellenden, Adam Bothwell and others, clergy and lay.[161] Robert had also to convey to the bishop the 'commoun seillis ... registeris and evidentis' of Holyroodhouse, and the plenishings of the palace of the Yards, with pieces of timber to be found there.

* * *

The bishop's letter to Sir John Bellenden of 18 April 1572 was followed by a short piece from William Henderson to Bellenden (letter no. 39, 1 May 1572). He had received a letter from Robert by the hands of John Graham; as a result, he could say to Bellenden that 'my lady' (Orkney) had direction from her husband to settle all matters between the two – 'swa ye be ressonable'. If not, Birsay and the Kerse would revert to their former holders. Henderson had no doubt as to Bellenden's reasonableness, and on Robert's part there was nothing in these negotiations that he would omit. Lady Orkney was coming south (in fact dates indicate she was already on her way), and John Gifford had been due to accompany her. In the event, he had missed the ship, but would probably be on the next boat south, with John Kyle, a servant of Bellenden's, whom he had sent north to negotiate with Robert. It was possible that Gifford's wife, Margaret Dunbar, might prevent him, since she was still pursuing her own dispute regarding her contract with Patrick Bellenden and Gilbert Balfour, assigned to Bellenden of Auchnoull and mentioned earlier. She was seeking to retain a portion of her inherited sister part which she had exchanged for a pension, to bequeath to her son, 'and Johne Giffart and sche is at ane daly stryfe thairfor'. On the other hand, if Bellenden settled his own disputes with the Lady Jean, which he could do easily, this would bring Gifford and his wife into line, 'or ellis thay will haif na thing of thame in Orknay'.

Four days later, on 5 May 1572, Jean Kennedy was in Leith, writing the first of three letters to Bellenden (letters nos. 40–1, 11 May 1572; 42, 23 May 1572). She too was seeking his mediation, in her difficult dealings with Bishop Bothwell. She had arrived in Leith that very day from Arbroath, where she had

---

[161] The dispute flared up again on 7 March 1571, when Robert received a commission from the Regent Lennox to pursue Bellenden for 'ungodlie and tresonabill interprysis', especially in the earldom of Orkney (OA D23/12/10).

landed after 'aucht dayis being veray seik upone the sey'. Even at four centuries' distance, anyone who combines regard for the north with indifferent sea-legs can sympathise.[162] Despite her trials, she contacted Bothwell as soon as she arrived. She received little comfort from him and wasted no time in writing her letter to Bellenden that same day. She wished that he could be present to act as mediator, since in his absence any negotiations were unlikely to make progress. So far as Bellenden's own interests in Orkney were concerned, she mentioned Gifford, who was due to follow her south, but had missed the ship's departure, accompanied by an individual whom she called Bellenden's 'pursevant', though 'I luke for thame bayth togidder yit'. The 'pursevant' was unnamed; he could conceivably be John Kyle, who has been mentioned earlier as delayed in Orkney. However, it is perhaps more probable that it was James Purdie, another servant of Bellenden, previously mentioned (letter no. 38, 18 April 1572) and as Kintyre Pursuivant, carrying heraldic authority. Styled 'officer of sheriffdom of Orkney and Shetland', he had been granted letters to enforce Bellenden's claims against Robert for delivery to him of the lands in Rousay and elsewhere, granted by Lethington's decreet of 1564.[163]

Jean quickly received a reply from Bellenden. Her response, on 11 May (letter no. 41), sought hard to mollify the justice clerk, whom she perceived to be 'nocht a lytill stomochak (annoyed)'. His heraldic representative had clearly arrived in the south complaining of ill-usage at Robert's hands. Dame Jean was at pains to defend her husband against this charge. She believed that Bellenden's man could have no complaint, but was 'weill interteneit', taken to John Gifford's house, and could 'execute his chargis on him but ony molestatioun of ony man'. He should repeat his accusations in person before her so that she could answer them 'or ellis I wil allege your lordship dois this of purpois to caus my lord be supponit to be the man that wil nocht suffir the kyngs thingis to haif place'. She emphasised the advantage of Bellenden's presence in her negotiations with the bishop 'for reformyng of my lords evidents'. Previous adjusted 'evidents' had been sent to Bellenden, and the bishop had told her that he had sought them from Bellenden. For herself, she was willing to do 'that thing that becummis me, quhairintill your lordship sal find na fault, hoipyng to ressaif the lyke also'.

She emphasised all this when she wrote again, on 23 May (letter no. 42). Leaving the letter's bearer to say more of her progress with Bothwell, she suggested that Sir John should send 'sum man of jugement with your commissioun' to address the points at issue between them all. She had her

[162] This first letter foreshadows the countess's ambivalent attitude to her husband's northern possessions. Their marriage was not an easy one, but Jean Kennedy in addition seems reluctant to spend time in the north. She was to return later in the year, and perhaps on other occasions. Later, despite Robert's urgings, she was to spend most of her time in or around the Canongate, latterly suing him for divorce (Anderson, *Stewart Earls*, 57–8).

[163] NRAS 1100, bdl 720.

own reasons for wanting an end to all this. Her husband had 'burdenit' her with the payment to the justice clerk of his arrears of pension from Orkney. She was willing to do this if everything could be settled as a result. She now wanted the relevant documents to be brought to Leith, together with the common seal of Orkney, so that all affairs might be settled. She would receive due caution for payment of all sums contained in the bishop's book of arrears, and a discharge from Sir John of his pursuit of pension, thus settling the dispute between Bellenden and Bothwell. If Bellenden was prepared to co-operate, he would find she and her husband would reciprocate in assisting with his own ongoing dispute with Margaret Dunbar.

Bothwell himself wrote to Bellenden the following day (letter no. 43), adding more detail. He had not personally been in touch in recent weeks, relying instead on John Graham, Bellenden's servant noted earlier, as intermediary as well as mediator between himself and Robert's wife. He had dealt as considerately as he could with her. She however had said that she could not conclude matters without 'perpetuall displesour' of her husband unless the bishop withdrew all his disputes with them. She had also emphasised that Robert would 'be na meynis' put any money on the table himself. There was nothing she wanted more than 'universall concord', but on this she was emphatic. Bothwell said that he had done his best, and had remitted much debt to bring matters as far as they had. He could do no more, 'And now give we sall schaik all louss agane it sall be occasioun of perpetuall pley amangis us.' The ball was in Bellenden's court. Mr John Dishington would soon be arriving in Leith at the lady's behest, and Bothwell urged his cousin to send the charter and seal, so all the wrangling could be concluded.

Jean Kennedy's next two letters to Bellenden, of 7 and 17 June (letters nos. 44–5), were little more than notes, but she was clearly concerned. On the one hand, it was her intention to return home to Orkney as soon as possible (she mentioned an initial departure date of 10 June, but was still in Leith a week later, the date of her second letter, and seemingly for considerably longer). On the other, she was still awaiting a response from Bellenden. She had written a previous letter to him, intending to send it with John Graham, but having missed his departure from Leith, she had given it to the bishop to send. She understood that it had duly arrived, and was 'mervelyng' that she had not had a reply, knowing that 'I tary upoun na uther purpois', and John Graham could have supplemented the contents of the letter and reported 'all our procedingis'. John Dishington had shown her Bellenden's latest position, with which she was satisfied, and looked either for his verbal response or his appearance in person, not forgetting delivery of the 'evidents' and seal, that would 'mak an end with me'. Her letter of 17 June was a single paragraph, in the same vein, and urging 'that all occasioun war takin away of the persute of my lord my housband for the pensioun quhilk ye acclamis, quharof ye knaw your self we haif sufficient warrandice'.

For the next month, the major players – Bothwell, Bellenden and Jean Kennedy (supported as commissioner for her husband by William Elphinstone and William Henderson) – were engaged in much activity. On 16 July William Elphinstone, as procurator for Robert, produced two instruments of resignation in the hands of the bishop. Both concerned bishopric lands all over Orkney, as well as in Fair Isle. The first followed upon letters of 30 March 1572, the second upon the contract of 27/30 September 1568; these were in favour respectively of Robert in liferent and his son Harry in fee, and (in the latter case) of Jean Kennedy.[164]

The following day, 17 July 1572, a detailed contract was concluded between the bishop and Jean Kennedy, Elphinstone and Henderson, seeking to resolve all matters relating to the bishopric.[165] Amongst its many provisions, Robert was to seek confirmation of the provisions of the 27/30 September 1568 contract, and exhibit before judges the letters of obligation of Gilbert Balfour, both concerning Westray and duties which he owed Bellenden. He should also pay Bellenden, by assignation from Bishop Bothwell, the sum of £2066 6s 3d, in arrears of pension, as well as of feu mails of lands in Birsay. Sir John had already received £80 in cash from Magnus Halcro of Brough, so provision was made for the payment of the remainder, £1986 6s 3d, in the form of 20 lasts and seven barrels of Orkney butter. On the same day, Bellenden (a witness to the contract) granted the bishop an acquittance for 3550 merks,[166] in accordance with a bond dated 4 June 1562, in final settlement of his pension demands.[167] There were numerous other provisions. The commissioners were to ensure that the bishop received all his arrears for 1567 (his last full active year as bishop), as set out in the bishop's book of arrears in William Rynd's handwriting, together with others in the bishop's own hand, due by a variety of other individuals, including Ola Sinclair and Patrick Bellenden. Robert, having obtained decreet against William Lauder and arrested his goods, should pay Lauder's arrears to the bishop. There were also such matters as the plenishings and munitions of the Yards and the castle.

All the charters had two places and dates of sealing, 17 July in Leith and [?] September 1572 in Kirkwall, after being brought north by Jean Kennedy for her husband's attention. There was also provision by the bishop to Robert and Jean, in liferent, and Henry, their son, in fee, for the bishopric lands in Shetland, notably in Dunrossness, not set in feu before the making of the contract, and a charter of the offices of bailiary and justiciary in the bishopric and regality in Orkney, Shetland and Caithness; also the constabulary and keeping of the 'castell of Yairds' (presumably the bishop's palace rather than Kirkwall Castle), both

[164]   NRS NP1/30, ff. 14–16.
[165]   NRS RD1/19, f. 95.
[166]   NRS RD1/14, f. 192.
[167]   NAS CS7/31, f. 64; NRAS 1100, bdl 1612.

to Robert in liferent and his son in fee. Besides 'ample' charters of these, there were also to be two letters of tack to Robert and Henry, the longer survivor and their heirs male, one each of the bishopric teindsheaves of Orkney and of Shetland. Regarding movables, Robert Stewart was to pay the bishop for the 'insight plenishings of the Palace of the Yards', with which he had intromitted. Adam for his part had delivered the palace to Robert and was thus relieved of any relevant obligations under the 1568 contract. With regard to the bishop's new dominions in the south, Bothwell was to discharge Robert of any actions against him concerning the teinds of Broughton and any other fruits of the abbey of Holyroodhouse before 30 September 1568. Robert was to secure appointment of curators for his children, who would advise them on renouncing their pension from the thirds of Holyrood according to the 1568 contract.

In the contract, the main conditions made reference to the provisions of that of 1568, in some cases modified, in others allowed to stand. Although Jean Kennedy had been sent south by her husband to expedite his affairs and was a party to the contract, yet to some extent she appears to have remained in the background and let the commissioners, Elphinstone and Henderson, do the talking. She does not witness or subscribe the document, though the bishop (accompanied by his servant Alexander Kincaid) and Robert's commissioners did so. The witnesses included Bellenden of Auchnoull, several designated servitors of the bishop, and three others who signed on Robert's behalf. Procurators for the two sides were Thomas Craig for the bishop, and John Preston for Robert's commissioners. But there was one matter, as we shall see, that Dame Jean, at least in the eyes of her husband, had signally failed to address: her own interest in the Kerse.

Following upon the contract, Bishop Adam granted three charters to Robert and Henry, both in liferent and fee respectively, the first of bishopric lands in Orkney[168] (which superseded that of 28 February 1570), the second of those in Shetland to be erected into a free tenandry called Grymbusta;[169] the third constituted them justices and heritable bailies of the lands and regality of Orkney.[170]

* * *

Some time in mid-September 1572, Jean and William Henderson returned to Orkney. On successive days, the 16th and 17th, they each appear to have been closeted with Lord Robert discussing what had gone on in Leith, some of it unfinished business. All three wrote to Bellenden immediately afterwards. On the 16th, William Henderson wrote (letter no. 46) concerning his part in

[168] NRS E14/2, ff. 146–7.
[169] NRS E14/2, ff. 147–8; RH6/2254.
[170] NRS E14/2, ff. 148–9.

ongoing disputes about money the justice clerk was expecting Robert to resolve for him – with John Gifford and his wife, Bothwell, Jean Kennedy, and Patrick Bellenden. In the first case, Robert had tried to get Gifford and Margaret Dunbar to sign contracts and 'evidents ... quhilk thai refusit alluterly quhil thay war payit'. This was no doubt complicated by the transfer of the bishopric land from Bellenden to Robert, together with responsibility for the payment of Mistress Dunbar's pension. All Robert could do was sign the documents himself and consign them to the keeping of Mr William Moodie. Robert had also made a personal contribution to the 200 merks-worth of pension which was deemed to be outstanding. Henderson would attempt to cause Robert to get the documentation sent to Bellenden 'bot the wyf is far war nor Johne Giffurds self is'. According to Henderson, Robert would do his best to get payment to John Gifford and to satisfy Bellenden as well as doing his best to ensure this was done.

Robert had sent forth precepts of poinding for debts owed by the bishop. Much had already been paid, which was resting in 'William Bothwellis buke', and more had been discharged. So far as Dame Jean was concerned, both Robert and she herself had written (or were in the process of writing) at length to Bellenden, and Henderson had nothing to add. Regarding Patrick Bellenden, Robert's already stated position was, and remained, that if he could be 'suir' of Patrick, he '... wald be gud lord and master to him in tyme to cum'. If not, then 'I wil tak it upone my soul that ... it salbe in Patriks default'. It would be better for both if they could settle their differences, and Bellenden could easily bring this to pass.

Henderson then moved on to what seems at first a completely separate issue, but was clearly another ploy in Robert's dealings with Bellenden. This was a proposed marriage between Robert Stewart's daughter Mary and Lewis, Sir John Bellenden's son – 'the bairne is of ane gud inclinatioun and appeirrand to be wyfe and ane gud lyk personage'. In such an arrangement, her tocher – the figure of £1000 was mentioned – would be sufficient to cover 'the difference of the Kers'. Robert added the further incentive that the 'bairn' had another suitor in Lord Livingston, but he would prefer the Bellenden match. Nothing came of this, though ironically Robert's son Patrick was ultimately to marry Lewis's second wife and widow, Margaret Livingston, daughter of Lord Livingston. Mary Stewart, who at the time could only have been about ten years old, in due course became Lady Gray, though not until 13 years later.

Henderson's final paragraph touched again upon the ongoing issues. Robert had written to Bellenden, seeking a discharge of Bellenden's pension from Orkney, which Robert required before agreeing anything with Bishop Bothwell, outside what his wife 'and hir colliggs' had concluded during her trip south. At Bellenden's command, Henderson had delivered to John Gifford six chalders of victual for the crop of 1569 for which Robert wanted £20 per chalder, whereas merchants had been charged only £16; Henderson wanted

Bellenden to write to Robert standing firm for £16. Otherwise, his lordship would compel Gifford to accept the payment at £20, with Henderson himself having to make up the shortfall of £24 from his own pocket. Such were the problems of serving a difficult master. As so often, the letter's bearer was left to fill in further detail.

On 17 September 1572, both Jean Kennedy and Lord Robert, her husband, wrote to Sir John Bellenden (letters nos. 47 and 48). In her letter, Jean regretted that her actions in the south had failed to please her husband, and since her return she had been told that things were 'utherwyis nor was schawin me in the sowth'. She herself was clearly not satisfied with the way things were proceeding. What follows suggests that, at least according to Robert, his wife had not entirely grasped what should be negotiated with Bellenden. It is probable that Robert's chief irritation with his wife was that the question of her interests remained unresolved, for whatever reason. Nothing in the letter concerning what transpired in Leith suggests that the matter was ever mentioned. Later comments suggest otherwise, but Jean had not received enough satisfaction to consent to any sort of deal.

Robert noted that Jean had written to the justice clerk on her own account, and hoped that Bellenden would keep him abreast of developments. In her letter, she sought to remedy matters, and not merely for herself. So that Bellenden might be satisfied 'and I nocht hurt' he should send her details of what he would have her do, which she said was contained in a contract that should have been agreed between them in Leith. By this, Bellenden should have discharged her, her husband and heirs of all intromissions with his pension as well as of security on the lands of Coilheuchburn and others specified in his charter of the Kerse lands. In exchange, Robert would accept Bellenden's process against him, letting him have warrandice from transactions with the bishop in recompense, while Jean would renounce her Kerse interests in favour of lands in Birsay. Repeating her husband's previous comparison of the Kerse and Birsay lands, she felt the former was 'als profitable and commodius' as the latter or could be made so 'in sic uther things as may redound to my proffeit and avantage'.

She finished her letter with an inquiry into what may well have been a ploy of her own – to seek a liferent far outside Orkney, over which she might exercise greater control as a source of income. She had identified a piece of property, a 'rowme', on the north bank of the Forth 'forgane (opposite) the Kerss', pertaining to the abbot of Dunfermline, as yet unfeued but possibly available. If Bellenden could arrange a deal at, say, 4–5000 merks for the feuing (based on an assumption of 32 chalders victual at 40d per boll), then she could persuade her husband 'to lay out all his silver wark and my chenis and all uther thing that we haf in plege thairfor'. She asked that, as soon as he received her letter, he should put the proposal to the abbot, and let her know of his answer. Nothing more is known of this.

* * *

Robert Stewart's letter of 17 September 1572 (no. 48), from Kirkwall, was his last letter to Sir John Bellenden of Auchnoull. It was lengthy, occasionally querulous, but covered affairs with a brisk comprehensiveness which suggested that, whatever his annoyances with his wife, all his complex affairs were approaching some kind of endgame, and that we are reading what is genuinely the conclusion of this set of correspondence, rather than the end of what survives. We have still to examine one further letter, addressed to Sir John's son, Sir Lewis, but this dates from ten years on, and is followed later still by a second, completely separate, run of correspondence which will be touched on presently. By then, Robert's problems were different.

Letter no. 48 was in response to one from Bellenden, courtesy of William Henderson. According to Bellenden, Jean Kennedy had complained that her husband had given her no 'contentation' for her renouncing of the Kerse lands. Robert's reply suggested that the two were at a stalemate. He had agreed to grant her 'ane part' of the bishopric lands of Orkney, but would not grant sasine until she renounced her liferent of the Kerse. However, the disagreement between the two appears to have been changing, even evolving, in the course of Robert's writing. At one point he puts down 'and now sche is content to mak renunciatioun' – then scores it out. Someone had to blink first. But now he noted that Jean's letter to Bellenden asked him to send her a copy of an agreement made between the two 'with sic uther thingis as sche hes ado'. At first he referred any response to Bellenden's own discretion, but then changed his mind and hoped Bellenden would do what she asked. It was perhaps this change of tack that had persuaded Jean to renounce the Kerse: 'Now sche wil do all thing to your lordships contentment.'

Robert also had a confirmation from the bishop of his daughter Mary's grant of lands in Birsay, of which Bellenden (who had made the original grant in 1568)[171] could have a copy at his pleasure. He also thanked Bellenden for his continuing negotiations with Bothwell on his titles, though there were still matters outstanding, of which he would send more details, courtesy of his letter's bearer. If these could be settled, then everything would 'tak perfectioun', even though he would be greatly the loser, due to sums owed by the commons of Orkney. William Bothwell had been busy gathering up income and arrears due from tenants and vassals to Robert, Bellenden and the bishop. He had amassed £600-worth, and given up discharges on it, but Robert implied that Bellenden would not receive any of this, since in his view the needs of the bishop and himself should take precedence. On the matter of the demands of John Gifford and his wife, however, he would pay them the sums agreed by them with Bellenden 'swa that ye gar send me letters of

171 NRAS 1100, bdl 1612.

the lords to that effect'. As we have seen, Gifford and his wife had agreed that the contracts made with Bellenden should be placed in the safe keeping of William Moodie, until the sums had been completely paid, 'utherwyis I culd get na thing done be thame [*marginal insertion*: 'and thai refusit to tak me souertie thairfor'].

Robert's disputation with Patrick Bellenden continued to drag on, but with seeming concessions on Robert's part. He was happy to submit their differences to the arbitration of four 'discreit men'. On Patrick's side, he suggested Bellenden himself and Sir Hew Kennedy (of Girvanmains, the Bellendens' father-in-law noted earlier); Robert would 'cheis uther tua'. This could only be done in person, all their differences 'tryit and endit', face to face. In the meantime, Patrick should send his servants north to visit his estates, put them in order, and settle outstanding financial matters. Despite this seemingly mollifying tone, Robert made clear his continuing rancour. He referred to Patrick's 'divers sinister reports of my using towards him' and 'his sclanderous toung'. His return to Orkney would require him to make amends for the offences he had done to Robert in the past, and find surety 'that he sal leif in quyetnes in tyme cummyng'. Any harm he had received in the past could be repaired by negotiation. On the other hand, 'gif he will continew in his malice towart me I haif thryss als mikle to lay to his charge as he hes ... quhilk he wil find gif he gangs to the uttirmoist wyth me'.

As for Sir John, Robert trusted that he would remain as supportive to him as he had been to him and his brother the elder James in the 1550s, particularly if he were pursued before the regent, council or session. He added, 'I tak your lordship to be ane of men in the warld that favours me best and hes ever hithertillis kythit the samin to me.' To assist their dealings, he had appointed William Henderson to keep him informed of events, his reports being given the same credit as if they were from Robert himself. He hoped that 'all things amangs us may be browcht to ane quyetnes ... thouch our inimeis wald wys the contrar'. He remained particularly wary of possible manoeuvres on the part of the bishop. He had 'eikit' a requirement to his contract with the bishop that Bothwell grant him warrandice on the justice clerk's pension from the bishopric, hoping to induce the bishop to conclude matters with Bellenden 'for I persaif he deilis fraudulently bayth your lordship and me', by the counsel he had given Jean Kennedy, and which she had shown to him.

One particular problem was the question of the thirds of Holyrood which might come before Bellenden in the session. He feared that the bishop would offer up 'smal defens', in the hope of receiving only minor demands from the kirk. Should he be spared the necessity of paying the thirds, then he could demand a guarantee of them from Robert and thus obtain a large part of the living of the bishopric 'quhilk wilbe my uttir wrak' if not anticipated and prevented. He hoped that if Bellenden perceived any danger of this he would intercede with the kirk and, in settling, he should make the bishop pay the kirk its due because he had already received thirds which would enable him to pay the pensions and had retained £400 of their worth, defrauding Robert in the process. For that reason, he had granted the bishopric half of the pensions which were due to him, and he would pay yet more, even if it were £100 or 200 merks, 'for it war bettir to me to gif out that nor fall in danger of the haill'. He had spoken to Mr James McGill on the matter 'to stand my gud frend heirintill quhilk I traist he sall', though he was not going to reveal the full details to McGill or anyone else, as he had to Bellenden, 'bot committis the samin to you to do thairin as your lordship thinks gud'.

Such was Robert's trust in Bellenden that he had already paid 200 merks to John Gifford of what Bellenden owed him, and would fulfil his demands for the rest 'howbeit I man pay ane gud part thairof of my awin purss'; this was why he saw no reason to pay the justice clerk from William Bothwell's gatherings – this, and the fact that 'the bischop is sa fraudfull that I can nocht deill wyth him'; Bothwell had inserted a clause in the most recent version of the contract between the two, absolving him from furnishing of security for any diminution of the rental, the latter being a longstanding complaint. This Robert had removed, and would not consent to it as long as the bishop lived. He interpolated a note that he would seek no security, but scored it out on second thoughts. He took the view that, since he now held the whole bishopric on a liferent tack, which obliged him to meet the cost of its thirds, then such a clause would be 'hurtfull to me and can do him na gude'. Bothwell also wanted a discharge for 'insycht' (plenishings) Robert should have received in the 'place' of the Yards; Robert's retort was that the bishop should actually give him in return a discharge for plenishings which he described as 'bot ane sort of auld rottin brewyng lomis (brewing vessels)'. He would then grant a discharge for the rest 'for I wald cut away all thing that may mak variance in tyme to cum'.

Finally he sought from Bellenden a discharge of any further liability for the justice clerk's pension. Bellenden was the 'principall actour' in the matter, acknowledged by both Robert and the bishop. Without this discharge, he would agree nothing further – 'I traist ye wil nocht gif me occasioun to complene of your doyngs, and that beine done ye salbe satisfeit of my wyf and al uther things.'

* * *

Thus ended Robert's last letter to Bellenden in the series. By the time of the last letter of all (letter no. 49, 2 September 1582), things had changed radically. Sir John Bellenden of Auchnoull had died, in 1576.[172] The late 1570s had been very difficult years for Robert, largely through the opposition of the earl of

<hr>

[172]  NRS CC8/8/6, f. 190.

Morton, now regent, prompted in part by Bothwell, and Bellenden in his last years. Morton supported complaints of oppression against Robert in Orkney (as well as the superbly detailed account of Bruce of Cultmalindie's misdeeds in Shetland, conducted by William Moodie and William Henderson)[173] which accused Robert of possible treasonable dealings with Denmark, wresting large sums of money from him in the process.[174] In 1577 Robert was in ward in Linlithgow and 'very poor and of no great judgment, party or friendship'.[175]

However, as Morton's popularity declined, Robert cultivated the favour of the king, who was approaching majority, giving him 'evell information' about the regent.[176] On 28 December 1577, Jean Kennedy granted to Sir Lewis Bellenden a ratification of the Abbotsgrange-Birsay exchange.[177] On 7 February 1578, Robert and Patrick Bellenden came to an agreement over their differences, at least for the time being.[178] By November 1579, Robert had returned to Orkney.[179] In January 1581, he and his wife concluded a contract with Bishop Bothwell reiterating the conditions of that of 1572, and settling matters with regard to the thirds of Holyrood.[180] Finally, the king's favour was at last demonstrated when, in August 1581, Robert was created earl of Orkney, lord of Shetland, 'knicht of Birsay'.

The last letter in the series (letter no. 49) was written by Robert from Kirkwall on 2 September 1582 to the late Sir John's son, Sir Lewis Bellenden. The tone was cordial indeed. 'I am persuadit of the guid will and favour your lordship beiris toward me, quhairof I thank yow in the maist hartlie maner I can, and will heirefter luik till have your lordship in the samin estait and conditioun as your father wes to me quhome I fand ever honest, gentill and kynd in myne adois Your lordships cusing Sir Patrik[181] sall for your lordships caus find sa favourabill ane dealing on my pairt as sall aggre to your lordships contentment.' This is misleading, as is Robert's description of the older Bellenden as 'ever honest, gentill and kynd'. Sir Lewis was to inherit his father's discontents, and in any case the late justice clerk's place in Robert's life was taken by another prominent figure of the time, Sir Patrick Waus of Barnbarroch, both as an adviser and general recipient of letters from Robert's relatives and followers. By the time of the first recorded of these, written by Robert in Kirkwall on 4 March 1582,[182] Henry Stewart, master of Orkney,

---

173 Ballantyne and Smith 1195–1579, 183 et seq., no. 237.
174 NRS B22/1/62, f. 151 (protest by Robert at having to pay 12,000 merks to Morton for discharge of a process against him concerning the admiralty of Orkney and Shetland).
175 CSP Scot, v, 252.
176 Melville, Memoirs, 263–4.
177 NRS RD1/16, f. 431, RD11/8.
178 NRS CS7/71, f. 229.
179 REO, 145, no. lxvii.
180 NRS, RD1/19, ff. 99–103.
181 Actually Sir Patrick Bellenden, Lewis's uncle.
182 Barnbarroch Corresp., 238.

was dead and Waus had become guardian of his brother Patrick, who was now master, as well as prior of Whithorn.[183]

All this brought to a climax the first part of Robert's great project of an earldom in Orkney, in time inherited, ominously, by his son. For someone described as 'vain and nothing worth', it seems an extraordinarily ambitious enterprise, particularly in his worsting of the Bellendens and Adam Bothwell. All might be thought of as abler men, and none ever forgave him, pursuing him by whatever means possible for the rest of their lives. On the other hand, in the face of this and other difficulties, Robert was never able, to the end of his life in 1593, to make his position wholly secure. His rule in the Northern Isles in the 1580s became notorious for oppression. The king came to revise his opinion of the earl of Orkney, feeling that he 'only serves his own ends'.[184] In 1587, there was a concerted attempt to wrest the islands from Robert's grasp – by the secretary, Sir John Maitland of Thirlestane, but perhaps more particularly driven by Sir Lewis Bellenden,[185] in which Patrick Bellenden played a leading role.[186] Their ostensible motive was the pursuit of Robert's misdeeds, but in the case of Bellenden, several of the old enmities re-emerged, and in these Maitland remained an encouraging but silent partner. The problems for Robert did not last however, perhaps due to his seeking support elsewhere by currying favour with Francis Stewart, earl of Bothwell,[187] and flirting with the Spanish faction during the tense times after the defeat of the Armada.[188] Robert survived this assault on his power, though it was diminished. In 1592, he received a grant of the lands of Orkney and Shetland on the king's reaching the age of 25, but it was in liferent, and to Patrick in fee.[189] Patrick was clearly poised to take over, and even used the title of earl himself, during what was left of his father's lifetime.[190]

But that is a later story. What we have looked at for the moment is a slice of Scottish history in the third quarter of the sixteenth century, where the participants in turbulent events and troubled times speak for themselves

---

[183]  There might be a case for reprinting of the correspondence of Sir Patrick Waus of Barnbarroch, to extend and supplement the level of contact with the players of the period. R. Vans Agnew's published transcription of the letters exists in a nineteenth-century edition; the originals were the victim of a fire, and do not survive among the Vans Agnew of Barnbarroch Papers held by the NRS (GD99). On the other hand, from the standpoint of study of the Stewart earls of Orkney, the relevant letters are a small part of the whole Barnbarroch corpus, which includes material regarding many other items, notably Sir Patrick's visit to Norway on the matter of James VI's marriage. For present purposes, the light thrown by correspondence on the affairs of the period must be restricted to the present collection.

[184]  *CSP Papal*, viii, 638–9.

[185]  *RMS*, v, no. 1354.

[186]  *CSP Scot*, ix, 485–6; NLS Adv. Ms 35.5.1.

[187]  *CSP Scot*, ix, 485–6, 532; *Salisbury Papers*, HMC, iii, 282.

[188]  NRS GD44/13/7/30.

[189]  *APS*, iii, 589–90.

[190]  *RMS*, vii, no. 247.

and to each other, and we can hear them do so. Some of their themes are personal, some concern the trials of the time, some are labyrinthine and legal. There are also bit players and plentiful noises off; but all are linked together by four principal characters: Bishop Adam Bothwell; Archibald Napier of Merchiston; Lord Robert, first of the Stewart earls, the collective 'Bad King' of Northern Isles history; and the one character, who has interests in the bishopric of Orkney, whose words in the correspondence are only alluded to, but round whom much of the writing revolves, that the others look to, rightly or wrongly, as a facilitator – Sir John Bellenden of Auchnoull.

# PERSONAL CORRESPONDENCE OF
# SIR JOHN BELLENDEN OF AUCHNOULL
# AND HIS CIRCLE, 1560–1582

## 1. The Yards,[1] 26 October [1560]
*Adam, bishop of Orkney, to Archibald Napier of Merchiston.*

Darrest brother, efter all hartle recommendation, pleis wit I ressavit ane wreting of youris fra James King,[2] be the quhilk ye schew me ye haid wretin dyvers tymes to me, and mervalet that ye haid gottin na anser. Trewle other na that wreting I gat naine fra you this gryt quhyill, quhairfor think not onkuith that I wreit na anser of that thing I ressavit not. As to the knawlege of my being quhilk ye war desyrus of, it hes bene in continuall trawell and labour of bodye and mynd and evill helth thairthrow continualle sene my cumming in this cuntray, as this berar can reherss and informe yow sufficiente. Alsua quhat cummeris sume frendis hes sterit oup unto us, and how the samin standis with us presentle, James Meinyes[3] will reherss yow. Prayand yow hartle to rekkin, that all the cummer that can be maid me sall not caus me to geif ouer that thing suld be my supple in tyme of neid, and that otheris weill deserving suld bruik efter me: bot gif thais that hes done me plesuir will resaiff sic thankfulnes of me as of thankfull mynd I am willing and glaid to do thame, I sall be abowt to do thame mair plesuir, and acquyt the benifet done to me mair thankfulle than ony in Scotland that ever ressavit sic guid deid. Prayand yow, that gif ye cum in commonyng with ony man thairanent, schaw how I haif offeret the justice clerk,[4] haiffand upone this benefice xi hundreth merk of pension yeirle to be geiffin owt of the quantite of xx chailder beyr, quhilk is mair than I haif to sustene me one behind, and gif the victuall com to sic

---

[1]  The bishop's palace in Kirkwall. For discussion of this name see Anderson, 'Cathedral, Palace and Castle'.
[2]  Servant of Bishop Bothwell (*RMS*, v, no 2265); notary in Edinburgh (*REO*, 342–3, no. ccxxi; OA SC11/86/12/2/3/5).
[3]  As bearer of the letter, certainly a servant of Bishop Bothwell. Otherwise unknown, this being the only reference to him.
[4]  Sir John Bellenden of Auchnoull.

pryces as it hes bene guid chaip within this schort spaice, I wald not haif sua mekil behind my pensionis as other mycht pay that or susteine my selff. Quhairfor pray him to be ressonable and ramember him that he that wald haif all, all is able to tyne. Alswa pray him to put ordur till his demanding, for gif he continowis as he hes begown I may find rameid thairfor sik as I best may, althocht it stand not with his plesuir, and I war laith thairto in respect of amite I haif hithertillis borne that I will be absolvit fra, gif he, as ye gait, castis doune with his fuit sic plesuir as he hes done me. And mak my hartle commendationes to my sister, quhem with yow and my navowis, your bairnis, the lord God mot eternalie preserve in weilfair of saull and body. At the Yairdis, this xxvi day of October.

Be your bruder at his powair
the bischop of Orknay.

'To his bruder, the laird off Merchinstoun, in Merchinstoun'[5]

NLS Adv. Ms 54.1.6, f. 1; printed Napier, *Memoirs*, 63–4.


## 2. The Yards, 1 December [1560]

*Adam, bishop of Orkney, to Archibald Napier of Merchiston.*

Rycht honorable schir and bruther, eftyr all hartle recommendation, pleis wit this present is to schaw yow off my helth and quhow all affairis standis with me quhilkis ar at syk punt that althocht freindis hes steret me owp mair cummer nor lyis in thair powair to lay to me againe that I remaine yit constant at my purpois, that is to do thaim plesour that newer deserwet ewill off me, off quhilk numer ye ar. Not dowbtand bot ye will continew and adverteis me quhatt is your opinion off all matteris, and quhairaway ye beleiff all sall turne. This ye may do sua weill awysetle, that I may haiff knawlege off my desyr, and ye na thing hairmet thairthrow, quhilk I pray you obmit not with the first that passis betwix, and be labourand to put off cummeris off me that otheris quhilk suld be frendis dois all thair powair to bring on, or at leist get me wit thairoff and mak me with the first ay adverteissement, and spair not to fee ane or twa futte fallowis to do the samyn with, quhatt ewir thai cost I sall pay it. Alsua get wit off my gossop Alexander King, quhat he hes doune anent the entrie off me unto the landis off Briglandis and Estown off Dunsyr, quhairinto I pray yow beyr help as I wald do giff I war present in ony causs concerning yow, and that becaus ye haiff enteres, and than I dowbt not bot I will furder the better, notwithstanding the iustice clerk reprochet me be wryt, sayand that my sairry frendis that I chairget with my bissines left all in the myrre, and culd do me na guid. Schir, this is litill off his ewill speiche. I

---

5    Merchiston Castle, near Edinburgh.

haiff not laissair to wryt off the laiff and off his unkind behavour towart me, quhilk sall newer vantaige hym ane d. as I tak God to witnes, for that is not the way to conqueis me, nor he sall never haiff me be that moyen. Treit my sister the berair° weill and hald hyr, sua far as ye may, in thai partis, for I haiff gottynne off hir word nor deid heyraway litill guid or eiss, bot continualle at debait with hir husband, becaus I wald not geiff hym all that I haid quhill I gat mair, be hyr caussing, and sua hes baynne hethirtillis be my awin maist hurt off ony. Commend me hartle to my sister, your bedfallow, and your sonne Jonne quhem with you and the remanent off your successioun God mot preserff. At the Yeardis, the first off December.

Be your bruder<br>the bischop off Orknay.

I pray you schir, schaw you kynd to Alexander King for my saik.

'To his bruder the laird of Merchinstoun thair'

NLS Adv. Ms 54.1.6, f. 2; printed Napier, *Memoirs*, 64–5.

## 3. The Yards, Kirkwall, 5 December 1560

*Adam, bishop of Orkney, to Archibald Napier of Merchiston.*

Rycht honorabill schir and brother, efter maist hartle recommendatione, pleis witt I haif send presentle with this berar sume power and commissione to your nyghbuir the lard of Rosling,⁷ your self, the schiref Olyfer Sinclair my guidfather,⁸ and Alexander King, coniunctle to commone, and, giff ye may, mak appoyntement anent sic differentis as ar happinnit betwix the justice clerk and me, quhairunto, schir, ye ar maid juge in your awin causs. Advyss gif be your jugement ye will condame your self for that thing quhilk is cumin to me throw my father, for ony weyr that may be maid me, withowt that chance of poverte compell me, sall not be me, godwilling, induring my tyme be put in fremmit handis. Quhairfor in this behalf I will put yow to cumir to labour concord, gif it may be haid upone sic heiddis as I haif geiffin power to yow and your colloggis to offer, quhilk gif beis refuset, I pray yow mak my pairt knawin till all honest men that happinnis to heyr of our debaitt; and, sa far as ye may, stay cummeris fra us, quhilk I wait thai folkis will not leyf to bring one us sa far as is in thame. Bot gif thai get thair intent thairthrou thai will haif the mayr caus to want thame thairof. Onlye, schir, do that is in yow to appoynt us gif the samin may be, failyeand thairof, lat

6   Probably Margaret Bothwell, Bothwell's half-sister, wife of Gilbert Balfour, the husband referred to.
7   William Sinclair of Roslin, nephew of Oliver Sinclair of Pitcairns.
8   Oliver Sinclair of Pitcairns and Whitekirk, sheriff of Orkney and stepfather of Adam Bothwell.

him be at his vayntage of me, for gif he continowis in the stering of me oup mair cumir thane he hes alradye done, I sall suyt help at sik ane as I wait will mainteine my just caus againis his violence, and all thais that will tak his part in wranging of me. I pray you, schir, to send your sone Johne[9] to the schuyllis, other to France or Flandaris, for he can leyr na guid at hame nor get na proffeit in this maist perullus worlde, that he may be savet in it, that he may do frendis efter honnour and proffeit as I dowt not bot he will; quhem with you, and the remanent of your successione, and my sister, your pairte, God mot preseve eternalle. At the Yairdis in Kirkwall, this v day of December, the yeir of God 1560.

> Be your bruder at powair,
> Adame, bischop off Orknay.

I pray yow, schir and bruder, to dress the laiff off your collegis to beyr you cumpanye for to dress thir affairis, becaus I may not laubour thairin in my absence.

'To his bruder the laird off Merchistoun, in Loudeanne'[10]

NLS Adv Ms. 54.1.6, f. 4; printed Napier, *Memoirs*, 66–7.

## 4. The Yards, 19 January [1560–1]
*Adam, bishop of Orkney, to Janet Bothwell, lady Merchiston.*

Darrest and best beluiffet sister, I commend me hartle to yow. I ressavit your wreitting fra this berar, maiking mention that thair is sume variance betuix yow and your howsband, and that ye ar not sua luiffet of him as ye war wont, and I am sorie that ye suld be at sic disease, and specialle I beyng sua far removet fra yow, and in sic tyme as I mycht haif worss supportet yow of ony tyme that hes passit sen my cumin in this rowme. Bot alwayes, sister, accompt with your self, that sic trubles as hes happinnet unto yow ar the visitatione of God to pruif yow, to try yow gif ye luif him; and ar, as the croce of the faythfull uses ever to be, the fatherle cheisteisment and maist speciall signis and evident taikinge of Goddis onedowttet favour and luif toward yow; quhome as he hes beyne protectour, guvernour and defendar of in tymes passit, sua dout not bot he will be in tymes cumming; and reconsall yow with your housband in gayning tyme, to your gryt contentment; geiffing your croce sik ane yschew and end of joy and glaidnes as ever the faythfulles croce uses till haif. Prayand yow to tak the samin thairfor in patience; saying with godle Job, gif we haif ressavit guid owt of the hand of the lord, quhai suld we not alsua ressave

---

[9]   John Napier, later of Merchiston, mathematician and inventor of logarithms (1550–1617).
[10]  This place-name was at first taken to be Loudon. Any reason for Napier's presence there is unknown, though there may have been a Campbell connection through Napier's mother, who was a Campbell of Glenorchy. However, it seems more likely that it is in fact Lothian.

evill, and geiffin him maist hartle thankis thairfor, attesting your godle and stedfast fayth in him, quhilk is maist evident in tyme of probane. And as for my part, notwithstanding my inhabilite that is happinnet throw frendis mysusing, quhilk this berar will schaw yow, ye sall ressave of him threte libs, and, as God furtheris me, I sall send sume taikin to your howsband for intertynement of amite. Committing yow in the protection of the hiest. At the Yairdis, this xix of January.

Be your bruther at all powair,
the bischop off Orknay.

'To his darrest sister, Jene Bothwill, lade of Mercheistoune'

NLS Adv. Ms 54.1.6, f. 3; printed Napier, *Memoirs*, 65–6.

## 5. The Yards, 5 February 1560–1

*Adam, bishop of Orkney, to Archibald Napier of Merchiston.*

Weilbeluiffet bruder, I commend me hartle to yow. Pleis wit, I ressaivet your wrytin off Merchinstown the xxiiij day off December lattin me knaw syk novellis as occurret, and sua specialle that I cunne yow verray meikill thank thairoff, and specialle off the adverteissement maid my lord James[11] quhill he was in Strathbogy[12] be aine off the Sinclairis, quhaironto that ye may be the habillair to mak answer. Pleis understand the caussis off thair setting fordeward off syk thingis, quhilk was that thai beand instigat be the justice clerk, quha maryet with thaime twa sisteris, to lowp in ane off my plaices callet Birsay,[13] quhilk thai kepit; and thaireftyr onbesset the way quhairbe I was to cum haime from my visitatioun, with gret nomber off commonis quhem thai pat than in beleiff to leiff frelie, and to knaw na superiouris in na tymis cumyn; quhilkis be Goddis graice haid na powair to hairme me, althocht thair uttir purpos was at thair hethir cumyn, to haiff alder slaine me, or taiken me. At quhatt tyme I caussed demande the said Henrie Sinclair, cheiff off that conjuratioun, quhatt mowet hyme to do syk thingis to me, and als quhat offence I haid doune hyme or any off the countray to provok thaime to syk thinkis in my contrair; quhaironto he promeisset to mak answer in wryt, and schortle he gaiff me certaine petitionis, in quhilkis I findand petitionis and not answeris or ressonis off the injury doune to me, I schew thaime to the schireff and said, schir, now ye sie thai haiff na just causs off taikin my houss or doyin me the uther wrangis thai do; quhairfor I requyr yow in the quenis name to do

---

[11]  James Stewart (1532–70), illegitimate son of James V, shortly to become earl of Moray and later regent.

[12]  Centre of the Huntly lands, where Moray was no doubt pursuing his fractious dealings with the earl.

[13]  One of the bishop's two palaces, the other being The Yards in Kirkwall. See 'Monsbellus' below.

me justice: quha, beand weill myndet to dress concord betuix us, wald use na chairgis apon hyme for delyvre off my houss, bot desyret me mak answeris to his petitionis, quhilk I reffuisset simpliciter quhill I haid my houss againe. Thir petitionis wes proponet be the said Henry and his bruder Robert, and certaine als weill geiffin as thaime self, not exceding the nomber off xviii or xx; to the quhilkis the said Henry fader gainestowd, calland hyme and the laiff fullis that wist not quhatt thai did, and said he wald on na sort consent the mess wer doune; lyk as sensynne he hes said, and biddin be with ane gret multitude off the commonis at the first heid court eftyr Yeuill, quhen thai wer all gatheret and inquyret be certain off my messingeris, send to thaime to that effek, giff thai wald be content off mutatioun off religioun, quhilk thai reffuset, and that notwithstanding I cloisset my kirk dorris, and hes thoilet na mess to be said thairin sensynne. Quhowbeit thai wer sua irritat thairbe, that eftyr thai haid requyret me sindre tymis to lat thaime in to that effek, at last gaderet together in gret multitud, brocht ane preist to ane chapell hard at the scheik off the schamber quhair I wes lyand seik, and thair causset do mess, and marye cetaine pairis in the auld maner. This was doune on Sonday last was, quhilk I culd not stoppe withowt I wald haiff committit slauchter. Quhairfoir thai falyet far informet the lordis sua, quhilk I pray yow hartle to put owt off thair heidis be contrair informatioun, and mak me frendis amangis thaime, for I am heyr detainet with seiknes, and may not do for my selff as now; bot as soune as I may, I sall mak to the gait fra I understand that ye haiff graipet the principal off the consailis myndis towartis me, and found the samyn ressonable; for I am certaine as my small frend the justice clerk hes steyret me owp all sorte of cummeris heyr that he culd be Henrie Sinclair and Thomas Tulloch, [14] sua hes he labouret thair my hurt sua far as he may; quhilk, schir, giff ye may persaiff, I pray yow mak me adverteissement, that I may provid for my affairis in caice thair wraith may not be mitigat, for I will not commit me to ane angry multitud.

Your wrytin was veray comfortable to me anent the frendis ye schew me ye haid to do for me, but leiff thairfoir to mak man, and the gretest rathest. [15] Schortle, bruther and schir, I commit my lyff and honnour in your handis. Quhattewer happin, I haiff maid ane charter to yow and your airis off syk thing I haiff, quhairfoir subscrive ye the reversion I send to yow be this berair, and put to your seill thairto; and quhatewer chancis, ye nor your airis sall not be defraudet off your portioun and part ye suld haiff off me. As to the landis off Briglandis quhilk I suld be enteret to, I pray yow bayth speik your selff, and causs Alexander King speik Michaell Nasmyth, that is with my lord

---

[14]   Thomas Tulloch of Fluris, former constable and chamberlain of the bishopric.
[15]   'and particularly the greatest'.

of Sanct Andross,[16] that is donatour to the waird and marigge off the laird off Maner, my superiour, quhem off I hald blench, and my superiour alsua off the queine blanch; and, giff neid beis, compone with hyme as ye wauld do for ony your awin landis; and quhatt ye promeis I sall keip. At the maist thair is thairoff bot twa yeiris to rynne off the waird. This, schir, ye may do giff the said Michael cummis to the town; failyeynne thairoff, witschauff ane servand apon my expensis, and I sall quyt it to pass to Paslay quhair he is. All uther thingis Mr Frances[17] and this berair kan reherss yow. Quhairfoir, I will not distaine yow with lang wrytin, bot commendis you with my sister, your wyff, and my awin bairnis, your successioun, in the kepin of the almytty. Prayand you hartle, schir, to mak my commendatiounis to thaime and all uther frendis. At the Yeardis, this fift off Februair anno lxo.

Be your bruder at his utir powair,
Adame, bischop off Orknay.

'To the rycht honorable and his best beluiffet bruther the laird off Marchinstown'

NLS Adv. Ms 54.1.6, f. 5; printed Napier, *Memoirs*, 67–70.

## 6. Monsbellus,[18] Orkney, 25 March 1561

*Adam, bishop of Orkney, to Archibald Napier of Merchiston.*

Rycht honorabill schir and brother, efter all hartle commendatione, pleis witt I ressavitt this day ane wreittin of Mercheistoune the ix of Marche, answer of ane other wreittin of myne the v of Februar, and hes understand thairbe your vigilant favour in the dress of my bissines, quhairof, schir, I bliss God and thankis yow. I can na wayis rameid, bot onefrendis sall saye the wors of me; bot I sall keip that thai sall not haif the moyane to saye trewlie ony evill of me. As to the first part of the complaint that is geiffin in to the lordis one me, I wreitt sik informatione to yow befoir, that I beleiff, gif ye plesit to informe the lordis in that poyntt, thai suld be thairby satisfeitt. As to the second poyntt, I nay it utterlie that the samin can ever be verefeitt, altoght I haid guid caus to haif done the samin to our soverane, and to all that mycht haif helpit or supportit my caus. I pray yow to mak and entertinye the moneast

---

[16]  Lord James Stewart, later regent, also prior (commendator of the priory) of St Andrews; Nasmyth is Michael Nasmyth of Posso and the laird of Maner is Thomas Lowis of Manor. Nasmyth was clearly waiting upon the regent, but both he and Thomas Lowis had interests in the lands of Briglands (NRS GD34/178, 180).

[17]  Mr Francis Bothwell, treasurer of Orkney, close relative of the bishop

[18]  The name of the bishop of Orkney's palace in Birsay. Erroneously 'Mousbollus' in Napier's transcription. Parts of a stone bearing the name are embedded in the stonework of buildings near its site (close to the ruins of Robert Stewart's palace) today.

frendis ye can, and mak my hartlie commendationes to my lord of Kylmauris,[19] assuring him that we salbe fund thankfull folkis for sik kyndnes as he hes schawin us. And the narration I maid you is veritable, and I will mak it guid, and of other mair sene syne, that may [infuse?] my caus amangis all men; and quhow evir it be, I sall be fund the honnest man, and my adversairis luid liearis. As to the wreittingis that ar send quhilk contenit plaintis, I did bot as I haid caus, and hes beyne thankfull to the gentill man ye waitt of. At this time gif he recompensis me with evill; I may weill tyne this, bot I sall tyne na mair. As to the inspectioun of my wreittingis quhilk he hes gottin, that was wreittin to my lord James, I regard it not, and farles his menaces, for and he war heir, and soght me be oneressonable wayis, he suld haif nathing bot evill will and sad straikkis, and his allya with him. As to the evidentis quhilk ye mak mentioun of in your wreittingis, I was in purpois at the wreittin of your wreittin to send thame; bot becaus I tuik purpois to cum till yow, I thocht not expedient till committ thame to ony messinger quhill I cum my self. Assuring yow, schir, that the mair onkyndnes I thollit for the keipin of favour to yow and youris, and the preserving of your ofspringis apperand rycht, the mair constantt am I at the samin purpois, and salbe godwilling, quha mot evirlestinglie preserve yow and my syster, your bedfellow, and your ofspring, my bairnis. At Monsbellus in Orknay, this xxv of Marche.

Be your bruther at all powair,

'To the laird of Mercheistoune'

NLS Adv. Ms 54.1.6, f. 6; printed Napier, *Memoirs*, 70–1.


## 7. Kirkwall, 20 April [1561]
*James Alexander*[20] *to Archibald Napier of Merchiston.*

Rycht honorabill schir and traist frend, efter my maist inwart and hartle recommendatione of service, it will ples your mastership wit at the wretine of this present, me lord, my maister and your brothir, was departit of his lordschipis ples of Kyrkwall and passyt to the schype quhairine his lordschip was myndit to depart into, and, be the grayce of God, to pass in France to vese the quenyis grace, our maistres; and is of purpos to remane at the schype quhill God provide the wynd and wadir, that his lordship may pass to the completing of his lordschipis voaig. And as anent the ocatione of his lordschipis voaig and interprys at this tym, is to lament his lordschipis extorsyone done to hym in the partis quhair his lordschip hes cur of, and in lyk manner, the

---

[19]  Alexander Cunningham, later fourth earl of Glencairn, prominent member of protestant nobility.

[20]  Servant of Adam, bishop of Orkney, also sheriff-depute (OA D23/5, 232) and commissary of Orkney (*REO*, 286, no. clxix).

oppressyone that is done to uthir frendis, the quhilk his lordschip beleifis that his maistres sall caus rameid to be put thairto as affeiris. And ye sall wit, that afoir his lordschipis departing, hes maid his device and legase, as it afferit to be done, and hes left your mastership ane of his lordschipis executoris, and hes left your sone his lordschipis air; and intendis, gyf God prolongis his lordschipis dayis to agment that airschyp to the gret weill and prophit of your mastership and your airis and his. Farder, your mastership sall reseif fra this berar ane aquytanis of Gylbart Balfouris apone the somys of mone the quhilk your mastership was akit in the buikis of cunsell for to the said Gilbart; and me lord hes dessyrit your mastership quho sone that ye haif reseifit this his aquytance, and that your mastership may be at laisser, that your mastership caus this acquytance be insert in the buikis, and the act quhair your mastership was actit to be distroyit. And as to the uthir affairis of this cuntra, the berar can schaw as me lord hes bene usyt, and as thai intend to us his lordschipis servandis efter his lordschipis departing, gyf thai may. Als me lord hes prayit your mastership to speik the justice clark, and the uthir lordis of sessyone as your mastership thinkis gud towart the mater betweix his lordschip and Tomas Tulloch. The said Tomas hes raissyt new sommandis and hes execut the letteris afoir hys lordschypis departing; I beleif the day be the xxv of May. And to his cusyng Jhone Kynkaid, he hes rafussyt to remane in this cuntra, for quhat caussys I kna nane, for I will assur your mastership that it was me lordis intent and mynd to haif done [him] gret honour and plesour gyf he wald haif remanyt, the quhilk your mastership and his uthir frendis will knaw quhen it plessys the lord God that his lordschip and frend meitis; the quhilk lord mot preserf your mastership in prosparete wyth gud heill. At Kyrkwall, the xx of Aprill.

Be your mastershipis servand and frend,
James Alexander.

'To the honorabill the lard of Marchyestoune'

Napier, *Memoirs*, 72–3.

## 8. Kirkwall, 20 April [1561]

*James Alexander to Janet Bothwell.*

Maistress, efter my maist hartle recommendatioun of service to your ladyschip, it wil ples your ladyschip wit that me lord, your ladyschipis brothir, is at the wretyng of this present blyth and weill in halth, thankis to the lord God, for all the havie trybbill and cumyris his lordschip hes had in tymyss past; the quhilk trybbyllis gyf your ladyschip had knawyne be quhat personyss thai war moifit, ye wald nocht beleifit. I wil expreme na namyss, bot the occasyone of the trybill that mufit his lordschip maist was nocht done be na Orknanaye borne. Albeit that the Synklairis maid insurrectioun agane his lordschip, he wald nocht haif regardit that one thyng gyf his lordschip had wantit the occatioune of displesour done to hys lordschip be thame that his lordschip confydit maist in to resentle for the warldis part; bot as now, thankis to God, his lordschipis mynd is releifit of the maist part of the occatiounis. Atour your ladyschip sall wyt, that at the tym of his lordschipis seiknes, as his lordschip was mervallis seik and beleifit nocht to haif recuverrit, thair was na speciall persone that his lordschip was myndit to haif left his lordschipis heretag, pois of sylver that his lordschip had for the tyme, allenrenlie bot to your ladyschipis housband, your self and your airis; and this I mak your ladyschip assurit of. And now presentle at his lordschipis deperting, his lordschip hes maid his deviss and lagese and hes nemyt your ladyschipis housband ane of his lordschipis executouris, and your sone to be his lordschipis air in all thyngis pertenyng to heretaig; quhairfoir your ladyschip may beleif surlie to haif ane faithful brothir and ane kynd lord, gyf God prolongis his lordschipis dayis, the quhilk your ladyschip and all his lordschipis gud frendis aucht to pray for. Farder, your ladyschip sall wit anent your cusyng Jhone Kynkaid, that me lord is varay myscontentit that he wald nocht remane in this cuntra; consyndirane that his lordschip send for hym affectuoislie bayth to haif done hym prophit gyf he wald haif remanyt in the cuntra and to set fordwart his lordschipis honor in his absence; bot I will assure your ladyschip that he wald nocht remane wythout me lord wald haif put awaye the constabill[21] Gylbert Balfour instantle, quha hes intrametit wyth this yeiris fruttis and can gef na compt of his lordschipis fruttis of this yeir, he beand put awaye, and to haif maid hyim chalmerlaine, the quhilk office, gyf me lord wald haif gyfin hym, is nocht gaynand for hym; bot nochtwythstanding he wald haif maid hym hail bailye, and kabtane of hys lordshipis pless; and promest, gyf Jhone Kynkaid wald us that weill, and remane quhill his lordschipis returnyng, that he suld haif his dissyris fulfillit. And gyf Jhone makis ane uthir rehairss to excus hymself, and to put the wit to me lord, belyfit it nocht, for I assur your ladyschip it is trew that I haif wretin; quhairfoir gyf your ladyschip speikis wyth his modir, or anie uthir frendis, schaw as I haif wretin, and lat nocht me lord be murmuryt wyth na frend. I will wrat na mair as now, bot the eternall lord preserf your ladyschip. At Kyrkwall, the xx of Aprill.

By your ladyschipis cusyng at powar,<br>James Allexander.

'To the ladie of Marchyestoune'

NLS Ms 1707, f. 1; printed Napier, *Memoirs*, 73–4.

---

[21]   I.e. of Kirkwall Castle.

## 9. Kirkwall, 25 April 1561
*Mr Francis Bothwell to Janet Bothwell.*

Darrest antt, efter hartlie commendatioun, ye sall understand that my lord, your broder,[22] hes tane purpos to pas in Franche, God willyng, and for the gud of hymself and all his freindis, sua that God almychty geif hym prosperite in his vaiage. And in the tyme of his departyng I spak hym effectuislie for to be gud unto you and your barnis, gif it chance hym inlaik in the tyme of his vaiage; quhilk he shew in deid, for he institute, nominat and ordinat your son Jhon[23] to be his undouttit ayr of all hes heretage, and your housband to be excecutour to hym also; and hes left to your dochter and Frances your son, in legasie, largile of his geir. And quhen he wes seik, I being absent with you, efferand of his lyff, he schew sic greit kyndnes to you and your barneis, that he leift and gaif outt of his handis the effect of the mony that he had than, before famois wittnes, and commandit it to be delyverit to you and your barnis; and this I have of hymself, and of thame that was maist secret than with hym. Thairfor ye aucht till have greit luiff to his lordschip, for I assur you his lordschip beris als greit luiff to your housband, your self and your barnis, as to ony that is in this present lyff; quhairfor I pray you speyk your housband effectiuslie that he await upoun my lordis besynes in till Edinbrugh intentit and movit contrar his lordschip be Thomas Tulloch of the Fluris, quhilk wil be upoun the xxv day of May nixtocum, and caus him requeist the lordis of the session that my lord gaitt na hurtt nor skatht in na matteris intentit befor thame, untill his lordschipis hame cummyng fra the quenis grace service. This I doutt nocht bot ye wil be diligant thairintill, as your partt is for to do. Attour I will nocht latt you gang withoutt repruyff, and this is it. I schew you sum thyngis anentis sum personis towart thair misbehavor towart my lord, quhilk he will schaw at the meittyng be you with hym; the quhilk thyng I bad you keip secrett, yit notwithstanding ye schew thame agane to your sister Mergratt,[24] quhilk scho vrait agane heir despitfullie, and causit cummaris to be amang us, of the quhilk my lord was gretlie offendat at you for the tyme. Quhairfor apardon me in tyme cummyng till schaw you ony secrett bot only that thing quhilk I sett no by quha heir it, for thair was nocht ane word that I said to you, and ye will keip the treuth, bot I will byd be thame and verefee thame in my lordis presence, quhan it will pleis God us till meitt all togethir. Of this repruiff tak in patience, for it was writtyn heir be your narration, and thairfor my lord bad me writt to you and repruiff you thairof in his name. Command my hartlie service to the lard, and Jhon, and my awn son

---

[22]   I.e. Adam Bothwell.
[23]   John Napier, the mathematician (1550–1617).
[24]   Margaret Bothwell, actually Janet's half-sister, wife of Gilbert Balfour of Westray.

Frances, and to the rest of my gud frendis. Nocht ellis, bot the leving lord keip you now and evir. At Kirkwall, the xxv day of Aprill the yeir of God lm vc lx ane yeiris.

> Be youris at powar,
> Mr. Frances Bothwall.

'To his darrest antt Jane Botwall, lady Merchyngstoun'

Napier, *Memoirs*, 75–6.

## 10. Kirkwall, 28 August [1561]
*Mr Francis Bothwell to Janet Bothwell.*

Darrest antt, aeftir maist hartly commendatioun, loving to God I haiff hard of the quenis grace cuming hame,[25] and off my lord your brotheris, quhairfoir I pray you that ye beir your self waisly and kyndly to his lordschip; inlykwiss your husband, in sic ane maner that your husband be never frai hyme, and that for your greit weill and profeit; for I feir, be rasone that I am frai hyme, that thair sal be sum that sall labour in your contrary for to obteine that thyng the quhilk ye haiff Goddis rycht of. It is nocht neidfull to expreim the personis to you, for ye knaw them; for giff I war present with hym, I suld keip hyme that na man suld do you hurt in to your rychtis, for I knaw weill thair greit deligence that thai will mak one the ane pairt, and my lordis facilite one the uther pairt; quhairfoir be ye deligent and waikryf, and gyf my lord cumis nocht haistaly heir bot is in purpois to remaine thair, labour ye, and caus for to labour, that my lord send about me to remain with hys lordschip, for your weill and uther fryndis; nocht that I desir to be in courtein or cummer, bot only for me lordis weill. Bot I prai you lat nocht my lord wit that I wreit to you for ony affaris, for I wreit to you as ane freind, warnand you of inconvenientis that maye chance excep ye be the mair deligent; and weit nocht me gyff it be utherwaiis nor weill, for quhene his lordship and I depertit, he was als weill gevin to you and your bairnis as ye or I wald haif desirit, as I wreit to you at lenth efter his lordshipis depertyng. And gyf it chansis me to cum in his cumpani, I wald trow in God that his lordship suld continew in the sam luiff and favour that he had to you and your bairnis quhene his lordship depertit, and thait na uther laboraris suld prevaill. The rest of this maiter I refar to your wisdom and your husbandis. I wreit to you oft tymes of befoir and gat na answer as yit; thairfoir be nocht sweir in tymes cuming, bot adverteis of all thyngis ye thynk necessair. I sall send your hors to you all sone as I get passingiairis cumand betwein, for this com awaye at the poist and your naik mycht induir to cum with hyme. And commend me

---

[25]  From France, earlier the same month.

hartly to the laird and to Jhone, and your sone Frances quhilk I trest in God salbe als gud ane man as ever was in Lowdyene. Nocht ellis, but the eternale God preserve you. At Kirkwall, the xxviij daye of August.

Be your cusyng at the utirmaist of his powar,
Mr. Frances Boitwall.

'To ane honorabill lady Jein Boitwall, lady off Merchestoun'

Napier, *Memoirs*, 76–7.

## 11. Kirkwall, 6 August [1565]
*William Henderson to Sir John Bellenden.*

My lord, efter humill commendatioun and service, pleis I traist or now your lordschip hes gottin word of sik thingis as hes occurit in thir partis at the wreting of this present, loving to God I wes nocht weill at eis. Nevertheless I haif send to your lordschip the extract of compt of your lordschipis portion of Orkna of the lx four yeires crop as your lordschip will consider be the samyn, and ye sall resaive ane wreting derect of Duncan Scolay[26] to caus him answer your lordschip of xx pundis. I haif nocht gottin compleit payment furth of the tenentis handis of Rowisay and sum of Sanday; nevertheless I hoip to get it and then, with godwilling, sall mak your lordschip compleit payment of the last yeiris crop becaus Duncan Scolay is presentlie thair. Ye sall caus requer him to mak your lordschip payment of the Wittsounday terme of Eglissay of the lx fyve yeiris crop becaus it is allrede bypast. Tweiching payment of your lordschipis portioun of the lx twa yeiris and lx thre yeiris I se na way to get payment thairof without my lord assing yow sum place to tak it up of, for thair is nane heir that will mak payment but his lordschipis precept and command. Thairfor your lordschip maun awyis and speik the bischoip to se how ye may best cum thairto. Tweiching the rest of flesche that is in this cuntre the tenendis makis ane hevy mane that all thair guidis ar deid, and I dreid thair be less payit this yeir than was farne yeir, bot I sall do guid, with God willing, to get sameikill as is possabill of thame, and I wald your lordschip gart some salt and creis for the butter and flesche for thair is nane heir to be gottin. Tweiching Margret Dunbar[27] scho hes na will to cum south becaus scho is with bairn and on nawayis will cum quhill scho be deliverit, and I knaw nocht nothir gif scho be purposit to cum than or nocht for schois, that scho will on nawayis adheir to the tothir man. For I resavit your last wretin I had delyverit to hir sax last of beir furth of Sanday, and in guid fayth the

---

[26] Duncan Scollay, burgess of Kirkwall and 'beloved servitor' of Adam Bothwell.
[27] Of the Dunbar of Loch family, widow of John Wemyss and wife of John Gifford. See Introduction.

carage, fraucht and inlaik be the get wes darrer to me nor aucht pundis and thair inlaikit that was skalit be the get and be difference of punderis, vii [in] beir, and odis, quhilk I buit to pay silver furth to John Gyffart,[28] and I trest your lordschip will nocht desyr me to pay that of my awin purss for I did it at command of the sherif to put thame in entres of payment, and he said he wyst weill your lordschip wald allow the expensis that I maid upon it, and bad me tak ane schalder thairof to mak the expensis and travell upon the rest, and he hes tane up ane uthir schalder of the said beir to him self. I find hir satisfeit with the sax last of beir that scho hes gottin and is not plentewis thairfor. I would your lordschip send me word quhat salbe done to hir in tyme cuming, for doutless or I cair it furth of Sanday yeirle to Kirkwa I had lever cair it to Leith furth of Sanday. Als your lordschip sall wit that Mr James Annand[29] purposis to mak impediment in the persoun of Sanday. Thairfor your lordschip maun caus John Grahame[30] provid remeid thairfor; and now at harvist the teindis wald be redy that he may knaw his awin and set the samyn to sufficient dettouris for ilk thre yeir anis all teindis ar ridden in this cuntre and set thairefter, and now the takis thairof is warkand. I can writ to your lordschip na uthir thing at this tyme for caussis as your lordschip will knaw afterwart. Prayand your lordschip to send me word in wret at lenth of all thingis that ye wald I did, and God willing I sall fulfill the samyn at the utermest of my power. Your lordschip will mak my humill commendatioun of service to my maistres your honorable badfellow. Committand yow and hir and all your houssald to the eternall God for ever. At Kirkwa, the vi day of Agust, be your lordschipis humill servitur, etc.

W. Hendersone, Dingwell purseveant.

'To my lord justyce clarke'

Roxburghe Muniments, Bundle 1104.

## 12. Kirkwall, 16 November [1567]
*William Henderson to Sir John Bellenden.*

My lord, eftir maist hummyll commendatioun of service, pleis I ressavit your lordshipis wrytting fra my brother togidder with your lordshipis discharge safar as I haif maid compt of quharintil your lordship hes gevin me sufficient allowance for my labouris. Nochtwythstanding I persaif that my lady is nocht

---

[28]  John Gifford, notary, first appears in Orkney in company of Adam Bothwell, acquires land in Gorn, Sandwick, and remains in Orkney, seemingly till his death in the 1580s. See Introduction.

[29]  Prebendary of St John, later chancellor of Orkney and co-commissioner for planting of kirks there. First appears in Orkney with Adam Bothwell.

[30]  Parson of Sanday, and servitor of Sir John Bellenden.

content with the pryces quhilk I gat for the victuall, and trewly I did that lay in my power, bot your lordship sall understand that albeit this cuntre be skant and deir at this present thair is na siluer to be gottin in it, and in gud fayth thair is xx li. or mair awand to me of the pryce of your victual yit be the wyffis of Kyrkwall that I trow neid to get payment of. For lyk as the cuntre is skant of victualis sua is it scant of all uther thingis that is worth, and sum thairof is restand in the commownis handis quhilk on force I man frist quhil thay may get siluer maid of sic wareis as thai haif presentlye, yit of the saidis restis I haif collectit ane hundreth pundis money and send with this beirar with sic uther grath as was in reddines befoir his departing. And as for your victual this yeir to cum advyss quhat ye wil do thairwith and send me word againe with this beirar for thair was nocht thir mony yeiris sa scant ane yeir of cornis as all men reportis for thai mene that it wil nocht sustene the peple gif thai saw the grownd and pay the half of thair dettis. God send remeid as he pleissis. And gif your lordship can get the siluer fra the bischop for Deirness and Holme I think it war not evill for I dreid thair salbe evil payment maid of this yeir. Twecheing the buttir and victual defalkit quhilk is in your lordshipis assignatioun I spak with the bischop towart the samin and desyrit his lordship to mak the samin furth in sum uther rowme, and his answer was that albeit the samin be nocht payit his rental beiris it and sayd that thair is mony uther thingis nor that quhilk he himself gettis na payment of quharof he can get na remeid, and beleiffis your lordship for sa smal a thing wil mak na deference. Thairfor your lordship may speik him your self towart that purpois. Quhar as your lordship wryttis to get the rentailis of the kyngis landis of Orknay and Yetland and siclyk the bischopis landis, trewly I can nocht haif thame presently to send to your lordship, bot as to the kyngis rental of Orknay I can lat you haif the just rental thairof as it payis now, and as to the rentale of Yetland your broder Patrik[31] tuk ane rental fra me thairof and presently I haif nane thairof. As for the bischopis rental I haif the soum thairof bot nocht in particular, bot gif your lordship plessis to haif the samin I sal do deligence to get the samin.

As twecheing this cuntre effairis I traist your lordship hes hard how my Lord Robert hes appointit with Gilbert Balfour, that is to say the said lord hes gevin to Mr James Balfour[32] x chalderis victual, and to Gilbert x chalderis victuall, to be payit furth of the Quhytkyrk[33] yeirly. And his awin broder the lard of Cultmalindeis[34] hes gottin v chalderis victuall. The person of

---

[31]  Sir Patrick Bellenden, later of Evie and Stenness.
[32]  Parson of Flysk, later Sir James Balfour of Pittendreich (c. 1525–83), brother of Gilbert Balfour of Westray. Politician and legal commentator.
[33]  Barony of Whitekirk. This was the subject of an action for payment by Gilbert against Oliver Sinclair in 1569 (*Canongate Ct Bk*, 22, 125–6, 132–4).
[34]  Laurence Bruce of Cultmalindie, half-brother of Robert Stewart, by his mother Euphemia Elphinstone and John Bruce of Cultmalindie.

Pennycuke[35] hes gottin for his labouris ane monkis pensioun and xl li., and the lard of Grange[36] hes gottin ane teynd besyd him self in Fyiff. And Gilbert attour all this hes gottin Westray and Papay Westray als frely haldin of the said lord as he haldis Orknay of the kyngis majestie. And for that Gilbert hes gevin ower the schirefschip and keiping of the castell, and at thair cummyng to Edinburgh all thir thingis ar to be endit and perfytit amangis thame and contractis maid to that effect for fulfillyng thairof.

Concernyng your broder Patrik he departit furth of this cuntre in ane strange maner, for I persaif that my Lord Robert is myndit to do him na plesour, and Gilbert Balfour compleinis greitly that he did nocht his dewtie to him, and thairfor gif your lordship mak nocht sum dress thairintil I desyir him nocht in thir partis. Farder in this purpois I wil nocht wrytt bot referis to the beirar.

My lord hes bene deligent in the furthsetting of justice and hes put gud ordour and rewle in the cuntre. God gif him grace to continew. And your lordship is brutit to be the caus of the summondyng of thir cuntre men sowth to underly the law for intercommonyng with my Lord Bothwell,[37] and thai purpois to gif you the hail wyit and the bischop thairof, and allegeis that thai ar innocent of all crymes and that it is bot of malice and evil wil that thai ar summond sowth, and this I thocht gud to advertiss your lordship of, that ye may haif ane reddy answer to thame gif thai propone the samin.

Als I spak wyth my Lord Robert anent the teyndis of Dalry,[38] bot I culd cum na speik at his hand. He allegeis ye mak him nevir gud payment. He is to cum sowth him self and than ye may assay quhat ye may do your self with him, bot now he puttis of and sayis he hes referrit all to his chalmerlane and wil nocht mel thairwith him self.

At the makyng of this wrytting I was to depart to the north ylis and commandit my wyf gif thair come in ony of your lordshipis geir affoir my cummyng againe that scho suld schip it to cum sowth, and samekle as cumis caus ressaif and gif your lordshipis tikatt to this beirar thairupon. I can wryt na uther thingis at this present, bot referris the rest to the beirar quha can schaw your lordship the samyn at lenth to quhom ye wil pleis gif credence. And sua committis your lordship to the preservation of almychty God for evir. Wryttin at Kyrkwall, the xvj of November, be your lordshipis servitour at his uttir power.

W. Hendersone, Dingwell pursewant.

'To the richt honorable Sir Johne Bellenden of Auchnowle, knycht'

Roxburghe Muniments, bdl 1634, no. 1.

35   Mr William Pennycuik, parson of Pennycuik, provost of Kirk o' Field and vicar of Urr; pension granted by Robert Stewart.
36   Sir William Kirkcaldy of Grange (c. 1520–73), soldier and politician. His estates were near Burntisland.
37   James Hepburn, earl of Bothwell (1534/5–78), magnate and third consort of Queen Mary.
38   The kirk of Dalry and its teinds were appropriated to the abbey of Holyrood.

## 13. Kirkwall, 4 February [1567–8]
*William Henderson to Sir John Bellenden.*

My lord, eftir maist humyll commendatioun of service, pleis I haif ressavit ane wreting of your lordshipis togidder with twa wryttingis of may ladeis, your bedfallows, in to the quhilkis mentioun is maid that sen my broder Cuthbertis departing fra your lordship ye nevir ressavit answer thairof nor wrytting fra me except ane wrytting fra Thomas Robesone, servand to my Lord Robert. Trewth it is that aucht dayis eftir Mertymes my brother Cuthbert had answer wryttin of me to your lordship and to my lady bayth concernyng all effairis in this cuntre, and your hail flesche and buttir samikle as I culd get reddy was schippit in Gilbert Balfouris bark togidder with vixx li. of money quhilk I traist be this your lordship hes ressavit. Bot I persaif be your lordshipis wrytting and mekle mair be my ladyis that your lordship takis sum suspitioun of my using, for my lady hes gevin me veray heych repreiffis in hir wryttingis quhilk I desarve nocht that I knaw, and menyng that war nocht your lordship stud my frend it had bene war with me as it is hable to be yit. My lord, gif ony man hes maid report of me that I haif nocht done my dewtie to your lordship in all thingis according to my habilitie and power I pray your lordship to lat me knaw it, and owther I sall mak amendis at your lordshipis desyir or ellis thair report salbe knawin fals, for I knaw your lordship wil nocht start without ane caus and in gud fayth, or your lordship suld haif occasioun to complene of my using I had rather be geirless. Tharfor my lord I pray you lat it cum to lycht and I sal cum and iustifie my awin caus gif neid beis for I loif God. I haif nowther done nor said that I mister to feir, nowther towart your lordship nor in na uther sort, bot I dar face the mater. My lady thinkis that hir geir cumis nocht sasone as sche wald desyir it. Your lordship sal understand that it is eftir Alhallowmes ony flesche or buttir is gottin furth of the tenentis handis, and this winter hes bene sa tempestuous that it culd nocht cum sa schortly as sche desyrit, and your buttir lyis in sundry ylis quhilk is veray cummersum to be gadderit in as thai that knawis the rowmes can informe your lordship. And lykwyss thair is yit of your lordshipis victual of the last yeir restand in the tenentis handis quhilk I can nocht get payment of, and yit my lady hes na consideratioun, bot as al was reddy and in my default only postponit. I beleif that I haif bene als reddy to forder your lordship to your dewteis heir as ever ony that had the handillying of samikle geir in Orknay. Speir how utheris ar answerit and your lordship wil knaw, and I wald nocht that your lordship tuk ane uther opinoun of me bot that I willit your proffitt safar as lay in my power. Als my lady is plaintuous of sum gold that I send to hir sayand that sche tynt xij d. of ilk pece, and siclyk of yopindailis that sche tynt ij s. thairof. Your lordship may requyr my brother Cuthbert gif he offerit hir nocht quhyt siluer in Edinburgh for every pece bayth of gold and yopindalis to that samin pryce that sche resaiffit thaim of, and thairfor sche aucht nocht to complene sa hevely upone me for, or I suld be suspectit or haif your lordshipis indignatioun I had rather want all proffitt that I culd haif thairthrow for I never menit bot to serve your lordschip trewly as God be my juge. As to this yeiris victual that is bypast I wald your lordship advertist me quhat ye wil I do thairintill, and I desyrit my broder to bring answer thairof fra your lordship. Tharfor gif ye haif nocht gevin him informatioun thairof I wald your lordship send word to me with the first that cumis betuix for the victuall is veray skarss in thir partis this yeir, and schew me gif I sal answer Margaret Dunbar and your broder of thair victuall and out of quhat rowm, and gif your lordship takis up the victual of Deirnes and Holme this yeir or nocht for the soner that we start we wil cum the bettir speid thairintill, and provyd the best way that it may cum to your lordshipis utilitie and profitt, and sa far as lyis in my power it sal nocht ly behynd.

Lat men speik quhat thay pleis of me, I traist, God willyng, your lordship sal knaw that I sal do my dewitie, and peraventur I haif deservit bettir report of thame that hes informit your lordship of ony ewill using that I haif done in the handillyng of your geir in thir partis. I wil nevir refuse to serve your lordship attour ony uther man for the greit kyndnes and favour that I haif evir fund of your lordship, bot or I suld haif your lordshipis indignatioun for ony profitt that culd redound to me I had rather want all gaines that I haif or can haif of the handillyng of your lordshipis geir in thir partis. And gif it be your lordshipis plesour that I continew in the handillyng thairof gif in ony sort your lordship be hurt I pray you lat me knaw and I sal do gud will to amend it. Your lordshipis rental is knawin bayth to your lordship and to the tenentis that I ressaif your dewiteis fra, and quharintill can I defraud your lordship seying that bayth ye that ressavis and thay that delyveris knawis quhat I may do, and gif your lordship wald say that be the sellyng of your victuall that I haif nocht gevin you the just pryce that I gat for it, my lord, I send my compt with my broder, and of the last yeiris victuall thair was sum thairof unressavit fra the tenentis and sum that was ressavit was unsauld at that tyme and your lordship upone ane hail compt condiscendit that the rest of your lordshipis victuall suld stand as allowance to me for xx li. the last victuall, and albeit that I haif done my deligence to haif gottin hail payment yit thair is restand in the tenentis handis mair nor twa last of that yeir quhilk of fors I man allow for my fie quhilk your lordship hes grantit to me. My lord, I pray your lordship tak your ganis quhar ye may haif it. God hinder thame that wald hinder you thairof.

Twecheing my Lord Robertis effairis quharof I wrait to you I haif schawin him all the maner how your lordship hes send me advertisment thairof, of the quhilk he is veray weill content, and offeiris to fulfill all thingis that I wrait to your lordship, swa that he may haif the samblable done to him, and consideris that it can nocht be perfyitit quhil ye meit all togidder. I haif alsso spokin his lordship for your teyndis, howbeit I haif wryttin wyth my broder thairof of befoir how I culd get na answer thairof bot referrit the samin to his chalmerlane, bot now his lordship is content and hes promisit to me to caus his chalmerlane overse you quhil he and your lordship aggrie thairfor, and he is content to tak victual heir for the samin as ye can aggrie. Alwayis he hes promist nocht to be regorous, and I wald nocht that your lordship suld think that I was slewthfull thairintil nor yit in na uther actioun that evir your lordship committit credit to me. I neid nocht presently to referis thame, bot your lordship may remember thame bayth first and last, and gif ye haif fund falt thairin or nocht I wil mak na man juge bot your lordshipis self.

Anent your broder Patrik I wrate inlykwys of befoir to your lordship wyth my broder lamenting his infortunat usingis in thir partis quharof yit I haif na less caus be the consideratioun of your lordshipis wryting quhar as he hes informit your lordship that my Lord Robert suld haif bene sa extreme aganes him and sa wrangus as to haif evectit his frendis and servandis furth of thair rowmes and bailyeries and his wyf and bairnis furth of Camstoun[39] thair heritage, and haif possessit Johne Houstoun[40] in the subdenrye, etc. I will testifie the trewth to your lordship and I will avow the samin in presens of my lord regent and hail consaill that my Lord Robert nevir thocht to do sik thing lat be the doyng thairof. And first anent the evectyng of ony man furth of thair rowmes the contrair is of trewth, for sen his lordshipis cummyng in Orknay he hes nevir removit ane tenent. As for the bailyereis, William Halcro being bailye of Fyrth and Harry, becaus he was convictit de crimine falsi he depryvit him of his office.[41]

As for Camstane, Robert Sinclair had ane precept of Gilbert Balfouris to put him in possessioun thairof quhilk he presentit to my Lord Robert, and he seying it subscryvit of befoir thocht that he mycht ratifie the samin and swa subscryvit the samin precept, yit howsone as it come to William Giffartis[42] eiris he schawand the mater to my lord he gaif ane precept in the contrar thairof, and swa thair was nevir na molestatioun maid thairintill mair. And towart the subdenrye the trewth is at Alhallowmes the puir commounis, occupyaris of

---

[39] Campston in St Andrews parish, in which Patrick Bellenden's wife, Katherine Kennedy, had interest as widow of Henry Sinclair of Strom.

[40] The new subdean of Orkney is elsewhere named as William Houston, temporarily supplanting Archibald Douglas, forfeited for a time for alleged complicity in the murder of David Riccio (*RSS*, v, no. 2757). This seems to be an error, as Douglas's replacement is mentioned as John Houston twice in the letter. John Houston was only briefly subdean, and is later designated as prebendary of the altar of St Peter in the cathedral and master of Kirkwall Grammar School (*REO*, 354, no. ccxxxi).

[41] Nothing further is known of this, though William Halcro was said to be a supporter of Magnus Halcro of Brough and Patrick Bellenden, and as such an enemy of Robert Stewart. See Introduction.

[42] Seemingly a relative of John Gifford; a William Gifford from South Ronaldsay had been implicated in an attack against Hanseatic merchants in Shetland in 1566. He, along with Peter Loch from St Reinold's Isle, claimed they were servants of 'Peter Ballenthun', presumably Patrick Bellenden (Ballantyne and Smith 1195–1579, no. 158; *REO*, 375, no. clxxxviii).

the subdenry and payaris of the dewiteis thairof come in affoir his lordship and maid ane hevy complaynt schawand how that threfauld poyndit for thair dettis com on thame, anis be Patrikis servandis, ane uther tyme be James Alexander, and the thryd tyme be Johne Houstoun, quhilk complaynt beand sa grevous and the puir folkis desyrand to be relevit of thair dettis, my lord causit collect the fat guddis of the said subdenry furth of the tenentis handis be his lordshipis officiaris to the utilitie and profitt of thame that obtenit the rycht thairof be the decreit of the lordis of sessioun, and send the samin sowth with Maister Johne Montcurr[43] in Dundie quhilk wil be deliverit to Patrik gif he hes gottin decreit thairupoun. And sua my lord allanerly did that bot for the releif of the puir tenentis that was sa hevely oppressit thair that sum of thame ar put fra thair houshald be the samin. I wait your lordship or ony gud man of conscience wald haif done as his lordship did thairintill gif he had knawin the maner. Now my lord attour all uther thingis I man lament the caus to your lordship of your broder Patrik quhom aboun all creatuir in erth I was willing to haif servit and did that lay in my power to him and gat the indignatioun of all his unfrendis for his caus quhilk I want nocht yit nor never wil salang as he and thay ar at variance, yit be quhat motyve or of quhat caus I knaw nocht, I haif fund him veray fremmit to me, and supponis that owther he or his wyf hes maid sum report to your lordship of me, and gif sua be I pray your lordship to lat me knaw the samin and albeit he haif done it swa your lordship knaw the trewth I wil put it clene furth of rememberance; and prayis to God that he may prosper weill nochtwithstanding ony caus I haif to complene for. And he never come in that stres or misfortune bot I lamentit the samin als hevelye as him self did and safar as lay in my power did for his releif. I wil mak him juge thairof himself. And now at last I haif commownit with my Lord Robert anentis him quha is veray heychly offendit at him for the sinister report that he hes maid to my lord regent, and yit I fand him of this mynd, that gif his lordship culd be suir of him in tyme cummyng for the effectioun and favour that my lord regent beiris towart him for the trew and afauld mynd that he hes fund evir of your lordship, and for the luf and kyndnes that Maister Nychol Elphinstoun[44] hes to him, he is willing to remit all byganis for fair play in tyme to cum swa that he lat my lord regent knaw that the complaynt that he maid of befoir is utherwys nor he informit his grace. And lykwys to caus his grace to schaw his lordship favor for his saik, lyk as he schew him self displesit for his caus, and this being done I traist my Lord Robert sal denay him na thing that he will requyr that is ressonable. I beleif my Lord Robert hes wryttin to your lordship his mynd and sic uther effairis as he hes ado with your lordship, quharfor I wil cess to wryt forder thairintill.

---

[43]    Presumably a Dundee merchant.
[44]    Servant of the Regent Moray (NRS B22/1/62, f. 151).

I lippin that your lordship sall send me advertisment at lenth of all thingis that your lordship will haif me to do. Praying your lordship to put the samin in wryt and I sall do gud will to performe the samin to my power. I can wryt na answer to my lady, your bedfallow, bot gif I schew my self impatient thairintill, tharfor it will pleis your lordship to excuse me at hir hand, for gif sche knew all the impedimentis that stoppis hir gudis fra hir at sic tyme as sche lukis for it sche wald nocht gif me sa heych ane repreif as scho hes done in hir wrytting, bot I knaw your lordship hes consideratioun and thairfor I beir wyth it. Commyttyng your lordship to the protectioun of God for evir. At Kyrkwall, the feird of Fabruar, be your lordshipis humyl and obedient servitour.

W. Hendersone.

Als I spak to my Lord Robert about James Menteth[45] quha is laitly cum hither, and said that it was by the conditioun that his lordship maid with you at his departyng, and he sayis that quhat assythment and mend that your lordship will devys to be done be him to Patrik he sal caus him to fulfill the samin, and desyris your lordship to speik Patrik thairintil, and as your lordship wryttis to him he sal caus James Menteth to do the samin or ellis he sal haif his leif fra him agane gif he refusis to do it. And my Lord Robert hes gevin me his hand upone his honour he sal fulfil the thing that I haif wryttin to your lordship. Tharfor I lippin your lordship wil send me advertisment thairof agane amang uther thingis.

W. Hendersone.

'To my lord justice clerk'

Roxburghe Muniments, bdl 1634, no. 2.

## 14. Kirkwall, 20 March [1567–8]
*William Henderson to Sir John Bellenden.*

My lord, eftir maist humyl commendatioun of service, pleis I wryttit to your lordship of befoir with ane servand of my Lord Robertis callit William Menteth, quhilk wrytting I beleif ye haif ressavit lang syne, quharintil I send informatioun of all thingis that your lordship had wryttin to me bayth towartis your awin affairis and your broder Patrik. Bot now haiffand greitar occasioun I thocht neidfull to send your lordship advertisment of the unhappy chance that is happinnit amangis us in thir partis that ye may find remeid for stopping of greittar inconvenientis to mak ane asythment thairintill utherwys it wil turne

---

[45]  Follower of Robert Stewart as a member of the Menteith family. Originally from the Kerse, the family, which later rendered its name as Monteith, settled in Orkney and flourished there until the mid-seventeenth century. See Introduction.

to the warss rather nor to the bettir. Thus it is happinnit that upone the xvj day of Marche instant my Lord Robert raid of the toun of Kirkwall accompaneit with Maister Gilbert Foulsey[46] and ane few number of his awin servandis and causit me to pas with him to Sandwyk to pas his tyme. And haiffand mynd of na ewill beand in ane place callit Gorne[47] with Johne Giffart, upone the morne thaireftir thair come word to his lordship furth of the toun that the men of the kyrk that was put in be the bischop to keip the samin and my Lord Robertis servandis war fallin in ane tulye, and that thai war segeand thame in the kirk and this beand about iij houris eftir nown or thairby his lordship thocht best to ryde to the toun to stay cummeris, and it beand ten mylis or thairby to the toun thairfra it was veray lait or he come to the toun of Kyrkwall, and be the gait he gat word how that thair was ane servand of his slane be the bischopis men and twa of the men in the kirk slane inlykwys. The name of my Lord Robertis man was callit Johne Brown, and the twa bischopis men war callit Nychol Alexander and James Moir.[48] And howsone he come to the toun he wald nocht pass to the castill nor suffir his servandis to speik wyth him, bot past to Hew Gordonis[49] and remanit thair twa dayis thaireftir; and send for the honest men of the cuntre and tuk thair consultatioun quhat thai thocht best to him to do and tryit the hail maner as was happinnit quhilk was reportit be thame to his lordship in this maner. That this forsaid servand Johne Brown quha was newly arryvit bot ane day affoir furth of ane schip passit to the mornyng prayaris in the kirk, and the prayaris beand endit he passit throw the kirk viseand the samyn and come to ane entres of ane turnpyk quhilk past up to the pendis of the kyrk and wald haif bene up; and thay that keipit the kirk commandit him to remoif or ellis thai wald cast at him. And he nocht knawand that it was keipit gaif thame scharp wordis agane and thocht that it was done in dispyt past and advertist my Lord Robertis servandis, and thay in ane angir ruschit furth of the castell in to the kirk, and als sone as thai was enterit the bischopis servandis that was in the kirk seand the man that thai had forbiddin befoir to cum to the duir at the samin thay schot at him and hat him in the heid and slew him. And he beand slaine my Lord Robertis men schot thair culveryngis up amangis the throwgangis of the kyrk, and chanceit to slay the said twa men, and thair beand bot uther thre fallowis in the kyrk thay past doun over the kirk owtwith upone ane tow and left the samin voyd and swa my Lord Robertis men enterit thairintill. And

---

[46]   Gilbert Foulsie, archdeacon of Orkney, first appears shortly after arrival of Adam Bothwell. With James Annand, he was commissioner for the planting of kirks in Orkney. He died before 1584.

[47]   Gorn, no longer a farm, south of the Loch of Skaill in Sandwick.

[48]   See Introduction; no further details about these individuals except Nicol Alexander who, as stated, seems to have been in the fourth degree of kinship to Robert Stewart – probably a Holyrood connection.

[49]   Little-known figure, probably with ecclesiastical connections, seemingly based in Kirkwall. Possible progenitor of the Gordon family, of Cairston.

now my Lord Robert hes desyrit me to wryt to your lordship the hail maner
quhilk is reportit to be as I haif wryttin of befoir; and becaus it is chanceit by
his expectatioun and sair aganis his will, his hail confidence is in your lordship
that ye wil tak travell to metigat the mater, and quhat ye think that his lordship
can do for assythment thairof he sayis he wil do it, his honour saif and his
servandis lyffis. And he lamentis sairest the deith of Nychol Alexander quha
was feirdis of kyn and his lordship. My lord I pray you to pondour the mater
and haif respect quhat gud may proceid upone the dress of this truble and quhat
inconvenient may follow gif the samin be nocht mitigat, for my Lord Robert
hes desyrit me to reduce to your memorie the auld affectioun and kyndnes that
hes bene betuix him and you, and siklyk betuix him and your broder Patrik,
and how that ather of your bairnis and his ar feirdis of kyne quhilk suld move
yow to lufe and favour uthers. And nochtwithstanding of the variance that is
presentlie betuix him and Patrik he is content to submit him hallely to your
lordshipis jugement sua that ye and sum uther landit man be souertie for him
to be his leil trew servand in tym cummyng and amend the thingis bypast. And
becaus that his lordship is bent to haif the superiorite of this cuntre alsweil of
the bischopry as the rest, tharfor or fardar trublis happin gif your lordship can in
ony sort dress the bischop and him, it war ane godly actioun, and I wait it wald
stay gret inconvenientis that is appeirand to cum. And nochtwithstanding of
this mischance I pray you to ceis nocht to performe the dress of the interchance
with the bischop puttand the maner thairof in sic heidis as your lordship thinkis
gud. And my Lord Robert sayis gif he may find you at this tyme his suir frend
ye sal nocht requyr that thing of his lordship that he wil na you, for he sayis
now in tyme of neid ane frend is best knawin. All thing that I wrait to your
lordship of befoir concernyng my Lord Robert he wil performe to you and
mair, ye doand your part to him in this mater. Your lordship is wyss anewcht.
I can wryt na forder perswasivis to put away inconvenientis, and gif it be nocht
schortly dressit I wald wyss my self with wyf and all that I haif furth of thir
partis for I luk for na rest gif it be nocht sone metigatt.

As concernyng your lordshipis victualis of this last yeiris crop of lxvij yeiris,
I haif gottin na advertisment as yit quhat ye wil haif me doand thairwith,
quharfor I lang to knaw your lordshipis mynd; and I beleif I sal be evil answerit,
and howsone the beir seid is sawin I beleif thair sal nocht be samikle as to fend
the tenentis till new corne, for God hes plagit this cuntre with mony plagis
this yeir. God for his gudnes to put remeid thairto. I omit forder wrytting
hoppand to get advertisment with my broder fra your lordship of all thingis.
As for your teyndis of Dalry quhilk extendis to sex chalderis aittis, beir and
quheit my lord is content to ressaif sex chalderis of your victual heir for the
samyn, and becaus I durst nocht interpryss to aggre with his lordship by
your lordshipis advertisment thairfor I haif postponit quhil ye send me word
agane quhat ye wil I do thair anent, for quhen I ressonit wyth him that the
chalder of aittis culd nocht be sa gud as the chalder of beir heir he said that

the aittis will gif xvij or xviij bollis of meill the chalder, and swa it standis til I get advertisment, and in the mene tyme his lordship hes causit Adam Bell to stay to persew your lordship for payment thairof. Twecheing your broder Patrik, I pray your lordship to stay him to cum in thir partis ay and quhil ye mak the appointment betuix my Lord Robert and him, utherwyis it wil turne to his detriment. And thus committyng your lordship to almychty God for ever. At Kirkwall, the xx day of Marche by your lordshipis servitour reddy at command, etc.

W. Hendersone, Dingwell pursewant.

'To my lord justice clerk'

Roxburghe Muniments, bdl 1634, no. 3.

## 15. Kirkwall, 20 March [1567–8]
*Lord Robert Stewart to Sir John Bellenden.*

My lord, eftir hartlie commendatioun, pleis wit that the present occasioun of my wrytting is to lament the unhappy chance of fortone quhilk is happinnit in my absens betuix the bischopis servandis quhilk war keiparis of the kirk of Kyrkwall and my servandis, quhar as but ony motyve bot of suddantye thair is ane servand of myne slane and twa of the bischopis, and that I lament maist of all the slauchter of ane man callit Nychol Alexander quha was feirdis of kyne and I togidder. And sen the menis lyiffis can nocht be recoverit the nixt remeid is to mak assythment to the narrest of thair kyne quhilk I am willing to do be your advyse be quhat maner of way ye think gud. Prayand your lordship thairfor to schaw your self ane frend at this tyme, and to tak travell and labour upone you to dress aggreance betuix the bischop and me anent this mater; and siclyk to mak the interchance and cois of his leiffing and myne, and of the landis of Birsay with your self and my landis of the Kerss. And thair salbe na plesour nor steid that lyis in my power that ye wil seik of me that I wil deney yow. And to bring the samin to effect it is neidfull that I and ye be present togidder; and gudly I can nocht wyn sowth bot wald ye tak the panes to cum to this cuntre to me to the perfectioun heirof I wald satisfie you thairfor of quhat thing that lay in my power, and gif ye wald cum be sey I suld send ane bark of my awin for you and my wyf togidder. Tharfor I beseik you effectuously to mak the dyat that ye wil cum to me and send me advertisment thairof, and mak you in reddynes thairto, and I sal nocht fail to caus my bark cum to you to convoy yow heir God willing saifly, and bring all thingis to ane gud fyne with the bischop, bringand wyth you ful commissioun with informatioun of all heidis that he wald be at, and at your discretioun I sal mak ane final end and securitie in all thingis. And this I pray you to travel intill that bayth I and your cousing the bischop may be at ane quyetnes and rest togidder, and ye sal nocht find your travell in vane, for I can nocht aventure my self to cum sowth as the chance is happinit without I war suir.

As for Patrik I wald ye causit him to declair to my lord regent that the report that he maid was be sinister informatioun, and that in tyme cummyng I may be suir of him to be my trew servand aganis all man, the authorite except, I am content to accept him. Utherwys your lordship wil nocht think that I can forgif sic offence as he hes done to me, and in that mater alsweil as the rest I wil refer my part to your lordship. Ane frend can nocht be knawin sa weill as in tyme of necessitie, and I knaw nane that can dress this mater bot ye. And gif I war sowth presently as I am heir I suld nevir be servit with thame that was the occasioun of the samin, bot in thir partis I haif na uther to be servit wyth. Prayand your lordship to haif my part in consideratioun. Nocht ellis bot referris the rest to your lordshipis frendly favour, and sua committis you to God. At Kirkwall, the xx day of Marche.

Be your lordshipis,<br>
Robert Stewart.

'To my lord justice clerk'

Roxburghe Muniments, bdl 1634, no. 5.


## 16. Kirkwall, 20 March [1567–8]
*William Henderson to Patrick Bellenden.*

Honorable sir, eftir hartlie commendatioun, this present is to certifie you how that thair is ane debait happinnit betuix my Lord Robertis servandis and the bischopis that was in the kirk, and thair is ane of Lord Robertis servandis slane callit Johne Brown, and twa of the bischopis, Nychol Alexander and James Moir. The kirk is now keipit be my Lord Robertis servandis, and he allegeis that ye ar the causs thairof for he is suirly informit that ye haif tane up ane cumpany of suddartis and purposis to cum in this cuntre in his contrar. Tharfor I pray you for your awin weill to mak satisfactioun to his lordship for ony offence that ye haif done to him, and schaw my lord regent that ye war sinisterly informit quhen ye maid the informatioun to his grace of his lordship, and tak your broderis counsal in the doyng thairof, for my Lord Robert hes writtin to my lord your broder to that effect, and that beand done he wil submit him to your broder in al thingis that is betuix you. And gif this be nocht done I persaif na rest to you in this cuntre. And quhar as ye man put away cummer for ane sobir thing I think ye wil considder it to be the best to metigat his lordship thairintill, for he sayis planely that all thame that wald displace him of this cuntre or assist thairto, that he wil declair him self plane inimie to thame, and sayis he wil nocht sinder wyth it salang as hes ane lyf. And considerand that he is desyrous to haif you to be his servand gif he culd be suir of you, quhat dishonour war it to you to serve him now as ye war wont and to haif gud deid thairfor. I pray you use your broderis counsale heirin and be wyse, and leif thair counsales that wald bid you do in the contrar, for gif I beleffit that it war nocht greit weil I wald nocht wryt safar to you in this mater. Referrand the rest to your awin wisdome, and so committis you to God. At Kyrkwall, the xx day of Marche, be yours at command, etc.

W. Hendersone.

'To ane honorable man Patrik Bellenden of Stenhous'

Roxburghe Muniments, bdl 1634, no. 4.

### 17. Kirkwall, 31 March [1568]
*Lord Robert Stewart to Sir John Bellenden.*

My lord, eftir hartlie commendatioun, I wrait of befoir laitly to your lordship anent sik thingis as occurrit heir amangis us desyrand you to stand gud frend thairintill as ye will evir I do the lyk to you or yours quhen ye requyir me thairto, referrand that mater haill to my formar wrytting. And now sensyne I haif ressavit answer of my wryttingis quhilks I send with William Menteth, my servand,[50] togidder with the heidis concernyng the excambium betuix the bischop and me and syklyk with your self. Ye sall wit that I haif considerit the samin and findis that ye haif delt uprychtly with me thairintill, and gif ye may bring it betuix me and the bischop to effect to modifie the samin as ye think gud to my weill, and gif it may nocht be reformit to the bettir to me at your jugement be your counsal I wil apply to the samin. And anent the coiss wyth your self I think my landis of the Kers is als gud as the landis of Birsay, and lykwyss the superiorite and bailyerie of the Cannogait to be als gud as the bailyerie of the bischopis landis of Orknay and Yetland, and to satisfie you thairintill I am content to augment you wyth the bailyerie of the landis of the Kerss in heritage to you and your airis, swa that ye haiffand thai twa bailyereis thair is na man in Lowtheane may do bettir service to thair prynce nor ye.[51] And as for the superiorite of Leyth I think it neidfull to caus my lord regent consent and ratifie the coss betuix the bischop and me to gratifie his grace thairwith, nochttheless gif ye may caus him consent thairto I am willing in lykwys ye haif it to your self, for presently I am swa superexpendit that I inlaik money to dress him thairto and man satisfie him

---

[50]  Edinburgh and Leith merchant and agent of Robert Stewart.
[51]  Further details, following on Robert Stewart's letter no. 15, of his plans to exchange with Sir John the lands of the Kerse for the bishopric lands of Birsay, now also the bailiary jurisdiction of the Canongate, in exchange for that of the bishopric, and also the teinds of Broughton (itself a bailiary, and justiciary of the whole Holyrood estates), Wardie and Inverleith.

utherwys to consent thairto wythout ye find remeid thairintill. And quhidder I appoint wyth the bischop or nocht alwayis I am willing to appoint wyth your lordship, and to that effect becaus I can nocht cum sowth wythout I war suir I sal mak ane commissioun to my wyf and my chalmerlane to do all thingis that apperteinis of the law for securite thairof as ye wil devyse, for wythout that my lord regent send me his wrytting to assuir me to cum and gang unmolestit in my body or possessioun of this cuntre I can nocht aventuir my self to cum sowth to dress ony besynes, bot as I haif wryttin in my last uther wrytting to your lordship gif ye mycht tak the travell to cum atour in this cuntre to me ye mycht bring all thing to ane perfectioun quhilk I wil beseik you effectuously to do for ony steid or plesour that ye wil requyr of me.

As to your broder Patrik I understand that he with certane of this cuntre men ar in band togidder contrar me to persew me in my body and to rute me and all myne perpetually furth of this cuntrie gif it may ly in thair power as I traist, God willing, it sal nocht be hable to thame. Quharfor considerand that he hes done me sa mony iniureis and continewis still thairintill I can nocht accept him in favouris wythout he schow him self to be my frend, als far as he hes bene my inneme, and to that effect lyk as he hes put me in hatrent and indignatioun with my lord regent and the consale that inlykmaner to schaw him self frendly he wald labour be him self, my Lord Mortoun and utheris his frendis to caus my lord regentis grace to accept my few mailis of Orknay. And that beand done sua that I may knaw him to do me alsmikle gud as he hes done me evill than I wil think him worthye of gratuite and favour, utherwyis nocht for I wil gif nor do na man gud for ewill causs makyng. Yit for your lordshipis caus I wald accept him in favoris he makand me sufficient mendis for the offences bypast, and your lordship and sum uther man bund for his trew and afauld service in tyme cummyng, bot I wil nevir lippin my body to him nor cum in his danger. And as for his frendis I beleif thai can nocht be plaintuous of my using sen I come in Orknay except it that I haif done be justice. And gif I and he aggre lat me knaw quha ar his frendis; thay salbe als tender to me as ony of my awin thai makand the samblablye occasioun to me. Bot sum that he haldis for his frendis hes bene greit oppressouris and becaus I caus justice to haif place and power, men that hes bene wrangit to get rycht thairfor, thai murmour that I do it in hatrent of him quhilk is nocht of verite for I haif done na thing sen I come in Orknay be way of justice bot I will answer for it bayth befoir God and man.

Twecheing your teyndis I appoyntit with your factour William Hendersone to haif tane owerheid vj lastis cost in this cuntre for the sex chalderis of quheit, beir and aittis, quhilk ye suld haif payit me for the teyndis, and was nocht content that ye had maid ony payment to my chalmerlane thairof. Alwayis for the aittis that ar unpayit I sal tak cost as ye haif wryttin fra William Hendersone. Sic materis sal nocht stand in differ betuix us swa that I may be suir to haif yow ane trew frend in neid.

Als my lord ye sal wit that I haif fund na frendschip done to me be the lordis of sessioun quhar as thai haif decernit me to mak payment to the persone of Pennycuke of his pensioun quhilk he hes gevin for service done and to be done, quhilk failyeing and he being requyrit thairto the said gift to expyir, and insafar as he refusit service I think the lordis hes done me sobir justice quhilk, God willing, I purpois to retreit; desyrand your lordship to forder me thairto safar as law will. And siklyk thay haif dischargeit me of my thryddis quhilk I haif ratefeit be vote of parliament and as yit unreduceit, quharfor in that as in the uther I think I am wrangit. Traistand ye wil help with your assistance and gud consail to caus the samin be amendit to my contentment, for gif the coiss gais fordwart it wil help to satisfie the bischop for ony thing that he dois to me attour the availl of my benefice and I may gratifie you the bettir for your labouris.

Your lordship sal wit that I haif bene falsly dissavit be ane callit Robert Boswall, skippar of the fouldis schip,[52] quha tuk upone hand to me to transport the lard of Benestoun to Leyth and nocht to suffir him to eschewe. Nevertheless how sone he come to the sowth schoir of Murray firth he pat him on land and the rest that was wyth him. And I send twa of my awin servandis to convoy quharof ane hes assistit thairunto, quharfor my lord regent is informit that thai ar eschewit be my moyane quhilk is nocht of trewth. Tharfor I wald ye causit my lord regent to gar Robert Boiswall and the twa servandis that I send with thame to answer for thame. And siclyk he tuke Edmond Blakatter away by my witting for quhom Gilbert Balfour tuk in hand to answer and would nocht delyver him to me. And this I desyir your lordship to do that my part may be knawin to my lord regent, and thai that ar fund in the wyte may be puineissit for thair away putting of thame.

Als I haif gottin knawlege that Mr Archebauld Douglas[53] hes set his landis of the subdenrye to Patrik quhilk was nocht his promiss, for he wil nocht sa bot that I had the first promiss thairof; and so evir Patrik is in my way, and I think nather of thame hes done thair dewite to me thairintill, bot I may beir wyth that as I do wyth uther thingis quhil I se forder.

Referryng all uther thingis to your lordshipis answer agane, and so committis yow to the protectioun of God. Wryttin at Kyrkwall, the last day of Marche, be yours.

Robert Stewart.

'To my lord justice clerk'

Roxburghe Muniments, bdl 1634, no. 6.

---

[52]  The ship of the *foud*, Shetland's senior law officer.
[53]  Scottish ambassador to England and subdean of Orkney. The lands of the subdeanery, granted by him to Patrick Bellenden (*REO*, 287–8, no. clxx), were a standing bone of contention between Bellenden and Robert Stewart.

## 18. Kirkwall, 26 April [1568]
*Lord Robert Stewart to Sir John Bellenden.*

My lord, eftir hartlie commendatioun, forsamikle as I haif ressavit wryttingis fra my lord regent in favouris of your broder Patrik, wyth ane wrytting of his awin quharintill he desyris certane gratuiteis of me, and for informatioun hes send the forme of ane contract to me to be subscryvit be me for fulfilling of the samin to him, with ane extract or abbriviatioun of twa assedationis quhilk he allegis he hes of certane landis within Orknay, your lordship knawis quhat impedimentis that your broder hes maid to me evir sen my first title and entres to Orknay. And now last (all formar offences being foryet be me) he ceissit nocht of now to mak wrang narratioun to my lord regent, quhilk hes offendit me mair nor all that he did of befoir. Nevirtheless, at my lord regentis desyir, and for your lordships caus and frendis, I am content that your broder frequent to this cuntre and, in seycht of the cuntre men, he makand me amendis of all offences bypast, and attemptand na thing in my contrare in tyme to cum, to use him self and his possesses at his plesour. Bot I can nocht contract wyth him, yit I am content to appoint and contract with your lordship in his name howsone we meit, ye beand gude and bund for his trew deiling with me in tyme cummyng, utherwyis I can nocht be suir of him. And anent the cummer that is happinnit betuix the bischopis servandis and myne I desyir your lordship effectuouslye to find him gud dress thairintill for satisfactioun of all parteis, and quhat ye wil desyir me to do for my part I am content to stand thairto, my servandis lyvis beand saif. And gif the bischop wil nocht stand content of gud wyis it wil put him to cummer and me bayth. Tharfor my lord as ye wald that I schow your broder kyndnes lat me knaw your lordships labour now, quhilk salbe ane recompans of your broderis offendingis in tymes bypast and be foryet with me. And as I wrait to your lordship of befoir that ye wil tak the travell to cum in thir partis to mak end in this your broderis besynes, and all uthir thingis consernyng the bischop and your self; or ellis that I may be suir to cum with my lord regentis licence to speik his grace and do my leissum effairis, with fre passage to returne quhen I ples, and to mak my awin part gud and all thais that hes spokin uniustly of me lyaris. And to that effect that I may haif my lord regentis hand wrytt to me, and all thame that hes nocht offendit in this caus to pass and repass but impediment, and swa sal I cum with deligence to the performance of the premissis. And so committis your lordship to the protectioun of God. At Kyrkwall, the xxvj day of Apryle, be yours.

Robert Stewart.

'To my lord justice clerk'

Roxburghe Muniments, bdl 1634, no. 7.

## 19. Scalloway, 1 June [1568]

*William Henderson to Sir John Bellenden.*

My lord, eftir humyl commendatioun of service, pleis I beand in cumpany wyth my Lord Robert in Yetland ressavit your lordshipis wrytting, daitit at Glasquo the xvij of Apryle, quharintill your lordship declaris how that the unhappye mischance that is begun betuix my Lord Roberts servandis and the bischopis is hable to turne thame bayth to greit inconvenientis gif remeid be nocht fund haistaly thairfor. I haif talkit wyth my Lord Robert and schawin him the effect of your wrytting, and I find his lordschip myndit yit as of befoir, that he is content to mak sic satisfactioun and mendis for the falt that is done as ever was maid for the lyk in Scotland, his servandis lyffis beand saiff. Bot as to thame to get skayth or yit to restoir the stepill he wil on na wayis condiscend thairto. And now he declairis the hail motyve and occasioun of the takyng of the kirk quhilk is this: Maister Magnus Halcro[54] wrait ane wrytting to his freind William Halcro schawand how that your lordships broder Patrik, and Gilbert Balfour, Maister William Mudy[55] and uther Orknay men was bund up in ane band aganis his lordship, and he was advertist in lykmaner be utheris how that Patrik was feand suddartis to haif cum in Orknay and to haif tane the stepill and constranit my Lord Robert to haif left the cuntre, and this to haif bene the bischopis devyss, quharfor he takand ane feir hierof causit his servandis to tak the kirk. Bot it was by his wil or wyttyng that ony slawchter suld haif bene maid, and sen the mennis lyiffis can nocht be recoverit, bettir is to tak satisfactioun nor to seik the uttir extremitie of the law, for I heir my Lord Robert menand that gif he can nocht get ane appoyntment of the bischop that he sal wair him self and all that wil do for him, or the bischop get his will of him. And he sayis that he knawis perfyitlye that the bischop can do na thing to his hurt by your lordships assistance, and that ye ar the man only that he feiris and nocht the bischop, and he wil lay the hail wyit upone your lordship gif ony inconvenient cumis to him thairthrow. And yit he is willyng to refer his part to his chalmerlane, Adame Bell, and your lordship swa that the bischop wil do the samin, and quhat satisfactioun that ye twa wil ordane him to do to the bischop or the mennis freinds that ar inlaikit he wil fulfill it, bot gif he persavis na thing bot rigour usit aganis him, he wil do all the displesour that he dow or may aganes the bischop and his parttakars, and wil caus him to be evil answerit of his lyffyng. And sayis planely that he douttis nocht quha cumis in his contrar gif my lord regent wil stand equal till him, and or he be put fra his rycht and title quhilk he hes of Orknay he will wair his lyff as he affeirmis. And all that wil pretend to depryfe him thairof he wil nocht spair to tak thair lyiffis

---

[54]   Chanter of Orkney, follower of Bishop Bothwell, client of the earl of Caithness, and long-time opponent of Robert Stewart. See Introduction.

[55]   Of Dounreay, later of Breckness (NRS RD11, box 12); chamberlain of the bishopric (*ER*, xix, 231), minister of South Ronaldsay and Burray, later of Hoy and Graemsay.

and he may. And he is ane man that wil get money assistars and it is dangerous deilying wyth him. Thairfor I pray your lordship, for your awin weill and the bischopis bayth, to wirk sum gud wayis betuix thame for uthirwyis, as your lordship hes wryttin, it wil cum to thair greit damnage on bayth the syidis and your lordship and freinds wil get na gud thairthrow. And I pray God that thai war fairly sunderit furth of uthirs way, that nowther thair bodeis nor leiffyngis was adiacent togidder in ane place, for I haif na hope of thair aggreance salang as thai ar macheit in ane rowm togidder. And your lordship knawis that it ane meritable turne to dress thair appointment and til cut of all occasionis that mycht hald thame at variance or in truble togidder, and thair is na way sa gud as to caus the bischop tak satisfactioun for the thing that is done and to lat the coss talkit of befoir pass fordwart to perfectioun, quhilk wald be to your lordships profitt and quyetnes and the bischopis bayth. For my Lord Robert is willyng to do your lordship bayth profitt and plesour gif ye wil bring it to pass, and he wil send to your broder Patrik and desyir him to cum till Orknay and speik him, and wil satisfie his desyir ressonablye swa that he wil caus you and frends to do for him to astablis him suirlye in Orknay bot ony molestatioun, and to caus his few mails be ressavit sua that he war admittit as fewar thairin.

And my Lord Robert wrait to your lordship schawand gif ye wald get him licence to cum saifly sowth to speik my lord regent and to pas and repass frely, that he was myndit to haif cumin sowth, bot he hes gottin na answer of his wrytting fra your lordship agane quharof he mervailis greitulye. And yit he desyris your lordship to get him the samin that he may cum sowth to my lord regent, quhar he purposis eftir that he returne furth of Yetland to cum, and to mak appointment with the bischope and satisfie him be your lordships advysing and mak ane end of all things bayth with him and you and your broder, and wyth my lord regent for his awin effairs. And in the mene tyme he wald desyir to get ane respett to his men in hop of appointments and to that effect to haif thame relaxit fra the horne, that he mycht aggre for thame. I pray your lordship to tak the best of this cummersum truble that is hapnit that it may be pacefeit, for it is ane godly purpois to aggre it.

Anent your lordshipis awin effaris I haif gottin na informatioun, and I beleif nocht to get samikle of your lordships victualis this yeir as to pay my lord of the sex chalders that ye haif wryttin to me to delyver him, for Orknay was nevir at sic ane poynt as it is this yer. And I can get na payment of Mr Magnus, and tharfor I wald wit quhat your lordship wil I do thairanent. Forder referris to your lordships advertisment, and so committis your lordship to the protectioun of God. At Scalloway, the first of June, be your lordships servitour.

W. Hendersone, Dingwell pursewant.

'To my lord justice clerk'

Roxburghe Muniments, bdl 1634, no. 8.

## 20. Edinburgh, 21 September [1568]
*Adam, bishop of Orkney, to Archibald Napier of Merchiston.*

Richt honorable schir and bruther, I haird the day the rigorous answer and refuiss that ye gat, quhairof I wes not wele apayit; bot alwayis I pray you as ye ar sett amiddis betuix twa grete inconvenientis, travell to eschew thame baith; the ane is maist evident, to wit, the remaining in your awin place quhair ye ar, for be the nummer of seik folk that gais owt of the toun, the muir is abill to be owirspred, and it can not be bot throw the neirnes of your place and the indigence of thame that ar put owt thai sall continewallie repair abowtte your roume, and throu thair conversatioun, infect sum of your servandis, quhairby thai sall precipitat your self and your children in maist extreme danger. And, as I se, ye hef foirsene the samin for the yung folk quhais bluid is in maist perrell to be infectit first, and thairfoir purposis to send thame away to Menteith, quhair I wald wiss at God that ye war your self, without offence of authoritie, or of your band, sua that your houss gat na skaith. Bot yit, schir, thair is ane midway quhilk ye suld not omit, quhilk is to withdraw you fra that syid of the toun to sum houssis upon the north syid of the samin, quhairof ye may hef in borrowing quhen ye sall hef to do, to wit, the Gray Cruik, Innerlethis self, Weirdie, or sic uther placis as ye culd chose within ane myle; quhairinto I wald supponis ye wald be in les danger than in Merchanstoun: and close up your houssis, your grangis, your barnis and all, and suffer na man cum thairin, quhill it plesit God to put ane stay to this grete plage; and in the meintyme, maid you to leve upon your penny, or on sic thing as come to you out of the Lennos[56] or Menteith; quhilk, gif ye do not, I se ye will ruine your self, and howbeit I escape in this wayage, I will nevir luik for to se you again, quhilk war some mair regrate to me than I will expreme be wreting. Alwayis besekis you, as ye luif your awin wele, the wele of your houss, and us your freindis that wald your wele, to tak sum ordour in this behalf, that howbeit your evill favoraris wald cast you away, yit ye tak bettir keip upon your self and mak not thame to rejoce, and us your freindis to murne baith at anis, quhilk God forbid, and for his guidnes preserve yow and your posteritie from sic skaith, and manteine you in holie keping for evir. Of Edinburgh, this xxi day of September.

Be your bruther at power,<br>
the bischop off Orknay.

'To the richt honorabill and our weilbelovit bruther the laird off Merchanstoun'
NLS Adv. Ms 54.1.6, f. 8; printed Napier, *Memoirs*, 110–11.

---

[56]   Lennox.

## 21. Kirkwall, 21 May 1569
*Lord Robert Stewart to Sir John Bellenden.*

My lord, eftir hartlie commendationis, I ressavit your lordships wreatting and considerit the samin, and quhair your lordship has maist earnistlie requestit me to caus your brutheris servand George Ballendene be answerit of ane Johne Houstounis escheit according to ane gift maid thairupon, your lordship as I understand is resolatt ineucht of my part thairof in that I am als frelie infeft with all eschetreis of Orknay and Yetland as the kyng or queine mycht gif the samin, and as to the bishopis part your lordship knawis my poweris gif I ony haf or nocht, quhilk I wilbe werreay layth to pas fra. I am assurit gif your lordship had bene myndfull of my undoutit rycht, as said is, your lordship had nocht chairgit me heirwith. And as towartis my awin besenes I will spend na mair peper and ink thairupoun in reiding missyves, becaus I find the samin takis and hes tane bot small effect. I belevit evir that your lordship suld haive done diligence to haive put me furtht of cummers, in that safar as I wes evir willing to haive fulfillit my part of the contractis maid betuex the bishope, your lordship and me, and gif the evidentis cummis nocht subscryvit and seallit to me now in Yetland swa that I may tak sesing, thay ar able to do me bot litill guid and wilbe to my great hinderance, and nathing to the bishopes nor your lordshipis fortherance. And forder I am informit that all my procuratoris hes refusit the office of procuratioun in my caussis, quhilk I may nocht presentlie mend, bot concerning ony proces led be the bishope in my contrar is nocht neidfull, for I my self at my suythcuming (quhilk wilbe als sone as I cum furth of Yetland againe) sall but ony proces of law fulfill all my part of the contract or uther conditioun maid betuex us at the regentis graces sycht and youris, and gif ony beis led wilbe of nane availl becaus of null defence. Now I will knaw gif your lordship be my assurit frend or nocht. Refarrand the rest to your lordshipis wisdome and forder adverteisment, and God preserve your lordship. From the toun of Kirkwall in Orknay, the xxj of May 1569 yeiris.

Be your lordshipis assurit,
Robert Stewart.

'To my lord justice clerk'

Roxburghe Muniments, bdl 1634, no. 9.

## 22. Kirkwall, 2 June [1569]
*Mr Magnus Halcro of Burgh to Sir John Bellenden.*

My lord, I commend my service unto your lordship in my maist hartlie maner. It mocht pleis your lordship to onderstand that angir and ane impatient hart hes bene the motive that I wrett nevir to your lordship sen this blak excambioun was maid, for my part thairin is mair hevyar nor I will expreme in wrett. For gif it had plesit God I desyrit nocht to have changit maistiris, and as it cumin in gud fayth my gud mynd and service sall nocht be changit fra my lord the bishope nochtwythstanding all biganis. And that my trublis is on recompansit togidder wyth my service done and bettir occasion in tymes cumin all is best acceptit. I luk for his lordships gud mynd and support quhairin he may nocht hurt him self, bot all that I have done and gif it war ane hundretht tymes mair I think it weill warit, and it war bot only for your lordships caus, for I had nevir samekle of ony mannis geir as I haif had of youris, and that wythout my deservings bot of your lordshipis meir liberality. Promittand to God and to your lordship thairfor I sall nocht be fownd the ingrait man, bot I think my self adettit to the nynt degre of youris that is in your lordships favouris, and sall nevir refus eftir my powar your lordships querrell and charge. Exhortand your lordship nocht to ressave thir wordis spokin throcht ony flattering bot fra the boddowme of my hart wyth ane faythfull mynd that wald recompans gud deid. And to haiff experience of the samyn put me to charges that I may do, and your lordship sall luk for the bigane kyndnes als mekle service as gif I had brukit that I had and thryss samekle till it, etc.

Pleis your lordship, I have wrettin to my lord of Orknay sobirly lamentand my caiss throcht this excambioun that I have lois him that wes my maister togidder wyth sik helpe that I wald obtenit throcht my gud service, etc. And fordir I had the takkis of the Ile of Rolsay[57] amangis the quhilk I have ten d. land liand rig and rendell wyth my conquest landis of Burgh,[58] and now I ondirstand that the samyn landis that lyis rig and rendell is promisit in phewis to my Lord Robart, quhilk gif swa be perfytit it will at schorttyme returne to my trublis and wrak. For your lordship it is nocht gud to me to be pertinar in rig and rendell wyth my Lord Robart gif your lordship knew quhat is and apperantlie wilbe amang us. Quharfor gif this ten d. land that is nixt wyth my land, that is to say five d. land in Scaill and five d. land in Vestnes,[59] may be reservit fra my Lord Robart to hald me out of trublis I satisfe my lord wyth geir and service to his plesour. And gif I may nocht obtene the haill x d. lands latt me have in phewis the five d. land of Scaill, and that is bot ane sobir mater quhilk I traist your lordship will assuir me quhat I may luk for. And gif your lordship will get me this landis reservit out of my Lord Robartis chartour I will cum south quhen my Lord Robert cummis, quhilk wilbe quhosone he retiris out of Yetland. Prayand your lordship to lat my lord of Orknay ondirstand the effeck of my mynd wyth your lordships ansuer. Committand your lordship in the protectioun of hiest. Of Kirkwall, the secund day of Jun, your lordships servand at powar.

Maister Magnus Halcro off Burght.

'To my lord justice clerk'

Roxburghe Muniments, bdl 1634, no. 10.

[57]  Rousay.
[58]  Brough, lands on the south-west coast of Rousay.
[59]  Skaill and Westness, lands adjacent to Brough.

## 23. Kirkwall, 5 June [1569]
*Lord Robert Stewart to Sir John Bellenden.*

My lord, eftir hartlie commendatioun, pleis your lordship to wit that I haif send Jonett Levynstoun[60] sowth with sic directioun as I had ado, and in speciall to bring Hary, my sone, to me. Tharfor ye wil pleiss to delyver him to hir; and quhat expenss that your lordship hes bestowit upoun him sal be recompensit, God willing, at your plesour. Als your lordship sall wit that I have put James Menteth fra me, and in speciall for Patrikis caus, for I was advertisit be George Bellenden that gif he had bene furth of my company that Patrik was content to do his dewtie to me concernyng all thingis quhilk I wald charge him with, and to the effect that I may haif Patrik, and be suir of him to be myne I haif put away that man that I beleif was the impediment that we war sa lang sindry, and Patrik preiffand the honest man to me sal find me to be ane gud maister to him, quhilk I wald your lordship be your dress causit him to do to me lyk as I am willing to do to him. And gif James Menteth cumis to my lord regent to mak ony sinister report of me, that I haif nocht rewardit him according to his deservyng I traist your lordship wil mak answer thairto, for gif he had bene worthy owther of reward or to haif bene mainteineit in my companye I wald haif dressit to haif maid appoyntment betuix Patrik and him and utheris quhom he offendit greitly by my will or wytting as I sal answer to God. Nevertheless he hes tane his reward at his awin hand for he is restand to me of his intromissioun with my geir, quhilk extendis to mair nor four hundreth pundis quharof I can get na compt, raknyng nor payment bot man on [force?] let him slip with the latter hand.

As twecheing the performyng of my evidentis be the bishop I heir say that he wil do na thing thairintill, and in special of the lands of Yetland quhilk he sayis is deminusion of the rentall. My lord, ye knaw that all few chartours ar maid contenand samony bollis or chalders of victual as the use was of befoir to be payit for ony land, and yit nevertheless the pryce is set of sobir siluer thairfor quhilk is deminussion of the profit howbeit it be nocht diminussion of the soum of the rentall. And siclyk is it of the chartour quhilk I haf causit mak of the lands of Yetland, for the land mailis of Yetland ar comptit in schillingis, pennyis and pundis of buttir and wadmell, and ane schilling of buttir in compt of land mailis is ij lispund butter in payment, and ane schilling of wadmell is sex cuttall wadmell, and thair is in the Yetland schilling xij d. lyk as is in our schilling. And swa quhar it is said in my chartour, *Reddendo, etc.,* *pro qualibet libra novendecim librarum et decem solidorum butteri et wadmell secundum antequam suppotationem et usitatem solutionis firmarum et debitorum Yetlandiae, summa treginta quinque solidorum sex denariorum unius obuli et tertiae partis obuli usualis*

---

[60]   Servant of Robert Stewart, not otherwise noticed in sources, but clearly attendant on Robert's eldest son.

*monete regni Scotiae*[61] thair is contenit the haill soum of the rental albeit the pryce of siluer be sett less nor may be gottin for it. And gif that be ane causs to reduce my chartor all the few chartours in Scotland that had wont to pay victual and ar turnit in silver wil reduce, [*interpolated*: and ony bischop that cumis eftir let thame reduce it gif thai can, I wil stand to my aventure]. And sen I am willing to fulfill all thing that I am oblist to the bishop I wald he did the lyk to me, utherwyis it sal be knawin that the stop salbe first on his syid, bot I lippen your lordship wil caus him to do his dewtie, and he doand that nowther nor your lordship sal haif caus to complene upoune ane jot that I am oblist to, bot sal fulfill it to the uttirmaist. Haffand na fordar occasioun to wrytt to you for the present, committis your lordship to the eternal God for ever. At Kyrkwall, the v day of Junij, be your lordships, etc.

Robert Stewart.

'To my lord justice clerk'

Roxburghe Muniments, bdl 1634, no. 11.

## 24. Kirkwall, 10 June 1569
*Lord Robert Stewart to Sir John Bellenden.*

My lord, eftir hartlie commendatioun, pleis wit I wrait to your lordship with Andro Williamsoun[62] ane answer of sic things as your lordship wrait to me. And now sensyn schawin me how the bischop will do nathing to my evidents and wald nocht delyver thame agane, nother sped nor unsped. Quharfoir I have writtin to my lord regent and hes schawin him the hale maner of the bischoppis refuiss, desyrand his grace to command the bischop to seill and subscryve my evidents and to delyver thame in his graces keping or in your lordships handis, thair to remane ay and quhill I fulfill my pairt of the contract to him. For gif the bischop fulfillis nocht that part to me, I have tynt the teynd of Brouchtoun, and four hundreth pund of male superplus by ony thing that I have ressavit in recompenss, and or I tyn that I sall rather pass to my awin and lat the bischop pass to his. Nevirtheless the thing that is appoyntit betuix yow and me I sall performe in all heids to your contentment. Bot I am informit that your sone Lwes[63] is seasit in the lands of Byrsay, and gif that be of treuth I can nocht be sicker thairof, for the quhilk ye man provyde remeid gif sua be, that I may have warrandice thairof, for your chartour can

---

[61] 'Paying, etc., for each pound of £19 10s of butter and wadmell following the ancient mode and use of payment of the fermes and debts of Shetland, the sum of 35s 6½d and a third part of a halfpenny usual money of the realm of Scotland.' The original charter is in *OSR*, i, 178, no. 69.

[62] Burgess of Edinburgh, and occasional transactor of business in Edinburgh for Robert Stewart.

[63] Sir Lewis Bellenden.

nocht be warrandice to me gif he be seasit as said is bot he may revoke it at his perfyte age. I wrait to yow concerning James Menteyth quha I have put away fra me for your broder Patrikis caus nocht doutand bot ye will dress the said Patrik to be myn lyk as he sall find me gude maister to him agane. And sua gif he plesis to cum to Orknay, and your lordship to be gude for him that he sall use him self towart me as becummis ane faythfull trew servand he sall be wylcum and have the fortificatioun and mantenance that he will requyre of me in all his just effairis. Gif James Menteyth cummis to the regent to mak ony complaynt that he hes nocht bein rewardit for his service I traist your lordship will schaw my lord regentis grace how that I inlaik iiij$^c$ li. of his intromissioun with my geir be just compt and raknyng by sindrie uther things that he hes done to me, yit gif he had behavit him self as it became him I suld have appoyntit your broder and him. Bot he is nocht wourthy to be done for as I sall schaw your lordship at meting. I will nocht cummar your lordship ferdar with langar wryting bot referris all uther things to your lordships meting and myn, quhilk salbe, God willing, sason as I returne out of Yetland. And credance to the beirar. And sua committis your lordship to God. At Kirkwall, the x day of June 1569.

Be your lordships,
Robert Stewart.

'To my lord justice clerk this be delyverit'

Roxburghe Muniments, bdl 1634, no. 12.

## 25. Holyroodhouse, 14 June 1569

*Adam, bishop of Orkney, to Sir John Bellenden.*

My Lord, eftir maist hertlie commendatioun, I have lukit eirnistlie frome day to day for your lordships anser annent my besynes bot as yit I have hard na word. Albeit that winderfull is the deligence and solestatioun of my partie adversar, to wite the Lard of Dundass,[64] quhome I culd hald of be na utheris way bot that I was partie, and that thair was deffence in the cawss, and that the lords wald not be ane nowmber gif I rais. Bot I understand my Lord of Colddingame[65] is to be heir within viij dayis to wit quha will fill the noumber, and than I ame assurit thaye will proceid in that mater to my gret hurte gif that thing quhilk I have socht for my deffence be nocht exped. Quhairfoir

[64] Probably George Dundas of that Ilk; Bishop Bothwell was granted the escheat of Robert Stewart for failing to present before the privy council a large number of his servitors, including Dundas's son George.

[65] John Maitland of Thirlestane, later secretary and lord chancellor of Scotland; in the 1580s he was a silent supporter of Sir Lewis Bellenden in his inherited dispute with Robert Stewart. In this case he appears simply as a privy councillor in the disputes involving Bishop Bothwell and the laird of Dundas, the nature of which is unknown.

I wald ernestlie desyr your lordship to trawell to get me that besynes exped in the convenient tyme unto me or ellis adverteis me quhairupon it standis, quharbie that I may tak uthir ordur with my selfe as effiris. I suppone that your progres making hes stayit the proponing of that, bot now I suppone your lordship to be at the fardest tryst and sa ye may do bettir on or of in the mater. And refferis to your lordships deligence and wisdome quhat sall be done thair annente. Sen your lordship deperting the toun of Edinburch having young men to thair bailyes that ar inexpart of sic officis hes thryss attentit to cum upone our jurisdictioun and pepile of the Cannoget[66] to reise men that war attechuit out of the handis of justice, quhilk wald have bein sic dishonor to me that I culd not have recowertit, and yit war nocht that my lord regent is thair awaye and wald find oncouth that ony thing suld be done that mycht cawis ony effect of ourdur I have rassistit be na way of deid bot be moyens brokin thair interpryssis swa that all thair menis hes tane na uthir effecte to our prejudice bot to opin thair evill will and get na thank thairfoir. Bot gud it war that your lordship suld mean the mater to my lord regents grace, and desyr his grace to wret ane wretting unto thame, and desyr thame that thay na wyis atempte to ony prejudice to me or ony of myne concernyng my juridicsioun and subjectis, ather of Leitht or Cannoget, nor parmit ony of thairis to do the same certifeing thame that gif thay did ony thing be the way of deid to me or ony of myne that he suld gif me the remed thairof upone the toun of Edinburch, for he understud that nane within thair toun durst attempt the doing of ony thing be way of deid unto me onless the officiaris, counsall and clarke ower saw the samyne.

Further the Dene of Murraye,[67] my gud freind, hes requestit me to wret to your lordship in his favour that your lordship will helpe his cawssis in thay partis, and get him sum relife of the gret oppressionis that [h]is eme the sherefe[68] and utheris hes attempit aganis him. He was myndit to have cumin hether, bot becaws without him we cowld nocht be ane noumber we have retenit him and wretting away to my lord regents grace in his favoris nocht dowting bot your lordship will do for him as for ane freind.

Your lordship is rememberit that I cawssit summound Lord Robert for releving of me of that quhilks he and his chalmerlane had intrometit of this yeiris leving, quhilk summoundis albeit dependit upoun the contract, yit have I bein constraynit to warne off new, and to that effecte hes raissit summounds heir to mak new warnying. And for that effecte I have send this berrer unto your lordship that he may be derectit awaye with expeditioun that he may be agane with the letters agane the last day of this month, and

---

[66] Burgh of barony, part of the lands of the abbey of Holyrood granted by Robert Stewart to Bellenden and, with Leith, clearly a subject of dispute with the bishop over relative powers.
[67] Alexander Dunbar.
[68] Uncle or close relative of Dunbar, possibly opposing him in his claims to the deanery of Moray.

becawss of his passing thethir it war gud your lordship suld with speid send ane letter with him to my Lord Robert adverteisand him that I have maid the evidents conforme to the contracte and to his gretest securite, and hes consignet thame in ane of the clarks of sessiouns hands to be furth cumand as effiris. And tharfoir desyre my lord that ye will do sic deligence incawssing my servandis be ansurrit of that that is awand me, that his securitie be nocht stayit bot fenissit and delyverit to his contentmente, as my will is that all things spokin sall tak end and effecte as effiris. And becawiss my uthir besynes reqwyris sic hest I will praye your lordship to lat nocht this berrar tarye aboife ane nycht with yow that he may be the schoner agane at me.

My lady your bedfallow[69] departit of this toun upone Sonday last was and send us word this day that scho is weill. Quhat scho sall have ado scho sall want na helpe that I can mak in your lordships absence in quhatsumevir your lordship cawssis your affairis. [*hand changes*] Your lordship sall understand that Edward Prestoun[70] hes caussit summond me beffoir the lords for hearing off letteris geiffin conforme to his pensioun off vij bolls quheit, v bollis beyre, for his office, etc. I haiff nevir ane off the chanonis heyraway to avyss with thairanent quhat wes in use of payment or quhat defense may be off[er]et in his contrair. Always I sall do that I kan to hald off quhill I may haiff your lordshipis answer quhow I sall use that matter. Prayand yow to se to the samyn answer with the answer off the uthir bissines with the boy I directit with your lordship for I feare thai cum bayth laitt ineuch. And giff this boy brings unto your lordship the letters in four forms upon the laird of [Dumbeath?][71] owt of Orknay your lordship will causs exequit the samyn upon hyme, for I wes nevir sua [grimpit?] with noune I haid to do as with hym for [his gottin?] be moyen off me twa acquittance upon ane thing, ane be his bruther and uther be hyme selff, and chaipps to mak thairby dowble payment be single, and hes supstraket hym selff this twelmonth bigane owt off Catnes that I mycht never get hym chargit be my letteris. Bot now your lordship will causs ony officer your lordships [servants?] supple that default, and lat not knaw that your lordship hes to do thairwith. All uther things referris to your lordships nixt advertissment, and sua makand end heyroff. Committs your lordship in Goddis most hele protectioun. Off Halyrudhowss, this xiiij day off June anno 1569 be

Your lordships cuseng at all
power
the bischop off Orknay.

---

69   Janet Seton, daughter of Walter Seton of Touch, Bellenden's third wife, m. 14 January 1565.
70   Barber burgess of the Canongate, concerning his pension as barber of the abbey and convent of Holyrood. See Introduction.
71   Possibly William Sinclair of Dunbeath, son of Alexander, son of William, 2nd earl of Caithness.

Your lordship plais understand that according to your lordships counsall I deferret to accept the matter upoun betuix my Lord off Newbottell and the laird off Traquhair,[72] bot be the avyss off bayth continewit the matter to the x day off this instant desyrand thame to be bayth present at that day, and to bring with thame twa off thair jugis arbitouris quhilk thai did, bot my thochtis tuik na effect quhairbe off the anseris, ressonis I supponit to haiff drawin into ane guid for all was in vaine. Thairfoir I declairit unto thame bayth I wald not accept the matter upone me bot wald remit the samyn to my lord regents grace agane, and in the meane tyme desyrit thame ernestlie in my lord regents name that na novation suld be maid quhill his graceis hame cumyn. The laird refusit prorogatioun, bot said he suld mak na trowble; not the less I am informet that samyn nycht he rid hame, to wit the xj day, at ewin [his?] brother James slew my Lord Newbottell scheiphyrd upon the stede debaitable callit Jonstoun.[73] Quhat succedis thairoff I fear, [etc. ?] Your lordship will adverteis my lord regent of all this.

'To my lord. My lord justice clerk to our souraine lord. In Innernes.'

Roxburghe Muniments, bdl 1634, no. 13.

## 26. Edinburgh, 8 July 1569
*Letter from Adam, bishop of Orkney, to Sir John Bellenden.*

My Lord, after all hartlie recommendatioun, pleis wit I ressavit your lordships wreting and hes understand the forderance that ye haif had in my bissines quhairunto I may weill lament bot nocht the bettir. Alwayis I am forwartis in that cace as I am in all uther belanging to my Lord Robert for the actioun that I sent Caldell[74] my man away for stayis throw his nother turning befoir the day appoynttit nor sensyne. Alwayis your Lordship did evill that send me nocht ane wreting of my lord regentis graces request to the toune of Edinburgh, for daillie thay haif molestit me sensyne and yit dois, that I haif na refuge bot *praeter protaxia*[75] befoir the lordis. William Boithwell[76] is cumin out of Orknay and arryvit heir the xx day of this last moneth quha assuris me that my Lord Robert hes nocht lattin him tak up ane sorte of ony thing perteining to me. And howbeit he speik fair wordis to him hes dischargit the commoundis to answer ony of myne of ony thing in Orknay, and supponis he hes done na less in Yetland, quhair he is now or this tyme, sua that I may be eittin up be my creditors sen na releve cumis of my dettis, and besidis this my servand culd nocht get ane notar in all

---

[72]　Mr Mark Ker, commendator of Newbattle Abbey, and Robert Stewart of Traquair.
[73]　See Introduction.
[74]　Otherwise unknown servant of Bishop Bothwell.
[75]　'Other than protection'.
[76]　(of Quhelpside), burgess of Edinburgh, notable follower of Bishop Bothwell, later chamberlain of Orkney.

Orknay that durst execute the offices geven him ony word of that thing that I sa oft requerit him be my wretingis, to wit my Lord Robertis answer quhither he wald poynd for my dettis or nocht, and mak me to be answerit thairof, etc., for he is becum terrable to all that is within that boindis. And quhen the last letters war execute upone him for the warrandice, etc., he bald my servandis in thir termes, put me to the horne quhen ye will, ye sall get na thing of me. Assuir your self he hes done that he can be revocatiounis for his self, his wyf and his barnis to annull all that is done. Ye knaw your man and his humour. Provid remeide for him as ye will be servit for your self and freindis.

Ye sall understand that I presentit ane supplecatioun to the kirk as commendator of Halyrudhous desyring thame to put to lybertie the channonis of the said place that thai mycht cum and serve at my kirkis quhilk was grettumle in mister, seing that for the penory of ministeris thai mycht lat me haif na may quhill thay mycht better. I desyrit the grant of thais, bot it is refusit be him that hes cuir of all, and planelie spokin that he wald plane to all the warld of my lord regent that war put in ony man in the gret benefice without adwise of the kirks, heirupon hes derectit ane artikill to him amangis uthir mony mar, quhilk becaus ye will heirof I omit to wret. Prayand yow to be the first advertesar and adverteis me of the answeris becaus I suppone to meit with your lordship in Sanct Jhonstoun. I will prolixt, bot committis yow in Godis most holy protectioun. Of Edinburgh, this viij day of July anno 1569 be

Your lordships cusing at power,
the bischop of Orknay.

Commend my humill service to my lord regents grace and to my lade his bedfallow. I am in ane evill cais for the kirk bostowis the reformet channonis that thai will not geiff that obedience as to cum to my kirkis and minister thair, and the papistis sayis thai sall sweyr obedience als soune to Mr Knox[77] as thai sall do to me, and betuix thir twa daits (?), subscriving on new maid to my inques (?) sua far as thai may, etc.

'To my lord. My lord justice clerk to our soveraine lord, presentlie in Aberdene.'

Roxburghe Muniments, bdl 1634, no. 14.

## 27. Dalquharran in Carrick,[78] 24 July 1569

*Patrick Bellenden to Sir John Bellenden.*

My lord, efter my maist hartlie commendatioun of service, I ressavit your writting and understands be the samyn, as alswa be letters ressavit fra my servands in Orknay, of my Lord Robertis desyr towart me, and how willing he is that I repair in Orknay, quharof I thank his lordship, wissing that your

---

[77]   John Knox, evangelist (1513–72).
[78]   Dalquharran Castle, near Dailly, Ayrshire.

lordship gif him hartlie thanks thairfor in my name, for in deid I do esteime (as of necessitie I man) Orknay to be my peculiar dwelling, swa that my lang remaning thairfra consistit nocht for feir of ony enemy I had in thay partis. And hopis, God willing, to be thair howsone oportunite sall suit for my uther effaris in thir partis. Your lordships wisdome can remember weill aneuche of the articlis subscryvit betuix my Lord Robert and me with mony uther promissis maid, quhairof na part as yit is performit althocht I haif sustenit greit lossis tharthrow and be his lordships occatioun, quhilkis man be redressit and reformit or ever I can promiss faythfull service to his lordship or bundin your lordship to be suirtie thairfoir. Tharfor my lord (sen ye ken the natour of the man, and how oft he is able to brek promiss) I wil refer sik suirtie as his lordship sowld mak to me (quharof the sum is that I be restorit to my officis and rowmis that I bruikit of befoir, and the articlis to be fulfillit war first maid as your lordship knaws) to be endit and devysit be your lordships self that may stand with our honour and commoditie. And quhatever your lordship sall promiss in my name that I sould do to his lordship, I promiss faithfullie to observe the samyn, wissing at God that I mycht be assurit laikwiss of his lordship. I man burdin your lordship heirwith concerning mony uther trubillis for my causs quhilks your lordship hes had, that your lordship desyr my Lord Robert to send the performance of sik articlis as your lordship thinks he sould do to me dewlie endit and subscryvit for my suirtie, and godwilling he sal have na causs to complene on my part.

Quhen I understuid of your deirest umquhile dochter Kathareinis[79] departing at Gods plesour I assuir your lordship I wes sa sare as in all my lyf I never wes sa havely oppressit. Bot thair is na remeid bot God to be prasit and all to be accepit in gud part as for the best; althocht I ken nocht the lyk of hir leving of our surname. Tak your lordship patience and think gud of all hoping that he sall send comfort as his godlie plesour sall fund you.

My lord, I haf hard sen my cumming in thir partis that Sanders Purves[80] is excommunicat, and being absent and your lordship alswa I knaw nocht quhat ordour is tane thairin, althocht I am determinat that Sanders sall never haf place to use the samyn herefter nor na uthers in his name. And sen he is deplacit in his awin defalt I will place ane uther in his roum, for that man never acknowlagit me nor wes never thankfull to me as became him thow quhat occatioun I knaw nocht, and sen the office is myne and I man answer for it, I will haf na man to serve the samin bot sik as salbe deput thairin be me and will do me sik service as apperteins. And I hoip your lordship will manteine my deputis and suffer na man to do thame wrang, for God willing I sal place sik ane tharin as sall content me in all things to my proffet and be reddy to serve your lordship and me at all tymes as he salbe commandeit. Quharfor I

---

[79]  Daughter by Sir John's first wife Margaret Scott (d. before 1554).
[80]  Alexander Purves, burgess of Edinburgh, custumar and clerk of the cocquet of Edinburgh.

thocht guid to advertis your lordship heirof that the man that I sall deput may
be set fordwart be your lordship to obteine possession, desyring your lordship
answer in writ quhat is the reddiest way to proced heirin, for I thocht I could
do na thing quhill I hard your lordships myind. Beleiving your lordship will
nocht suffer ony man to usurp that office by my guid will, sen it perteins to
me during my lyftyme as ye knaw, for gif law haf place I sall sek remed as
uthiris sall do as I can to provyd the best nixt remeid. Referring the rest thairof
to your lordships answer. Your lordship, and my gud fader Sir Hew[81] and my
wife hes thame hartlie recommendit to your lordship, your bedfallow and
haill company. And God preserve your lordship lang on lyff with gud helth
and prosperitie, and be assuirit sa lang as ye be, swa na thing can cum wrang
to me, for God willing I sall ever continew as I haf done to this hour reddy
to employ my lyf, lands and guds to do your lordships plesour and service.
Off Dalquharran in Carrik, this Sunday the xxiiij of July 1569, be

Your lordshipis bruther at command with service.

P. Bellenden of Stenhous.

My lord, I pray your lordship to writ this my mynd effectuislie to my Lord
Robert with the frist, and desyr his answer that I may adress me the samin
in Orknay, for in the menetyme I sall mak me reddy. Alis it will pleiss your
lordship to send me ane ticket subscryvit be your lordship direct to Master
James Hamiltoun[82] to caus me be answerit of my pensioun, for I haif bene
lang fra hame and hes mekill to do thairwith.

'To my lord and bruther, my lord justice clerk'

Roxburghe Muniments, bdl 1634, no. 15.


## 28. Holyroodhouse, 26 September [1569]

*Adam, bishop of Orkney, to Sir John Bellenden.*

My lord, efter all hartlie recommendation, pleis wit the minister of the
abbay befoir my lords departingis furth off Edinburgh complenit to my lord
of me that he culd nocht haiff his stipend payit him quhilk he travellit for,
and beand demandit of me gyf I was awand him ocht for my parte of this
yeiris pensioun, and he schew it was nocht of that he complenit bot that he
had modefeit to him twa hundreth merks and that I payit him bot sax schoir
merks thairof, and that in tymes past the collectour was wont to pay the
rest. Bot laitlie be the kirk, so termet he, John Knox and ane off his collegis
had inhibit ony payment to be maid to him thairoff, bot ordanit him to seik
the samyn at me in quhais kirk he did the service. To the quhilk I answerit

---

[81] Hugh Kennedy of Girvanmains.
[82] James Hamilton had responsibility for a pension due to Patrick Bellenden from the chantry
of Glasgow (NRS CS7/63¹, f. 126); possibly reader at Glasgow, 1567 (*RPC*, i, 498–9).

that quhatsumever my predecessour wont to pay I belevit he culd nocht be plenteous of the payment off it, bot my leving was mekle less than it was in his tyme quhairby I culd nocht be mair liberall than he was for agmenting of charge than requerit agmentatioun off proffeit for uphald thairoff, quhilk I saw nocht alwayis. Beand urgit be my lords grace to tak ane ordur thairwith I come to this that I schew it was nocht me that he suld bindin bot the burgh of the Cannogait quha ever of befoir, ya in the middis off papistrie, contributit large als mekle in thair peace fynis and in sustentatioun off thair curat and sick uther chargeis ordinar as mycht haiff helpit the minister, and thairfor desyrit my lord to superseid, and I suld tak sick ordur thairwith as that my lord mycht be out of glamour. And becaus your lordship was away I thocht guid to wret to my lord generall[83] and tak his advise thairanent becaus he is ane of the eldars in the abbay kirk this yeir desyrand quhat he thocht maist convenient to be done thairanent, quha hes planelie wretin to me that it is nocht possiabill to do na thing thairanent without my lord regents grace derect ane certane commissioun sick as the quenis grace, the kings moder, derectit to my Lord Galloway,[84] your lordship, the clerk register,[85] me, the advocat[86] and the generall, to cognos quhat the borrowis suld contribut to the sustentatioun of thair minister, quhairin alsua your lordship knawis we pledit to the help of dyverss sick as the minister of Glasgow and Sanct Johneston[87] quhill thai aggreit with him, and this commission beand purchasit to the haill or ony twa I dout nocht bot we sall get ane guid ordur thairanent. And the soner the samyn may be procurit and send hither wilbe the occatioun that the puir minister be the soner satefeit quhom I assur your lordship I petie for povertie and can nocht mend it becaus I am litill better my self be the gud using of my servandis. Your lordship hes mony argumentis to perswaid my lordship heir to sick as the samyn redound to the weill of the puir man and to the releif [of] the kings majesty of samekill of the thrids.

Quhen I sall get ony word out of Orknay your lordship salbe enformet thairof. I pray yow adverteis us of your lordships weilfair and commend my humill service unto my lord and my wyfis. I ressavit at the wreting of this your lordships wretingis derect to Orknay and thankis your lordship of your gret deligence usit thairinto, bot the man your lordship ordanit to be our messinger hes na haist, upon quhat occatioun I knaw nocht and gud it war your lordship suld walk him with ane wreting wretin in maist effecteuis maner and schaw as that tendis to his honour to justefie his restis sa will it be to his exoneratioun quhilk he can never obten, and he wald naver se fair compt

[83]   General of the Mint, at this time David Forrest. See Introduction.
[84]   Probably the bishop of Galloway; the earldom of Galloway is a seventeenth-century foundation.
[85]   James McGill of Rankeillour Nether (1567–77).
[86]   King's Advocate (jointly John Spens of Condie and Robert Crichton).
[87]   Glasgow – Mr David Wemyss (1562–1615); St Johnstone – John Row (c. 1526–80).

seand he hes omittit the ordur that I had comandit him quhilk your lordship
knawis without he gang thair and gather thame in, and now it is nocht my
bissines bot yours for he hes growin sa cankrait he will do na thing for …, and
rafars the rest to your wisdom. At Halyrudhous, the xxvj day of September.

By the bischop off Orknay.

Your lordship sall understand that we dwelling heir ar in maist extreme
dainger off our lyf throw the licentius using of tham that hes the pest upone
tham, and yit laifis nocht of to repair in all cumpaneis as thocht thay had na
infirmetie. I haif deprehendit thir in this falt, bot I can get na punischement for
tham be ressoun that Mr David McGill[88] that usis the office of bailyearie sayis
planelie thair is na law that may judge sick persons to deith, bot hes desyrit
that my lord regents grace will derect ane publik proclamatioun chargeing
all men that knawis tham selfis infirme in that siknes to uther the samyn to
the magistrats within sa mony hours under the pane of deith, and be this
boist carll he thinkis he sall caus men to feir to mak sick entepris. Alwayis I
pray your lordship acording to your wisdome to tak ordur thairwith to our
maist commodetie that ar your frendis heir away. The pest was never war
sene it begouth nor it is in this toun about it presentlie, And God preserve
your lordship.

Be your lordshipis cusing at all power<br>
the bischop off Orknay.

'To my lord. My lord justice clerk in Kelsoch.'

Roxburghe Muniments, bdl 1634, no. 16.


## 29. Holyroodhouse, 27 September 1569
*Adam, bishop of Orkney, to Sir John Bellenden.*

My lord, efter all hartlie recommendatioun, pleis wit efter the closing off
my last wretingis unto your lordship thair occurit ane certan cace mair
urgit be mene for the punischment thairof thane ony uthir that had precedit
concerning the last heid that I wret to your lordship for remeid thairof. For
efter the closing of my wretings and the departing of the berer the haill honest
men off the gait of our burgh of the Cannogait assemblit togither, cam to
me and menit tham self veray haivelie that nather thair awin nor thair barnis
lyffis was in ony souertie sa lang as thair was na punischment for thame that
left nocht of for inhibitioun publik maid to go attourlie beand seik, and said
gyf that I wald nocht put ordur thairto, it behufit thame to reteir tham to
other partis quhair thay wald be better preservit be guid ordur, etc. As your

---

[88]  David McGill of Nesbit and Cranstoun Riddell (c. 1532–95), later lord of session and
Lord Advocate.

lordship knawis ane angre multituid will burst furth with, thay brocht me ane notabill falt to wit that John Hartis sister, quhais conversatioun your lordship knawis, hes of the lait bene instrument of the infecting of his hous, the deith of his thre barnis and the gret gypertie of him self with marvellus gret skath of his movabill as your lordship knawis that in the said infecting will occur quha as thai allege hes this moneth reparit to and fra with honest men nochtwithstanding that scho had the pest upone hir and hes gyffin in presentis fruit to dyverss leand infirme thairin. Thair is uther thir that ar in the lik falt bot nocht of sa lang tyme, and as I wret to your lordship nane of us can be suir bot our domestik sal betray us onles punischment follow heirupone. Quhairfor prayis your lordship, seand we haiff na law quhairby sick exampill may be maid that our nychtburs the toune off Edinburgh with guid ordur hes preservit thair pepill and towne sa that thair haill foull folk ar to enter in the toune the monie with thair clengeour, and no man left ma upone the muir, and that be sum help thai gat of my lord regents grace at his departing to Ingland quhairby thai had ane wreting for thair warrand, that it suld be imput unto tham na falt gyf sick faltours as I haif spokin of war punissit to the deith nochtwithstanding thair is na law for the samyn, and we be the contrar hes within our regalitie of the Cannogait outwith fourte foull personis in Leith upon our syd, outouth four schoir besyd your awin toune of the Cannomillis, and utheris sugit to the regalitie quhilkis all ar infectit be sick lawless and godless persons. Quhairfor prayis your lordship to provid us ane remeid sick as our nychtburs hes, and send the samyn spedelie to us for I assur your lordship I am pressit to put tham to ane assise the morne or ellis to tyne all the sugetis of the Cannogait and the regalitie besid the glamour of the haill nychtburs thair about quhom findis tham self in resait and domage thairby, bot yit I will nocht suffer na sentance nor dome to be gevin quhill I gait my lords mynd thairin. And your lordship knawis quhat cost it wilbe to me to keip sick persons that we dar nocht put in commoun presoun, quhairfor it will pleis yow to speid us the anser agane gyf it be possiabill Thurisday at evin.

    Anent the bissines of my Lord Robertis that your lordship wretis and desyris me to consult with wyiss men thair is never advocat in to this toune bot Mr Clement Litill[89] quha will nocht gyf adwisis in sick caus less that it sall cum befoir him, nor hes bene this fyftene dayis nor thre oulkis bigane. And as to consultatioun I wait nocht quhair I culd consult nor adwise upoun thairin thai behalfis for the granting of me to haiff ressavit sowmes of money as he desyris, and is sa prejudiciall that I knaw nathing mair, and that thing that I can never be astrictit in to, as alswa the augmentatioun of the pensioun for the houss sustentatioun, the assignation of the frie tennentis thairfor, the

---

[89]    Advocate, later commissary of Edinburgh, sometime procurator for Robert Stewart and his wife; his book bequest forms the core collection of Edinburgh University Library.

diminusioun of the proffeit besid that the tother gyffis to the tane half in availl, quhilk gyff that woid as he sall pleis for his securitie can infer I report me to your lordship. Ye ar of als guid judgment as ony of the eldest practisars in Edinburgh, and prayis yow to send me rather your advise than to bid me suit otheris thairanent. All uther thingis reffars to our meting. I pray your lordship desyir my lord regentis grace to find na falt with me that the schakar is nocht set down for I was redy for my parte and the clerk off register[90] wald not haif the samyn beginand afor the secound of October upon quhat caus I knaw nocht, bot I haif awaitit heir still thairupon, and upon quhat service my lord wald command me gyf his grace hes no quhat to do with me I will reter me out of this ... to the cuntrey quhill it sall pleis God to put sum stay unto this devoring plage, and prayis your lordship to gyf me your guid informatioun thairanent as in all uther thingis, and adverteis us off your newis. The secretar[91] and the capitan of the castell[92] hes tham hartlie recommendit unto yow. Nocht ellis bot committis your lordship in the protectioun of the leving God. Off Halyrudhous, this xxvij of September anno 1569, be yours, etc.

Your lordships cusing at all power,<br>the bischop off Orknay.

'To my lord. My lord justice clerk to our souraine lord, at Kelso.'

Roxburghe Muniments, bdl 1634, no. 17.

## 30. Holyroodhouse, 1 October [1569]
*Adam, bishop of Orkney, to Sir John Bellenden.*

My lord, efter all hartlie recommendatioun, pleis wit yesternycht James Hay[93] come to me hame out of Yetland quha hes bene marvellous bissie, bot hes nocht gottin gret expeditioun for Maister William Lader[94] had ressavit and tane up all the restis, and my Lord Robert hes bene sa favorabill to me that he hes takin him and kepit him maist suirlie, and hes send him heir be his awin servandis William Gyffart, the laird Penicuik *(sic)*,[95] James Kennathie, my ladeis brothir,[96] and uthiris dyverss, quhat pat thair ship in Munrois[97]

90  James McGill of Rankeillour Nether.
91  William Maitland of Lethington.
92  Sir William Kirkcaldy of Grange.
93  Servant of Adam Bothwell, later of Robert Stewart.
94  Mr William Lauder, vicar and minister of Yell and Fetlar, chamberlain of Shetland.
95  Possibly kinsman of the parson of Penicuik, holder of a pension from the Airth lands of Holyrood.
96  James Kennedy is noted several times as a servant of Robert Stewart, but this is the only reference to him as his brother-in-law. The *Scots Peerage* makes no reference to Jean Kennedy having a brother called James; it is possible he was an illegitimate son of the earl of Cassillis.
97  Montrose.

upon Monnowday last was, and is luikit for to be heir this nycht, quha quhen
he sall cum I knaw nocht how to use him *salvis legibus*, and be suir to haif
compt, rakning and payment of him as I haiff na uthir way to cum thairby
bot the keping of his persoun. And your lordship knawis that thairto seand
no decreit is gevin nor captioun past be the ordinar justice bot I man haiff the
supplie of the exterordinar be my lord regentis grace wreting subscrivit with
his hand gyffand me captioun upon him, quhilk I wald pray your lordship to
get exsped and send me the samyn with speid, for thairby I hoip to bring him
to this poynt that he sall mak sum way for my satisfactioun, for all the gair
he hes that is knawin will nocht be the outred of saxt parte that is awand to
me bot or he be presonit he will find utherwayis to our contentatioun. Sua
prayis your lordship to be ernest thairinto and send me that letter with all
expeditioun, togither with the commissioun to do justice upon tham that hes
sa traterouslie exponit us all to the perell of our lyvis be cumin amangis thai
haifand the pest upone thame, for all the nychtburis of our gait ar determet to
leif the samyn in cace that ordur be nocht put thairto. Als gyff William will
nocht gang to Orknay for the thing ye wait of quhat your lordship neddis
me to do towart the in craving and gettin in of the samyn, for I assuir your
lordship James Hay sayis me that the honest men of Orknay schew him that
Williams wilfulness in uptaking boll for boll hes caussit me to haif samekle
restis, and trowis that and we had William Rynd[98] thair allanerlie suld get us
all that is awand. This I am put to gret cost, and cumis litill forder throw the
evill willit folischenes of my servandis. I haiff urgit him to comptis and trowis
to get the samyn ane of thir dayis. Thairefter sall communicat the samin to
your lordship gyff ye think it guid to wret the wreting that I wret for to your
lordship unto him, it war nocht evill done. And God preserve your lordship.
Of Halyrudhous, this first of October be your lordship.

Your lordships cusing at power
the bischop of Orknay.

I am veray sair craiffit be all that I am awand to and kan get na thing of all thir
parts to the outtred thairof, and mair I am [constrenit?] off the small thing I
haiff gottin out of Yetland outred ane part of the det I am awand in Ingland,
quhilk cummis to ic li. Striveling [lest?] that I suld haiff [maid our ration?]
to haiff bene cryet out upon.

'To my lord. My lord justice clerk.'

Roxburghe Muniments, bdl 1634, no. 18.

---

[98]  Inhabitant of Kirkwall and sometime servant of Adam Bothwell.

## 31. Holyroodhouse, 3 October 1569
*William Bothwell to Sir John Bellenden.*

My lord, eftir mast hartly commendation of service to your lordship, quhom pless your lordship to wit I haf resavit your lordships writting, that quhar your lordship dessiris me to pass till Orknay for ingattyn of me lordships rests, I am rady till do my utter deligence and service thairto. Sabeand that I gat obedience, assistance and fortification to the samin that I may haf William Rynd, quhilk I schaw your lordship wos rasavar fra the bounds me lordship directs, and that he mycht be creat officer to poynd and strenye quhar thai wor restand awand, with scharp chargis to me Lord Robert till caus me be abayit and assurit of the rests. Utherwayis I knaw perfitlie that I will gat bot littill, for I ken how I wos handellit afor with fair words, promessis, and com na fordur. And in caiss that William Rynd can nocht be gottyn I haf schawin to me lord our master till gat me Peter [Loch?][99] quhilk wos with me at the compttis makyng, for ane officer of armes may be haid with me Lord Robert officer, and writ to William Henderson to assist me for ingattyn of the rests. I sall laif na thing undoun that lyes in my power or possebellitie for me lord our master and your lordschip. I will nocht molest your lordship with farder writting bot commendis your lordship in the preservation of the ewir lestand God. At Hallirudhouss, the iij day of October anno 1569.

Be your lordships servetor at powir,
William Boithuill.

'To my lord, my lord justice clark of Auchinowll, knycht'

Roxburghe Muniments, bdl 1634, no. 19.


## 32. Holyroodhouse, 6 October [1569]
*Adam, bishop of Orkney, to Sir John Bellenden.*

My lord, eftir maist hartlie recommendatioun, I hef bene earnestfull with William Boithwell upon that your lordship and I condiscendit suld be directit away to Orknay, and albeit thair hes bene mony thortours amangis us quhair as gif we had commonit face to face we wald nevir aggreit be the mediatioun of Maister Frances.[100] We ar cum to this point that gif I will get him the armis to Malcome Sinclair that he may use the office of messinger or pursuvant, and send him with him upon my coist, and with that letters of poinding for sic thing as is awand he sall bring me in all that is restand, and sall do sic expeditioun that, God willing or Yule nixtocum, he sall ather be at me with the samin or hef ane guid parte of it at me. Quhairfoir your lordship man

---

[99]  See Introduction.
[100]  Mr Francis Bothwell, treasurer of Orkney.

tak the paine to procuir at my lordis hand that my bissines be not retardit be that occasioun bot that I may hef thai samin unto him, and I sall do diligence to haist thame baith away that na fawtte be fund in us. And for the letters of poinding I will se quhat moyen I can hef to obtene thai samin quhairby na excuis may be justlic pretendit, and gif I may hef thame in your lordships name exped I will send thame in that sorte thair.

I assuir your lordship it grevis me mekle to be sa mekle in det and to hef sa litle moyen to owtred my self be the wicked using of my chalmerlanis and the latheanes of thame that ar awand me. To obviat the quhilk I mister your lordship and all my guid freindis counsellis, quhairof I pray your lordship maist hartlie, and alsua for the commissioun and captioun that I send to your lordship for be Williame Inglis[101] upon Mr Williame Lawder, for I am far behind the hand with him and I get not that to renye him. Your lordships wisdome may considder the samin, quhilk I pray your lordship employ in this present. Thankand your lordship maist hartlie of the newis your lordship send me for thair wes nane in this toun that had the lyke or sa certane, and prayis your lordship to continew as occasioun servis. Margaret your dauchter is verray seik and hes hir hartlie to your lordship, bot I trw it be hir moderis seknes.[102] And God preserve your lordship. Of Halyruidhous, this saxt day of October be

Your lordships cusing at power<br>
the bischop of Orknay.

'To my lord. My lord justice clerk in Kelso'

Roxburghe Muniments, bdl 1634, no. 20.

## 33. Holyroodhouse, 13 October 1569
*William Bothwell to Sir John Bellenden.*

My lord, eftir maist hertlie commendatioun of service, pleis your lordship to wite that I have ressavit your lordships wrettings conserynyng my passing to Orknaye for in getting and gathering of my lord my masteris dewiteis and restis, and is all redy to depart in my Lord Robertis scheip within viij dayis. My lord, ye being rememberit that your lordship promessit to me affoir my lord my maister for to get me all provesioun nessarie for to be had for the gathering of the said restis, and specialie to provyde ane officiar of armes quhome I pleissit to name and cheis. And all redye my lord and I hes convenit upone Malcum Sinklar, my lordis servand. He was borne in the cuntre and hes knawlege of the samine, and will eftir my jugment do best and be maist

<hr>

[101] Seemingly servitor of Adam Bothwell; otherwise unknown.
[102] See Introduction.

movit for to do our besynes in to the said cuntre. And this I praye yow that
ye be verraye delegente to get this done suddartlie that I be in redenes to pass
away in this scheip. Als your lordship sall not faell to get speciall schargis fra
my lord regentis grace to my Lord Roberte that he may concur, assiste, and
his officiaris with me, to get in the foirsaid restis, and speciall to charge my
lord regentis grace that na man tak upone hand to mak no impediment na
trublenes, bot I may justlie tak up the rests of my chalmerlenrie of the yeiris
bypast. For gif that your lordship be sluthfull or negligente of this besynes
your lordship will be behind the hand of that thing that is assignit to your
lordship, for gif I pass nocht at this present tyme ye will be evill anssurit
eftirwarde, and I will not pass thair eftir this for that caus, gif I sall not this
tyme and passage of this scheip. Thairfoir your lordship I dout not bot ye
will mak sufficient provesioun, and I sall do me dewitie, and nathing sall ly
behind sa far as my possebilitie may serve. I will not fass your lordship with
langer wretting bot committe the rest to your lordships wisdome. And sua
committis yow in the protectioun of the leving God. At Halyrudehous, the
xiij day of October 1569.

                    Be your lordship at power,

William Boithwell.

'To my lord. My lord justice clerk of Auchnoule, knycht.'

Roxburghe Muniments, bdl 1634.


## 34. Holyroodhouse, 14 October 1569
*Adam, bishop of Orkney, to Sir John Bellenden.*

My lord, eftir all hartlie recommendatioun, I ressavit your lordships writing
fra Johnne Grahame, of Kelso the vij of October. I understand thairby that
your lordship lippynit the redemptioun of your landis to the silver that wes to
cum owt of Yetland, and that my Lord Robert had send your lordship word
that all wes payit that wes awand me thair. Suirlie I am verray sorie that on
ather syid we ar in that povertie that nather of us may help uther, and your
lordships distres in that point is mair grevous unto me than my awin, quhairby
I am brocht to that that I mon gif up my hous for answering can I get nane of
this leving. And albeit my Lord Robert hes said that thair is no thing awand
me in Yetland the treuth is that I hef futtit comptis with Maister Williame
Lawder and he is declar(it?) awand thre hundreth angell noblis and sex, besyid
parte of the thre scoir sevin yeir that is restand in the commonis handis. And
trewlie my lord I ressavit sex scoir angell noblis and fourtie yopindalis, the
quhilk I hef send away with uther mair that I behovit to fyne at my creditoris
handis to pay the hundreth pund starling quhilk I wes awand at London, and
that for the inaportune sute of the man I wes awand to, quha wes abill to

hef schamit me and myne gif I had not the mair spedalie provydit remeid. And sa my lord wes that thing that I ressavit owt of Yetland onhabill to hef servit your lordships turne, and I wait or I had bene blamit and detractit be men your lordship wald rather and ye had had it of your awin gevin it owt of your purs. And upon this occasioun I tuik the bauldnes to help to owtred my self thairwith, bot will ye hef the securitie maid to you that Mr Williame suld mak me in parte of payment of sic thingis as I am awand your lordship, and alsua ressave the assignatioun of sic thing as is awand me in Orknay and send away as Williame hes devysit with speid, and I trw your lordship sall gat that will do you mair guid than ony that I hef gottin yit will do me or hes done me ony guid.

It is ane meane thing to my lord regentis grace to grant me ane armis to ane that I will answer for as accordis, and howbeit the mater war na thing to your lordships commoditie, as I am determit it salbe haill for your lordships caus gif ye will accept it. I think your lordship wald obtene it for ane word, and lyon herauld quhame I hef spokin hes assurit me that upon my lord regents graces writing he sall do that I salbe satisfeit, sa thair restis na mair unto your lordship bot that parte to be done. And the declaratioun of your lordships mynd quhat ye will hef done thairanent as towarte the thing that he hes requyrit me to do, albeit that it be verray difficill yit sall I indevoir my self that your bissines hef no impediment nor the said Williame hef ony occasioun of substracting of his persoun fra ingaddering of that quhilk I wald assigne your lordship. Praying your lordship till interpete all of me in guid parte as I mene and evir sall to your lordship, and help me to acquyte my self as thair is moyen anewch be the dettis foirsaid gif thai war recoverit, not onlie of the thing that is awand to your lordship bot alsua sum of my uther creditours. And gif forby I sall hef ony thing afoirhand it salbe furthcumand to your lordships honour and avancement for I hef nane uther in the world I am samekle addettit to as your lordship. And think not bot it is als grevous to me to wit your lordship in that distres that your servand Johnne Grahame hes reportit to me as the present povertie that I am into, quhilk is sic that I may assuir your lordship sen evir I had ane leving I wes nevir sa abusit to get my sustentatioun and my fameleis as I am at this present, for I can get na thing of the tennentis or firmoraris handis, and my credite quhilk sustenit me sen I come owt of Ingland hes haillilie refusit to mak me ony mair furnesing. And your lordship knawis quhair ane furnesar refusis and ar plenteous of thair dettour how na uther will furneis again. This point am I at, and yit beris it patientlie as alsua the uncourtes dealing of my servand James Alexander quha will not gif me compt quhill I mon call him thairto be the law, nor yit lat me wit quha is restand or not, bot I mon hef your lordships counsell and support heirinto or ellis I wilbe at the worse parte.

Your lordship will pleis send me the commissioun I requyrit for helping of the minister of the abay. Alsua it will pleis your lordship wit we hef convenit

samony as wes appointit be my lord daylie to the chakker this viij dayis, bot nane
ar comperit for ony calling that we hef usit. And the custumar of Edinburgh
quhais bukis suld controll the remanent of the custumaris can not be had be
ressoun that Alexander Purves quha hes the keping of the cocket under your
lordship and alsua of the bukis is away, and that be excommunicatioun usit
aganis him for non adhering to the religioun, quhame your lordship suld caus
cum heir becaus he is your deput and presentlie is besyid you in the Merss.
And thai hef requirit me to wryte this unto your lordship that ye wald caus
him be heir gif it be possible again Sonday at evin that on Mononday we may
begin and do sum thing in that quhilk appertenis to the kingis propirtie. Thair
is heir awaitting on the thesaurar,[103] the clerk of register, the advocat, Mr
Henry and I. Quhat uther novellis your lordship heris I pray your lordship
communicat thame unto me, for the last wes verray thankfull. Committing
your lordship in the protectioun of the leving God. Of Halyruidhous, this
xiiij day of October 1569 be

Your lordships cusing at power
the bischop of Orknay

Margaret your dauchter, my wyif[104] hes hir hartlie recommendit unto your
lordship.

'To my lord. My lord justice clerk.'

Roxburghe Muniments, bdl 1634, no. 21.

## 35. Edinburgh, 17 October 1569
*Adam, bishop of Orkney, to Sir John Bellenden.*

My lord, eftir maist hartlie commendatioun, I ressavit your lordships writing of
Kelso the xv of October togidder with ane copie of my Lord Robertis writing
writin to your lordship, be the quhilk I understand the leathenes that he hes to
schaw your lordship or me ony favour onles he get his evidentis subscrivit as
he desyris. Quhilk how prejudiciall war to me your lordship is wyis anewch to
consider, seing he can be content of na thing bot that quhilk will wraik the
small heretage that I heff, for he will hef me, my aris, obleist to pay him ten
thwsand punds gif ony successour that I salhef sall intent actioun of reduction
aganis him, and in the menetyme will hef me gevand thame occasioun to reduce
it as that that may not be justifeit be na law, and that onles thai do the samin thai

---

[103] Mr Robert Richardson (treasurer, 1564–71).
[104] A very curious comment. Bothwell's wife (d. 1608) was indeed called Margaret, but she
was in fact the daughter of John Murray of Touchadam (*ODNB*). Since this is the second
reference to her as Sir John Bellenden's daughter, although he is not recorded as having such
a daughter (see letter no. 32 and Introduction), then the inference is that she was Bellenden's
god-daughter.

will not hef watter kaill to leve upon, with the astrictioun inlyikwayis of all the
fre haldaris unto him the quhilk na law can compell thame to. And albeit that
I hef conferrit with sum wyis men that wald my Lord Robertis wele yit thai
think it can nevir be maid in that maner, and I hef maid certane charteris levand
owtte thai claussis and as apperis to me sufficient anewch. And I hef taine diverss
wyis mennis awyiss thairanent gif of law or practik I can be compellit farther,
quha eftir the sicht of thame and the copeis of your lordships first charteris
wes maid hes thocht thame richt ressonable, and thinkis that gif he can not be
content with thai I can mak na thing that will pleis him bot it wilbe to do again.
Quhilks I hef reddy kepand again your lordships hidder cuming to lat yow se,
and hopis the schip sall not pass away quhill ye may be heir.

And as concerning the directioun of Williame Boithwell I will not dispesche
him quhill your lordship be at the ane end of the directioun, for it mon be your
lordships bissines he mon do and na thing of myne. And anent the officiar of
armes quhilk I desyir to be creat I assuir your lordship I haif spokin with lyoun
herauld quha wes contentit, and my lord will send him ane writing schawing
that he is desyrous that he gif him the armes to serve my turne at this tyme
that he sall do the samin albeit that thaireftir he will reduce to the accustumat
nummer him and all utheris. And becaus my lord hes not bene informit heirof
I suppone that hes bene the caus of his refusall, bot fra understand this I hoip
he sall grant the samin. The caus quhairfoir this is socht rather than to tak ane
commoun officiare is be ressoun that thai wilbe sa coistlie baith in thair fe and
alsua in thair expenssis, for it will not be *opus unius mensis*, for thai mon abyid
langar upon it and travell in sic pairtis, quhair as men that ar not accustumat
will not jeopard and induir Heland bedding and Hieland feding, quhilk na
man heiraway, nor uther nor ane Orknay man, will not tak wele with, and
besyid that he being ane cuntrey man will obtene mair favour than utheris.
And sa it war maist necessar for wele of the caus that he war send, and sa gif
your lordship may be ony meane obtene this, albeit that he suld be revokit
within ane moneth eftir his hame cuming it will help your lordships caus and
myne verray mekle, and this I pray your lordship hartlie unto. Committand
the rest to your lordships meting and myne, and praying the lord ye preserve.
Your lordship, of Edinburgh, the xvij of October 1569 be

Your lordships cusing at power
the bischop of Orknay.

'To my lord. My lord justice clerk.'

Roxburghe Muniments, bdl 1634, no. 22.

## 36. Holyroodhouse, 30 October [1569]

*Adam, bishop of Orkney, to Sir John Bellenden.*

My lord, eftir all hartlie recommendatioun, I wrait your lordship ane answer of your lordships writing writin to me of Kelso the xv day of October, bot be ressoun of your lordship going with my lord at this present I suppose your lordship culd not mak me na answer. I send the said writing to the thesaurar quha directit the samin unto yow quha I trow hes causit your lordship ressave the samin or now.

I wrait earnestlie to your lordship concerning the officiar quhilk I desyrit to be admittit and the caussis quhairfoir the samin wes, quhilk assuritlie movis me marvelouslie to insist in the samin, and passis not howbeit he war dischargit within ane day eftir his returning sa that my turne micht be servit quhilk utherwayis can not be remedit. I schaw your lordship that this wes lyoun herauldis opinioun that gif my lord regent wald wryte tilhim thairanent he suld satisfie my desyir and violat na statute. Becaus I culd haif na end in this it behovit me to lat my Lord Robertis ship pas away without ony of myne being in hir, bot that is tollerable becaus thair is ane uther to pas away within viij dayis in the quhilk I wald send William Boithwell and the said Malcolme gif I micht hef that quhairby thai micht be dispeschit, and sua prayis your lordship earnestlie to help thairto, etc.

Your lordship is in the pairtis quhair your lordship may help me greatlie anent thame quha hes maid me veray evill payment this haill yeir bygane, to wit the laird of Closburne,[105] the laird of Bombe,[106] James McClellane of Nuntoun and ane Gordoun that hes the kirk of Balmagy of setnes of the laird of Richardtoun,[107] for persute of the quhilk I hef maid utouth xl li. of expenssis, for I hef had sex sindrie tymes baith men and boyis in the cuntrey to that effect, and nevir to this houre culd get ane penny bot that quhilk the laird of Blairquhan[108] answerit me at the first. I committit the cuir of the creaving in of the samin to our cusing Thomas McClellane of Blakcraig[109] bot I suppose for fear to displease men he hes lattin me sing perqueir, and sa am I abill betuix the auld evill answering and the new far worse not onlie to skaill my hous bot alsua to be schamit be thame that hes furnesit me all yeir, to wit my baxter, browstar and flescheour, to quhame I am awand without five hundreth merkis. I pray your lordship caus call the said Thomas befoir yow and bid him deliver ather of the silver of thai kirks unto my servant Thomas

---

[105]  Roger Kirkpatrick of Closeburn.

[106]  Thomas Mclellan of Bombie.

[107]  Balmaghie, kirk formerly appropriated to the abbey of Holyrood, and now leased by 'Gordon' from the laird of Richardtoun. Gordon was clearly little known to the writer; 'the laird of Richardtoun' was Henry Drummond of Richardtoun (NRS GD24/1/145; RH6/2100, 2453).

[108]  John Kennedy of Blairquhan (some miles inland from Girvan) (NRS GD49/570; RH6/2231).

[109]  ?Blackcraig, near Minnigaff and Newton Stewart.

Kincaid,[110] or ellis the letters of horning dewlie execute and indorsat, or at least the saidis letters with samony executionis of chargis as he hes causit gif. And your lordship will owirsie that being done, that the remanent chargis be usit and horning in lyikwayis gif thai continew disobedient. I am marvelous sair put at be the kirk quha will hef me payand the minister of Libertoun,[111] and lxxx merkis mair than evir wes gevin to ony of the rest of the ministeris. Upon Mononday nixtocum thai will hef the actioun ressonit of the third and I war laith it war in your lordships absence bot yit I can not get delay.

I hef presentit my rentall to the lordis of the chakker reformit as it payis me, bot thai will not ressave it without ane writing of my lord regentis grace to that effect as use is. Your lordship will procuir the samin and send it with Thomas to me. Your lordship will alsua help me thairanent as ye helpit me in the last rentall of Orknay, etc.

I hef ressavit ane obligatioun of Mr William Lauderis registrat in our bukis of regalitie of the forme heirof that your lordship will ressave. He is wele willing to pay bot he desyris lang dayis, and upon that occasioun is content to gif cautioun for his entres betuix this and this tyme tolmound, and will find the laird of Cultmalindy and Andro Williamson, burgess of Edinburgh, cautionaris of the samin, bot not for the sowme, for thai will not be for the sowme, bot for his entres. Awyiss your lordship thairfoir quhat ye will hef done and send me word thairof as ye think expedient for your lordships awin wele and myne, for I hef no thing to releve me of my det bot that quhilk is awand me, and this your lordship seis is ane guid parte of the thing is awand me, quhilk with the remanent I wald bestow glaidlie to the owtred of my principall freindis dettis that I am awand daylie gif thai wald accept it. Becaus that heirupon and uther materis I mon confer with your lordship at greatar lenth I will superseid the samin unto our meting. Committand your lordship in the meintyme in the protectioun of the leving God. Of Halyruidhous, this xxx day of October be

Your lordshipis cusing at power
the bischop of Orknay.

I pray your lordship to get the commissioun fra my lord regent to cognosce upon the ministeris stipend, for you and I hes gottin alreddy the indignatioun that we will get thairfoir, for thai hef strikin up the bill that ye send to the minister, etc.

'To my lord, my lord justice clerk.'
   [Appended note, on separate sheet:]
   The kirkis belonging to the abay of Halyrudhous un payit within Galloway

---

[110] One of a number of Kincaid servitors of the bishop of Orkney, notably Alexander Kincaid, vicar of Walls. Possibly from the Kincaids of Warriston.
[111] Liberton, kirk formerly appropriated to the abbey of Holyrood.

The kirk of Dalgarno[112] set to the laird of Closburne, the parsonage payis
xx [Li] and the vicarage xl merks

The Kirk of Urr[113] set to the laird of Bombe for lxxxx [Li] The kirk of
Corcormo [Kirkcormack] set to him for xxi [Li] xiii [S] 4 [d] and the kirk of
Kirkcudbrycht set alsua til him for Liii [Li] vi [S] viii[d]

The kirk of Keltoun set to James McClellane of [?] for xxxii [Li]

The kirk of Balmage set to the laird of Richardtoun and [?] Gordoun of
[?] suld pay the dewitie xl [Li]

Roxburghe Muniments, bdl 1634, no. 23.

## 37. Edinburgh, 24 February [1569–70]

*Adam, bishop of Orkney, to Sir John Bellenden.*

My lord, eftir hartlie recommendatioun, I hef lukit mony luik for your lordship
sen my departing bot all in vaine, and I am oncertane gif ye sall get sa oportune
ane tyme to attend upon our bissines as now quhill the sessioun is onset doun.
Thairfoir I wald wis ye suld tak the travell to cum heir and gif sum attendance
to put my effaris in ordour. I assuir your lordship that we hef travellit in
vaine quhatsumevir thing we hef done for the wele of thir men that ar of the
convent for thai ar reddy to gratifie all men bot onlie me. And your lordships
requeist and promeiss followit be thame thairupon hes hed na farther effect than
howsone as evir thai ar requeistit in the contrair thai expeid all thingis that thai
ar requyrit of, sa am I disparit to ather hald bak or remeid in tyme cuming ony
thing that is done amiss. Gif I had your lordships self heir I suld schaw your
lordship mair nor I will commit to wryte. Praying your lordship to adverteis
me quhat ye hald convenient to be done for the nychtbouris of the Canyget[114]
to stay thame that thai mister not to gang furth at this present tyme, and inlyk
maner adverteis me howsone ye luik to be heir. And se that ye mak ane feling
of my lordis mynd quhidder he wil that the folkis of the baronie await upon
him self or upon the ane of us tua, or that we may remain heir and await upon
the sessioun. Ye ken I hef not mister of mair [oisting?] than I hef maid. I am
far anewch behind the hand alreddy and misteris not to be put farther. I pray
yow schaw my lordis this alsua that I can not be answerit of the small leving I
hef throw the cummeris that ar in the cuntrey, quhairupon men takis occasioun
to hald all in thair awin hand that letters in four formes is als litle regardit as
the wind that blawis. Quhat cumis heirof God knawis. I hef commandit my
chalmerlane to caus answer my taxt thair, and the laird of Ayrth[115] suld pay thre

---

[112] 1¼ miles south of Thornhill.
[113] North of Castle Douglas and Dalbeattie.
[114] Canongate.
[115] Alexander Bruce of Airth, relative of Bruce of Cultmalindie, and holder of Holyrood lands
in Airth.

scoir punds thairof and Johnne Leisheman[116] the remanent. Your lordship will adverteis me gif it be not thankfullie answerit. And sa committis your lordship in the protectioun of the almichtie. Of Edinburgh, this xxiiij day of Februar, be

your lordships cusing at power
the bischop off Orknay.

'From the bischop of Orknay concernyng the [service?] of the regalitie'.
'To my lord, my Lord Justice Clerk'

NLS Adv. Ms 22.3.14, f. 54.

## 38. Leith, 18 April 1572
*Adam, bishop of Orkney, to Sir John Bellenden.*

My lord, eftir all hartlie recommendatioun, I ressavit your lordships wreitting frome Johnne Grahame, your lordships servand, upoun Twysday last was, quhairinto your lordship declairis the evill estait that your lordship is at throw the trublis of the cuntre, and thairfoir desyring me that I wald mak your lordship support of sik thing as I am awand your lordship, and that your lordship man put at me in cais I will nocht amangis uthiris your lordships creditouris. Treulie my lord my awin pouertie greiffis me nocht litill causit be thir present trublis that God hes laid upoun us all, bot it is no litill eik unto my trubill to undirstand your lordships skaith that ye have sustenit of the lait, and give it lay in my possibilitie be ony thing that I had in hand to do I wald be glaid to do the thing that mycht stand in your lordships commoditie and present asiament. Bot your lordship knawis how I am delt with this instant yeir, baith be the laird of Innerleith[117] tennentis of Brochtoun quhilk was as your lordship knawis ane grait part of my leving, and als be the leave of the tennents that dwellis about the toun quhome of I can get na answer bot that thai have payit the prior of Coldinghame.[118] This makis me my lord the mair unabill to do that to your lordship that I wald with all my hart do, that is to releif your lordship bot yit that your lordship may the schortliar supportit seing that I have it nocht of my awin to do the [torn] bot man do it of the dettis that is awand me. And quhat mistir that evir I have quhilk your lordship may knaw is nocht littill, yit I sall speane my self thairfor at this present for your lordshipis supplie, and sall mak the coist alsua upoun the getting in of the samin sa that your lordship will spair Jamis Purdie[119] to the craiffing thairof, quhilk I dout nocht may be brocht in schortlie, and luik quhat way your lordship will divyss may furdir the payment thairof, it salbe usit for

---

[116] John Leishman, otherwise unknown; probably, like Bruce of Airth, a vassal of Holyrood, Leishman being a common name around Falkirk.

[117] John Towers (Towris, Touris) of Inverleith and his tenants of the lands of Broughton.

[118] Francis Stewart, later earl of Bothwell.

[119] Servant of Sir John Bellenden, as well as Kintyre Pursuivant (NRAS 1100, bdl 1091; RD1/11, ff. 262–3).

your lordships commoditie, quhome God knawis how glaid I wald be to support your lordships mistir give I had it my self to do it thairwith. And that quhilk I have nocht I sall do that I can to have that I may schaw the part of ane freind to your lordship, and give I had the haill soume that I am awand your lordship in hand I wald be als glaid to deliver it to your lordship as to keip it in my awin hand.

I have gottin na answer fra Orknay as yit frome my servand that went thair bot that he hes bene evill intraittit for the cuming that erand, and wald have bene war give he had nocht bene ane cuntre man.[120] And yit my ladie hes send ward to me be tungue that scho salbe heir hir self and satisfie me with all possibill haist, quhilk give scho dois I will promeis your lordship to mak the supplie that is convenient. And in the meyntym your lordship sall ressave the copie of the compt quhilk I maid with my chalmerlane in Galloway quhane he was last heir. Give your lordship thinkis gude I will rais letters upoun thame all for productioun and reductioun of thair taks be ressone thai have nocht payit at the terme appointit according to the claus contenit in thair saids takis quhilk is xl dayis immediatlie eftir entry terme, as I am informit, annulling the samin in caice of non payment as nevir ane of thame hes maid ane yeir eftir and sum nocht to this hour. Nocht ellis bot prayis your lordship send me your answer heiranent quhat ye will farder that I do that lyis in my power. For uthir moyane I thank God I have nane at this present, bot put to actioun for the thing that was wont to be my best sustentatioun. Committand your lordship to the protectioun of the leving God. Of Leith, this xviij of Aprill 1572.

Be your lordships cusing
at all power,
the bischop off [Orknay].

I pray your lordship mak my hartlie commendatiouns to your bedfallow.

'To my lord justice clerk this be deliverit'

NLS Adv. Ms 22.3.14, f. 17.

## 39. Leith, 1 May 1572

*William Henderson to Sir John Bellenden.*

My lord, eftir hartlie commendatioun of service, I ressavit your lordships wrytting fra Johne Graham. As for answer thairof your lordship sal understand that my lady[121] hes directioun of my Lord Robert to appoynt with your lordship upoun all heidis that stands in debait betuix his lordship and yow, swa ye be ressonable, utherwyis to suffir your lordship to ressave your awin lands of Birsay, and sche to enter agane to the Kerss. Bot I dout nocht bot your lordship will evir be aggreand to that thing that is ressonable, quhilk beand done thair is na thing that

---

[120] I.e. a Northern Islander. Suggests he is talking of Malcolm Sinclair.
[121] Jean Kennedy, countess of Orkney.

may be forderit in your lordships effaris that my Lord Robert wil pretermitt as I haif informit the beirar at lenth. As to Johne Giffurd he wes in reddynes to haif cum sowth with my ladie and slippit the schip, bot I beleif he salbe heir in the first schip that cumis fra Orknay with your man Johne Kyle, or ellis Margaret Dunbar, his wyf,[122] makis him stope, for sche will on na sort grant to sell the last sisters part that fell to hir, bot wald leif it to hir eldast sone, and Johne Giffart and sche is at ane daly stryfe thairfor. Yit gif all things succeid to ane gud fyne betuix my lady and you, thai will caus Johne Giffurd and his wyf to aggrie with your lordship or ellis thay will haif na thing of thame in Orknay. Your lordship knawis the heidis that is betuix you and thame quhilk ye can dress esaly gif ye war heir, bot your lordshipis presens it can nocht gudly be done. Refferryng all uther things to the beirar to quhom I haif gevin information at lenth. Sua committis your lordship to eternale God. At Leyth, the first of May 1572.

Your lordships servitour to command
W. Hendersone.

'To my lord justice clerk, etc.'

NLS Adv. Ms 22.3.14, f. 40.


## 40. Leith, 5 May 1572

*Dame Jean Kennedy to Sir John Bellenden.*

My lord, eftir hartlie commendatioun, pleis to wit I come to this toun upone this day aucht dayis being veray seik upone the sey and landit at Arbrocht, and sen my cumming heir I haif bene at the bischop for my lords evidentis and can find na fortherance thairintill at his hand. I haif gret neid of your lordship at this present to haif bene mediatour betuix him and me, and I trow without ye may be hable to cum heir I sall get smal thing done with him, bot I heir that ye ar evill at eis quhilk I am rycht sorye for, yit I sall do my deligence quhil I get your mynd quhat ye call best I do with him gif ye may nocht travell your self. As to your lordships awin effairs your pursevant remanit in Orknay eftir me to the effect that Johne Giffurd suld haif cum with him, and haif maid ane end with your lordship, and I luke for thame bayth togidder yit, for Johne Giffurd was purposit to haif cumit with me and slippit the schip. Referis all uther things to your lordships meityng and myne; and sa committis you to the eternall God. At Leyth, the fyft of Maij 1572.

Be your lordship at power
Jane Kennedy.

'To my lord justice clerk'

NLS Adv. Ms 22.3.14, f. 19.

---

[122] John Kyle is an otherwise unnoted servitor of Sir John Bellenden. Margaret Dunbar is, of course, the wife of John Gifford.

## 41. Leith, 11 May 1572
*Dame Jean Kennedy to Sir John Bellenden.*

My lord, eftir maist hartlie commendatioun, pleis I haif ressavit your lordships wrytting quharby I persave your lordship to be nocht alytill stomochak, and hes consavit the samyn be the opeinioun that ye haif tane of my lord my housbands doyings anent the handillyng of your officiar quhilk ye send in Orknay for executioun of your letters, etc. My lord, I beleif that the officiar can nocht put ony reproche to my lord anent ony charge that [ye?] gaif him to that cuntrie, bot that he wes weill interteneit and fortifeit in all effairs, and convoyit to Johne Giffurds houss and mycht haif execute his chargis on him but ony molestatioun of ony man. And gif he will report utherwyis I desyir him to verifie the samin befoir me that I may mak answer thairto, or ellis I wil allege your lordship dois this of purpois to caus my lord be supponit to be the man that wil nocht suffir the kyngs thingis to haif place, quhilk sall nocht be fund in him bot to be obedient at all tymes as salbe weill knawin, God willyng. Yit quhen your lordship is cum to your self agane I traist ye will consave ane uther opeinioun of my lord and housband. I schew your lordship in my last wrytting that I wes commownyng with the bischop for reformyng of my lords evidents, quhilk wald haif bene mair eisaly dressit gif your presens mycht haif bene had thairat, yit I hope we sal aggrie for it standis bot upone ane smal variance. Tharfor the evidents that was last maid and consignit in your lordships hand wald be send heir with the chapters seill that we may be advysit thairwith, for sum of thame wilbe reformit. The bischop schawis me that he hes wryttin to your lordship for thame. As to the effairis concernyng your lordship I wilbe willyng to do that thing that becummis me, quhairintill your lordship sal find na fault, hoipyng to ressaif the lyke also. Swa restis my letter, with my hartlie commendatioun to your lordships bedfallow, till we meitt. And so committis your lordship to eternal God. At Leyth, the xj of May 1572.

Be your lordship at power<br>Jane Kennedy.

'To my lord justice clerk'

NLS Adv. Ms 22.3.14, f. 22.

## 42. Leith, 23 May 1572
*Dame Jean Kennedy to Sir John Bellenden.*

My lord, eftir hartlie commendatioun, pleis to wit I haif directit this beirar to schaw your lordship how neir apoynt I am with the bischop anent all thingis that hes bene in variance betuix us, and the performyng thairof consistis in your lordships hand only, as ye will knaw eftir that ye haif hard the beirars report with quhom your lordship wil pleis to confer. And sen your lordship hes bene the first dressar of thir effairs quhilks we haif in hand, quharof a part thairintill concernis your lordship, I dout nocht bot ye will be the mair willing to haif thair cummyng to ane gud fyne for all our weillis, and gif your lordships presence mycht haif bene had it wald haif bene the mair esaly done. Nevertheless gif your lordship may nocht travell I wald your lordship send sum man of jugement with your commissioun to dress in your lordships name sik things as ye haif ado with us or we wyth you, for my lord of Orknay hes burdenit me with his restis of Orknay quhilk he wil haf me burdenit for payment to your lordship and to find your lordship souertie thairfor, quhilk I am willing to do gif I may be quyt of cummer in tyme cummyng, that is to say that al variance that is amangs us may be cuttit of, and that I may haif my lords evidents hame to him perfytit be the bischop. And your lordship to be satisfeit and giffand us ane discharge of the pensioun quhilk your lordship hes callit my lord for, as I traist your lordship will do, for your lordships awin hand wryt testifeis that my lord my housband hes that pensioun comptit to him, lyk as he hes the rest of Orknay pertenying the bischop and possessis the samin be ane gud rycht, quharby of your conscience your lordship can nocht accuse him nether as ane spoilyear nor wrangus intromettour thairwith. Sua I wald wis your lordship to appoint and aggrie with the bischop for sic things as your lordship is be hind the hand in that part and nocht to trubill my housband causles, and now is best tyme. Desyring your lordship thairfor that our evidents may be browcht to this toun and the commoun seill of Orknay that we may be advysit thairwith and reform we think gud; and that I may find cautioun to your lordship for payment of sic sowmes as is contenit in the buke of rests of the bischopis detts of Orknay, and get your lordships discharge of the persute of the pensioun befoir spousyt; and that the variance betuix the bischop and you, gif ony be, may be pacefeit. And lyk as your lordship schawis your forderance heirintill to us now, your lordship sall luke for the lyke at our hand gif it pleis you to burdin my housband and me with the mater betuix you and Margaret Dunbar, or ony other thing that your lordship will charge us wyth. I wil nocht trubill your lordship wyth langar wrytting bot referris the rest to the beirar to quhom it wil pleis your lordship to gif credence. And so committis your lordship to the protectioun of God. Of Leyth, the xxiij day of May 1572.

Be your lordship at power<br>Jane Kennedy.

'To my lord justice clerk, etc.'

NLS Adv. Ms 22.3.14, f. 24.

## 43. Leith, 24 May 1572

*Adam, bishop of Orkney, to Sir John Bellenden.*

My lord, eftir all hartlie recommendatioun, pleis wit I have nocht writtin to your lordship this quhyill bygane becaus Johnne Grahame, your servand, was cumand and gangand to and fra betuix us quha could informe your lordship sufficientlie of all proceidings, becaus he was mediatour betuix my ladie, fewer of Orknay, and me. Alwayis my lord I have utirlie put my said ladie frome all uthir schiftis with sik ressonabill dealling that all thingis is cleirit amangs us. Unto this hir saying that scho can na nayis without perpetuall displesour of hir husband end furth and mak my securitie requeirit onless I will red hir at your lordships handis of all pley and mak hir and hir husband quyt thairof, I schaw that that stude nocht in my hand, and that give I mycht mak hir and hir husband to be fre in ony wayis I wald be glaid thairof safar as law or justice permittit, bot I supponit nocht that I could be burdenit thairwith. Alwayis hir conclusioun was that be na meynis hir husband wald give geir to pley him self with. Your lordship seis how all gangs thair can be na falt imput to me, bot your lordship may se the gud will that I beir to mak your lordship be compleitlie payit. I have remittit mekill dett to bring that small thing to gud payment. And now give we sall schaik all louss agane it sall be occasioun of perpetuall pley amangis us. And to remeid it I knaw na way bot mane remitt to your lordships jugement quhat your lordship thinks maist meitt in that behalf. My lady appeiris to schaw hir self as thocht thair war na thing scho wald mair earnistlie be at thane universall concord. It will appeir to your lordship be Mr Johne Dischingtonis [123] awin speiking as I suppone quhome scho sendis hidder. Praying your lordship to tak sic ordour with it as ye may ressonable haif your awin and all cummeris may ceis. And give sa beis send hiddir the chartour and seill with sik as your lordship will give credeit to that we may end as ye sall devyss. Nocht ellis bot committis your lordship in the protectioun of the eternall. Off Leith, this xxiiij of May 1572.

Your lordships cusing at power
the bischop of Orknay.

My wyff hes hir hartlie recomendit to your lordship and your bedfallow, etc.

'To my lord, my lord justice clerk, etc.'

NLS Adv. Ms 22.3.14, f. 28.

---

[123] Mr John Dishington, later chamberlain of Lord Robert Stewart and commissary of Orkney. Related to the Dishingtons of Ardross. There had been Dishingtons in Orkney since earlier in the century, notably Margaret Dishington, who married Edward Sinclair of Strom, before 1549 (NRS GD106/330). As contemporaries of Bishop Robert Reid, it is possible they were ancestral servitors of the bishops of Orkney.

## 44. Leith, 7 June 1572
*Dame Jean Kennedy to Sir John Bellenden.*

My lord, eftir hartlie commendatioun, I had my wrytting maid to your lordship reddy befoir that Johne Graham departit furth of this toun of Leyth last, and seand him absent I delyverit it to the bischop to send it to your lordship quhilk I beleif ye haif ressavit. Mervelyng that your lordship hes send na advertisment thairof agane, knawing that I tary upoun na uther purpois, and gif your lordship had nocht gottin the wrytting Johne Graham can report all our procedingis, quhilk I stand content with provyding your lordship byid at that ye offerit to Mr Johne Dischingtoun quhilk he hes schawin me. It is nocht neidful it be rehersit heir, quharfor I wald desyir your lordship effectuously to owther cum your self, gif ye may travell, or ellis to send with expeditioun and mak ane end with me, for I can tary na langar thairupoun nor Tuisday nixt cumis. Nocht forgettand to send the evidents and seill with your haill mynd for the performyng of our effairis. I beleif the bischop hes wryttin to the samin effect. Haiffand na farder occasioun, committis your lordship to the protectioun of God. At Leyth, the vij of Junij 1572.

Be your lordship at power<br>
Jane Kennedy.

'To my lord justice clerk, etc.'

NLS Adv. Ms 22.3.14, f. 29.

## 45. Leith, 17 June [1572]
*Dame Jean Kennedy to [Sir John Bellenden].*

My lord, eftir maist hartly commendatioun, now being neir the end of all my effairis I purpois hamewort, God willing, schortly. I wald gif it war your lordships plesor that all occasioun war takin away of the persute of my lord my housband for the pensioun quhilk ye acclamis, quharof ye knaw your self we haif sufficient warrandice. I wald verray eirnistly haif that mater at sum quyetnes and rest, quharin I durst evir fallow your lordships awin devyse in ony ressonable maner. I can wrytt na thing mair speciall till I knaw your lordships awin opeinioun and jugement, quhilk I sal follow gif it be nocht to my lords inconvenient. I pray you in this errand or in quhatsumevir uther thing ye will burding me towart my lord that I may be advertist of your answer be this beirar. Swa eftir my hartly commendatioun to your self and to your bedfallow I commit you to the eternall God. Of Leyth, the xvij day of Junij.

Be your lordshipis assurit frend at power<br>
Jane Kennedy.

NLS Adv. Ms 22.3.14, f. 31.

## 46. Kirkwall, 16 September 1572
*William Henderson to Sir John Bellenden.*

My lord, eftir my maist humil commendatioun of service, as tuecheing your lordships effairis wyth Johne Giffurd, my lord my master hes laborit at thair hands to haif gottin the contracts subscryvit, and the evidentis quhilk thai refusit alluterly quhil thay war payit, and all that his lordship culd dryve thame to was to subscryve thame and delyver thame in Master William Mudeis keiping. And now sensyne thair is tua hundreth merks gottin quharof my lord hes furnessit ane part himself, quhilk is to be delyverit to thame, and at the delyvering thairof I sal caus my lord to labour at thair handis to get the evidents send to your lordship and the contracts, bot the wyf is far war nor Johne Giffurds self is. My lord hes directit furth precepts to poynd for the bischopis dettis, and thair is mekle payit that is in William Bothwellis buke, and uther pairt dischargeit as your lordship wil gett knawlege thairof heireftir. Alwayis my lord will do his deligence to get Johne Giffurd payit and your lordship satisfeit sa far as he can, and I sal leif na labour undone to the fortherance of the samin and sal be souertie as your lordship wrait to me, gif I can get the evidents sowth to your lordship.

As twecheing the effaris ye haif ado wyth my lady, my lord hes wryttin to your lordship thairin at lenth and hir ladischip inlykwys, sua that I neid nocht to truble your lordship with farther wrytting thairanent. And lykwys my lord hes wryttin concernyng Patrik sufficient informatioun of his mynd, and I knaw that gif my lord mycht be suir of Patrik, that for your lordships caus he wald releif him of all the skayth he hes gottin and wald be gud lord and master to him in tyme to cum, and I wil tak it upone my soul that gif thai aggrie nocht it salbe in Patriks default and nocht in my lords for I knaw his mynd thairin. Patrik can sobirly ruse him of ony advantage that he hes gottin be the discord, and my lord hes bene drevin to gret expenssis be his caus and bettir is for baith thair weillis to aggrie in tyme nor to continew thairin. And your lordship I think may bring it to pas at this tyme eisaly.

My lord hes declarit his mynd to me in ane purpois, and biddin me wrytt to your lordship the samin, that is his lordship is content to marie his eldest dochter with your sone Lues, and will gif ane ressonable tochir wyth hir to put away the difference of the Kers, for my Lord Levyngstoun is desyrous of hir, yit his lordship wil rather wair hir upone your sone nor thair, that he may be suir of your lordship to be his frend and his bairnis. And your lordship knawis that it is ane honorable allyance and ye wil get ressonable tochir, and the bairne is of ane gud inclinatioun and appeirrand to be wyfe and ane gud lyk personage. Thairfor I think your lordship suld ressave the offir hartfully. How evir it be your lordships wil, pleiss to wrytt your mynd agane and the forme of the contract that ye wald aggrie upone concernyng this mater, for I beleif my lord wil gif ane thousand punds in tochir with hir, and I trow Mr Johne Dischingtoun hes credence referat to him in this behalf.

Als my lord hes writtin to your lordship for ane discharge at your hand of your pensioun, and quhat releif that he can mak to your lordship be warrandice he wil lat your lordship haif it, bot gif he want your lordships discharge he wil aggrie na thing with the bischop bot wil do sufficient till all that my lady and hir colliggs did in the sowth, and wil denay that he gef ony power to mak resignatioun owther in my ladeis favouris or his sonis. And swa at he lyk to cum to ane intentement without your lordship handill the mater the mair wysly. Als I delyverit to Johne Giffurd at your lordships command of the thryds of Orknay sex chalders victuall for the lx nyne yeirs, quhilk my lord causit answer heirof. And my lord wil nocht be content to tak sexteine punds for ilk chalder of allowance thairof, bot wald haif ane burdinging your lordship with xx li for ilk chalder, quharfor I wald ye wrait to his lordship to stand content of xvj li for the chalder as he sauld to [uthers?] merchands, utherwys he wil gar me accept it in payment for xx li, and sa sal I pay xxiiij li of my purs without your lordship releif me. I can wrytt na farder to your lordship of ony thing, bot referis this beirar to declair the maner of all things, bayth anent my lord and my lady as towart uthers, quha can schaw your lordship the haill at lenth. And so committis your lordship to the tuitioun of God. At Kyrkwall, the xvj day of September 1572.

Be your lordships servitour at command
W. Hendersone

'To my lord justice clerk, etc.'

NLS Adv. Ms 22.3.14, f. 34.

## 47. Kirkwall, 17 September [1572]
*Dame Jean Kennedy to Sir John Bellenden.*

My lord, I commend me hartly to you. Your lordship sall wit that eftir my hame cummyng I schow my lord my housband of all our procedingis in the sowth, and amangs the rest quhat travell your lordship tuk to forther his effairis and wyth quhat difficultie we gat the samin exped. Yit becaus that I haif nocht maid ane finall end wyth your lordship anent the Kerss I am the war hard of his lordship, bot sen my cummyng heir it is gart me understand utherwyis nor was schawin me in the sowth. Bot now my lord to the effect that your lordship may be satisfeit and I nocht hurt, your lordship sal send the forme of that thing that ye wald haif me doand, quhilk I beleif was contenit in ane contract that suld haif bene perfyitit betuix your lordship and me in Leyth quharintill your lordship suld haif dischargeit my lord and me and our airs of all intromissioun with your pensioun, etc., and of the warrandice of the lands of Coilheuchburn[124] and utheris that ye ar plaintuous of contenit in your chartour of the K[erss]. And my lord on the uther part suld haif sufferit your lordship to haif had proces ag[ane] him anent your pensioun, and ye to haif tane the bischopis warrandice for recompans, and I to haif maid my renunciatioun of the Kerss, quhilk I am willing [torn] to do, and sall fulfill your desyir ye makand me sickir of the lands of Birsay as your commownyng was to me, [marginal insertion: the samin beand als profitable and commodius to me as the uther lands of the Kerss, or that the samin may be maid als commodius in sic uther things as may redound to my proffeit and avantage] and sal subscryve quhat securi[tie] thairof that ye will desyir, and consigning the samin in ane sufficient newtral mannis hand to be keipit quhil ye performe your part agane to me.

Bot thair is ane thing that I may requeist you for, and as ye wil haif my kyndnes and frends that wil do for me to labour heirintill, that is to say thair is ane rowm pertenyng to the abbot of Dunfermly[ng][125] lyand upone the north syd of Forthe forgane the Kerss[126] quhilk as yit is unsett in few, and I hard that gif he culd haif gottin silver he wald haif fewit the samin. And gif your lordship culd haif gottin the samin drawin to ane ressonable compositioun, and it had bene four or fyve thousand merks for the fewyng thairof I wald haif perswadit my lord my housband to haif maid scheift for the samin, and it war to lay all his silver wark and my chenis and all uther thing that we haf in plege thairfor that I mycht haif lyfrent of the samin, for thai gart me understand that it wil be twa and threttye chalders of victuale yeirlye, quhilk gif it culd be had for fourtye penneis the boll wald be worth the labouryng for, as I traist your lordship may bring the samin to pass gif ye will insist eirnistly thairintill. Thairfor, howsone your lordship gettis my wrytting, with all gudly diligence I wald your lordship put the mater to assay and confer wyth the abbot gif the samin may be had of him, and gif ye can get ony grant thairof send me advertisment with expeditioun thaireftir, that we may provyd to satisfie him thairfor. Referring the reist to your lordships judgment, and so committis [your] lordship to the eternall God. At Kirkwall, the xvii day of September [torn].

Jane Kennedy

NLS Adv. Ms 22.3.14, f. 36.

---

[124] Coalheuchburn (Colloch Burne in Blaeu's *Atlas*), near Hallglen, south of Falkirk; the 'uthers' included: Abbotsgrange, in the Kerse; Bowhouse, in modern Grangemouth; Newbiggings, near modern Polmont; and the unlocated Luderis Aikeris, Cowperland and Ponderlands in the same general area.
[125] Hewitt, 'Robert Pitcairn' (c. 1520–84), *ODNB*.
[126] Probably west of Culross.

## 48. Kirkwall, 17 September 1572
*Lord Robert Stewart to Sir John Bellenden.*

My lord, eftir my hartly commendatioun, I ressavit your writting fra William Hendersone quharintill the complene of my wiffis using towart your lordships effairis, and that scho allegis that I haif gevin hir na contentatioun for to renunce the Kerss, etc. My lord, albeit that I haif consentit to put hir in ane part of the bischopis lands of Orknay for that caus in speciall, yit I wald nocht suffir hir to get sesing thairof bot upone that conditioun that sche sal renunce hir lyfrent of the Kerss, quharupoun I haif tane instrument, sua it stands ower betuix us quhil sche condiscent thairto [*interpolation, scored out*: and now sche is content to mak renunciatioun]. As to the confirmatioun gevin be the bischope of the lands of Birsay to my dochter Marie, etc., I haif the samin, and quhen your lordship plesis ye sal haif the auctentik copie thairof. I heir be the report of my servands quhat diligent labour and travell your lordship tuke to the furtherance of my evidents at the bischopis hand, bot yit thair is sum things contenit in the last contract quhilk your lordship man caus be reformit be the bischop, as I haif send informatioun thairof wyth the beirar quhilk your lordship man labour to caus the bischop condiscend to. Sua sal all thingis tak perfectioun amangs us, albeit it be to my greit hinder for the half of that sowm that suld be delyverit to your lordship wil never be gottin furth of the commownis hands of Orknay. And as to William Bothwell it will extend to mair nor sex hundreth punds that he hes tane up and gev[in] his dischargis upone, and hes schawin tua sindry sufficient commissionis of the bischopis to that effect and was never dischargit as yit, thairfor on na wyis wil I tak him in my hand for I was oblist be the first contract to caus the bischop and his factours to be payit, and sua samikle as he hes gottin payment of aucht to be releif to me. As to your appointment wyth John Giffard I sal mak him to be payit of that sowm that ye and he hes aggreit upoun [*marginal insertion*: swa that ye gar send me letters of the lords to that effect]. And he and his wyf hes condiscendit that Master William Mudy sall have the contracts maid betuix your lordship and thame togidder with your lordships evidents subscryvit be thame in keiping till thai be compleitlye payit thairfor. And utherwyis I culd get na thing done be thame [*marginal insertion*: and thai refusit to tak me souertie thairfor].

Twecheing the deference betuix your lordships broder and me, etc., for your lordships caus I am content to submitt me to four discreit men, that is to say your lordship and Sir Hew Kennedye, for your broders part, and I for my part sal cheis uther tua, quhilk can nocht be done quhile I may (?in) put my self quhar he and I face for face may declair our awin partis. And thair all things betuix us salbe tryit and endit. And in the mene tyme your lordship sal caus him send his servands to this cuntrie to visye his rowmes and to put ordour thairto, as also to mak compt with me of sic dettis as is

restand amangs us, and the samin beand calculat quhat I haif intromettit with
of his as escheit salbe allowit thairintill, and that for your lordships gud will
only. And albeit your broder hes maid divers sinister reports of my using
towards him, yit quhen we cum present personaly ye wil knaw the contrar
in mony things. And thairfor ye sal keip ane eir to me quhile I cum to schaw
my awin part, and in the mene tyme all actionis betuix him and me to be
suspendit on ather part and principally of his sclanderous toung. And gif he
be desyrous to cum in this cuntrie to remane I am content thairof, sua that
he will mak me amends honorable for the offencis he hes done to me and find
me souertie that he sal leif in quyetnes in tyme cummyng. And this I offir for
your lordships caus, traistand to haif your lordship the samin man to me in
tyme cummyng as ye wes to my broder the abot of Kelso and to me befoir
my entres to this cuntrie. And quhen ony persewis actioun in my contrar,
owther befoir the regents secreit counsal or sessioun, that I may find your
lordship to answer for me. And to mak your lordship the bettir occasioun to
be weill willing heirunto I haif gevin declaratioun of my mynd to William
Hendersoun, my servitour, to mak your lordship advertisment at this present
to quhom ye sall gif credit as to my self quhat his wrytting reports, for be the
performyng thairof all things amangs us may be browcht to ane quyetnes, as
I traist sal cum, thouch our inimeis wald wys the contrar, quhilk sall nocht,
God willing, ly in thair power.

My wyf hes wrytting to your lordship anent sic effairis as sche will desyir
your lordship to do to hir, and gif ye find hir desyir resonable your lordship
wil send me advertisment thairof agane, for I wil refer that to your lordships
awin discretioun. Als I haif eikit in the contract last maid that the bischop
sall warrand me and my airis of your lordships pensioun of Orknay, and that
to caus him be the mair willing to aggre with your lordship thairfor, for I
persaif he deilis fraudulently bayth your lordship and me be the consele and
persuasioun that he gaif to my wyf quhilk sche hes schawin me. And becaus
I feir gif the questioun of Halyrudhous thrydds cum in ressonyng befoir
your lordship in the sessioun that the bischop sal mak smal defens gif he trow
to get eisye compositioun of the kirk thairfor, and the saids thrydds being
evictit than sal he haif place to call me for warrandice thairof, and sua obtene
the maist part of the leiffing of the bischoprye fra me, quhilk wilbe my uttir
wrak gif the samin be nocht wyisly forsene and remeid providit thairfor. And
becaus I tak your lordship to be ane of men in the warld that favours me best
and hes ever hithertillis kythit the samin to me, thairfor I oppin this mater
to your lordship desyring you maist eirnistlye gif ye persaif ony appeirand
danger of this mater that or it tak effect your lordship will rather mak sum
eisye dress with the kirk and lat thaim haif sum compositioun thairfor,
and lat the bischop pay ane part thairof becaus he may weill do the samin
in respect that he hes gottin the thryds of the pensionis [*marginal insertion*:
quhilk I never gat, and he hes four hundreth £ of superplus be the chance,

and four hundreth punds that the thrydds of Orknay extends to mair nor he hes gevin up, quhairin I am defraudit]. And for that caus I haif grantit him the tua part of the pensionis that suld haif fallin to me, and I am content to pay ane uther part, and it war ane hundreth punds yeirly or tua hundreth merks as your lordship will modifye, for it war bettir to me to gif out that nor fall in danger of the haill. And I sal ay be in ane cummer quhil that be done. I haif wryttin to Mr James McGill to stand my gud frend heirintill quhilk I traist he sall, bot I dar nocht oppin the danger heirof to him as I haif done to your lordship heir nor wil schaw na uther creatour heirof, bot committis the samin to you to do thairin as your lordship thinks gud. And as my haill traist is in you, I haif gottin alreddy tua hundreth merks to Johne Giffurde, and he salbe satisfeit of that thing that your lordship hes promissit, howbeit I man pay ane gud part thairof of my awin purss, bot your lordship sal nocht start that I haif refusit William Bothwell, for the bischop is sa fraudfull that I can nocht deill wyth him, and I haif left owt that clauss of the lattir contract that the bischop sal nocht be bund for the warrandice of the diminutioun of the rentall, quhilk I wil nocht condiscend to becaus sa lang as the bischop lyffis [*scored out*: I wil seik na warrandice] the questioun of the diminutioun of the rental will nevir be movit betuix us, becaus I haif the hail bishoprye be the lyfrent tak, and I am bund for the thryd thairof be the formar contra[ct], and sua that clauss may be hurtfull to me and can do him na gude. And quhar the bischop desyris ane discharge of thai things that I suld haif ressavit in the place of Yards, lat him gif me ane discharge of his inseycht that he seikis, quhilk was bot ane sort of auld rottin brewyng lomis, and I sal discharge him that uther, for I wald cut away all thing that may mak variance in tyme to cum. Mairowir, my wyf hes wryttin to your lordship to send hir ane wrytting that was maid betuix your lordship and hir with sic uther thingis as sche hes ado, quhilk your lordship pless to do safar as ye think ressonable, for I haif causit hir condiscend now to mak renunciatioun, and quhil than thair was lytill rest amangs us bot now sche wil do all thing to your lordships contentment.

Als concernyng your broder Patrik yit as of befoir for your lordships caus I wil schaw all the favour that I can of my honour sua that he wilbe the honest man in tyme to cum, and howbeit that I am requyrit be sindry to gif furth precepts of poynding conform to letters of the lords upone him yit I will nocht gif ony fortificatioun aganes him bot will oversey the samin I hope as said is. And for ony skayth that he hes gottin in tymes bypast I sal find the way that he sal gett als mikle advantage agane gif he wil use your counsale and myne till his awin weill. And gif he will continew in his malice towart me I haif thryss als mikle to lay to his charge as he hes to lay to myne, quhilk he wil find gif he gangs to the uttirmoist wyth me, quhilk I wald nocht wys him for your caus to do. Forder gif your lordship wil haif al things aggreand ye man send me ane discharge of your pensioun, for without that I will aggrie in na heidis, and your lordship was the principall actour thairof, quhom to bayth the bischop and I gaif credit. And sen your lordship hes ane honour I traist ye wil nocht gif me occasioun to complene of your doyngs, and that beine done ye salbe satisfeit of my wyf and al uther things. Referryng the rest to your lordships jugement, and so committis your lordship to the eternall God. At Kirkwall, the xvii day of September 1572.

Be your lordship
Robert Stewart.

'To my lord justice clerk, etc.'

NLS Adv. Ms 22.3.14, f. 38.

## 49. Kirkwall, 2 September 1582

*Robert, earl of Orkney, to Sir Lewis Bellenden.*

My lord, efter my verray hartly commendationis, I ressavit your lordships letter be the quhilk I am persuadit of the guid will and favour your lordship beiris toward me, quhairof I thank yow in the maist hartlie maner I can, and will heirefter luik till have your lordship in the samin estait and conditioun as your father wes to me quhome I fand ever honest, gentill and kynd in myne adois, quha salbe ever rady till acquyt your lordships greit guidwill with all thankfull plesour lyand in my powar. Your lordships cusing Sir Patrik sall for your lordships caus find sa favourabill ane dealing on my pairt as sall aggre to your lordships contentment. I have directit the berar, my servand Johne Cavertoun,[127] towart the south for addressing myne adois, quhome your lordship will supplie as myne erand sall craiff, and amangis all utheris that your lordship will becum cautioun to my lord of Rothois[128] for the thousand markis promesit be your lordship, quhome I sall, godwilling, convenientlie releif. Quhairin as your lordship will plesour me, and thairby mair and mair procuir my favour, sua may your lordship employ me to all guid office yow belanging. Ever haveing your lordship the almychtie in his protectioun. Frome Kirkwall, this secund of September 1582.

Your lordships verray guid freind to powar
Orknay.

'To the rycht honorabill and my verray guid lord, my lord justice clark, etc.'

NLS Adv. Ms 22.3.14, f. 43.

---

[127] Servitor of Robert Stewart, first referred to 13 November 1573 (NRS CS7/50); later of Shapinsay (1584, *REO*, 157, no. lxxii).

[128] Andrew Leslie, earl of Rothes (c. 1530s–1611).

# APPENDIX

## MR GEORGE BELLENDEN

Mr George Bellenden was a younger brother of Sir John and Sir Patrick Bellenden. He appears to have been illegitimate, though documents place him in line of succession after Sir John and Sir Patrick.[1] He had an early interest in the north. In 1561 he granted a tack of the vicarage of Dunrossness to Ola Sinclair of Havera for three years from Lammas 1560;[2] he was appointed chanter of Glasgow in 1564.[3] He was in Scotland in March–June 1564,[4] but by 17 October of that year he was writing from Paris describing his life there, as outlined in the letter below. This fascinating missive explicitly designates him as a brother of Sir John. Already a graduate, he had gone to France for further study. He sought to improve his Latin and French, and also heard lectures in Greek from 'P Ramus', the notable renaissance scholar who had had Lords John and James (the later regent) under his tutelage. It is not known whether he returned to Scotland as the only subsequent reference to him is on 21 March 1569 when Sir John Bellenden was granted a gift of the escheat of his goods, as he had died unlegitimated without lawful heirs of his body or disposition of his goods.[5] The following letter, though not part of the main body of the correspondence, gives an interesting perspective on the whole, on the Bellendens' part in it, and a picture of the times.

### Paris, 17 October 1564
*Mr George Bellenden to Sir John Bellenden, his brother.*

My lord, efter my humble commendatioun of serwice. Althoe I have writtin at lenth to your lordship with the Scottis merchauntis quhom with I come in thir partis quhatsoever thing at this present I had to wrytt, yit remembering on your lordships commands quhilk was that I suld nevir lippin your lordship suld ressave ony wrytting that I wrytt, and that with sindry handis I suld evir wrytt

1  *RMS*, iv, nos. 1710, 2472.
2  Ballantyne and Smith 1195–1579, no. 128.
3  *Fasti*, 207.
4  NRS RD11/3; NAS 1100, bdl 1612.
5  *RSS*, vi, no. 561.

the sammyn think. And understanding also that this berar was cummit of court and bound to Scotland in poist, and that he suld prevene our merchantis, I thocht gude to assure your lordship of your lordships cousing Williamis gude helth and weilfair,[6] and of his placeing in Rowane,[7] quhilk I understude your lordship was maist earnest with the first to knaw. As to my self I have adjoynit my self in chalmer with ane Scottisman, Mr David Cunynghame, [8]and ane other Frenche man, student heir for the tyme, quhair I assure your lordship I am best than els quhair in this toun bayth for that I am best cheip in pensioun, as your lordship sall understand of my other letters, and also of Alexander Moreis, merchaunt, quho was factour at this present to ane Mr James Hammiltoun, and thairfor hes the knawlege quhat he payit for him and quhatt is the leist pensioun in this universitie, and also of James Nisbett, servand to my lord thesaurar; and by this our conference in the Greik and Latin will profit mekle to us bayth, seing we bayth employ our selfis to the studie of the toungues and humanitie. So that I assure your lordship I wald not wishe to be better placed. As to the Frenche toung, I assure your lordship thair is na other spokin in our chalmer under ane certaine paine quhilk we have injoynit thairto. I heir at this present under P. Ramus[9] the Physices of Aristotle in Greik, the Oratioune of Aeschines contra Cthesiphontein under Dionisius Lambinus; I heir also under Guillonius[10] sum Epistles of Budeus, and payis thairfor a testoune in the moneth. Thair is na Latin at this present teachit be ony of the kinges lectoris. Thair is na thing sa dear in this toun as bukes, the derth quhairof daylie incressis in so mekle as thai bukes in Greik, quhilk was sauld for ane lyard the feture before the lectouris began to reid, ar now hichted to four denneris;[11] the Latin also in lyke maner. And thairfor this first yeir the furnesing of bukes wilbe derrest to me, as I sall advertiss your lordship of quhatsumevir I sall by, as I sall chaunce to by thame. I hae wryttin to your lordship in my other letters the compt of the claythis quhilk I was compellit to by this wintar with also the compt of my expenss in

[6]   This was William Bellenden, son of John Bellenden of Pendreich (Lasswade) who was described
     as Sir John Bellenden's cousin in an obligation dated 30 September 1565 (NRS RD1/8, ff.149-
     50). William is listed as a student the University of Paris in 1568 (*Scottish Historical Review*, 43,
     p.70). He went on to have a distinguished career (Durkan, 'William Bellenden', *ODNB*).
[7]   Rouen.
[8]   George Bellenden and David Cunningham are both listed as students at Collége Royal,
     Paris, on 17 October 1564 (*Scottish Historical Review*, 43, p.85).
[9]   Petrus Ramus (1515–72) was an influential French humanist, logician and educational
     reformer who published more than 50 works. A Protestant convert, he was one of the most
     prominent victims of the St Bartholomew's Day massacre.
[10]  Renatus Guillonius (1500–70), otherwise known as René Guillon, was a teacher of ancient
     languages at the University of Paris. He published several books.
[11]  No definite meaning is attached to the word 'feture' in *The Dictionaries of the Scots Language*,
     nor for 'denneris', other than the obvious. Tentatively, the following meaning for the
     sentence where they appear is suggested: books sold for a lyard in the period before the
     lectures began are now at a price equal to that of four dinners.

the jorenay. I have nocht spokin my lord of Ross[12] as yit, for his lordship sen his schearing hes bene evill at eass, bot, God be praysit, as I heir, he is in na danger, as this berar will assure your lordship. I have send your lordshipis letter to my lord of Glasgw, with ane letter of my awin also praying his lordship nocht to be miscontent, althocht I, unknawin to his lordship, darre be so bold as to present and recommend my service unto his lordship, quhilk I doubt nocht bot his lordship will of his humanitie ressave in gud part. I understand be this berar his lordshipis gude mynd anentis your lordship, and how his lordship had approvit quhatsoevir thing the quenis majestie had causit my lord of Ross to doe, quhilk he will schaw your lordship at mair lenth. I have nocht the laser at this present to wryt to the rest of my freindis be ressone of this berar haistie departing, quhilk in deid is sa haistie that I doubt nocht thair is sum hicht mater he is to advertiss the quenis majestie. And thairfor I doubt nocht bot your lordship will appardone and tak in gude pairt this in haist my wrytting, and heirefter, godwilling, I sall amend. And so I commit your lordship to the presevatioun of God, with the rest of your lordshipis gude company. At Parishe, the xvij day of October 1564.

> Your lordshipis humble obedient servitour,
> Mr George Bellenden,
> dwelling in the Rew of S. Jacqe at the south
> port thairof, under na sing.

'Fra Mr George Bellenden'
'To his verie good lord and broder my lord justice clerk of Scotland, this be delyverit'.

Edinburgh University, Laing MSS, I.350. Printed in *Laing MSS* (HMC), i, 20–1

---

[12] The bishop of Ross (Henry Sinclair), who was given leave to go overseas in 1563, for treatment of a kidney stone in Paris by 'schearing'. Despite his being described as 'in na danger', he died there early in January 1565 (*Fasti*, 351).

# SELECT GLOSSARY

**afauld**   sincere
**affeir (effeir)**   pertain
**akit (actit)**   entered in a record
**allenrenlie (alanerly)**   only
**apayit**   satisfied
**assythement**   compensation
**attour**   over
**avail**   value
**bald**   commanded
**begouth**   began
**beyr (bere)**   four-rowed barley
**blenche (blanch)**   purely nominal feu or rental
**boist carll**   threatening ploy
**bostowis (bostis, boistis)**   threatens
**bruik**   to have or enjoy the use or possession of
**cankrait (cankarit)**   ill-natured
**chailder, schalder (chalder)**   measure of capacity, particularly of grain
**chaipps**   escapes
**clengeour**   a cleanser of infected persons or places; a disinfecter
**conjuration**   sworn conspiracy or league
**coss**   exchange
**cost**   mixture of ⅔ malt and ⅓ meal
**courtein**   curtain, curtain wall (?)
**creis**   grease, fat
**culveryngis (culverin)**   early form of handgun
**cummer**   trouble
**cunne**   render (thanks)
**cuttall (cuttell)**   measure of *wadmell*; equivalent to Scots ell
**effectuouslye**   earnestly
**effiris**   appropriate
**eme**   uncle
**expreme**   name (verb)
**fat guddis**   meat goods
**forgane**   opposite

**fould (foud), foudrie**   chief law officer in Shetland, equated with sheriff
    in Orkney; his jurisdiction
**fremmit**   distant (personally)
**gainestowd**   resisted
**glamour**   clamour
**gossop**   godparent
**grimpit**   troubled (?)
**guidfather, gud fader**   father-in-law
**gypertie**   risk, jeopardy
**horning**   judicial outlawry
**inlaik**   lack
**kythit**   displayed
**lagese**   legacy
**last**   measure of goods
**latheanes**   unwillingness
**lever**   more willingly
**liart (lyard)**   small French coin, worth the fourth part of a sou;
    generally a small coin
**lippin**   to trust
**mister**   (noun) situation of difficulty or distress in which help is required;
    (verb) require
**murmuryt**   grumbled about
**navow(is)**   nephews, younger male relatives
**oisting**   assembling (of persons)
**onkuith, oncouth**   ill-mannered
**owtred**   to free or clear oneself
**perqueir**   by heart
**poinding**   seizing and selling goods of a debtor
**pois**   funds set by
**probane**   proving; trial
**quhill**   until
**reddendo**   charter clause specifying duty payment
**reise**   stir up
**renye**   put in order
**resentle**   recently
**rowmes**   portions of land
**ruse**   boast
*salvis legibus*   without breaking the law
**samblablye (semblable)**   of the same sort
**schakar**   exchequer
**schearing**   surgical removal
**segeand**   besieging
**setnes**   under lease

**slewthfull**   negligent
**sped**, **unsped**   completed, uncompleted
**stomochak**   angry
**suddartlie**   in a soldierly manner
**superplus be the chance**   surplus by chance
**supple**   support
**supstraket**   withdrawn; variant of *substractit* (withdraw, take away, remove)
**sweir**   reluctant
**thinkis**   variant of *thingis*
**thortours**   difficulties
**throwgangis**   aisles
**tolmound**   (twelvemonth) year
**tyne**   lose
**umquhile**   deceased
**uther (letter no. 28)**   variant of *utter*
**vese**   visit
**wadmell**   coarse cloth
**waikryf**   alert
**weyr**   hostility
**witschauff**   employ
**wyte (in the)**   at fault

# INDEX